don't try this at home

don't try this at home

Dave Navarro

AND NEIL STRAUSS

itbooks

Some of the photographs in this book have been moved out of sequence so as not to incriminate anyone pictured. Thus, just because a subject's photograph appears next to a particular section of text does not mean that the person was involved in the events described therein. In addition, some names and identifying characteristics have been changed to protect the innocent.

Photographs on page 238 courtesy of David LaChappelle; page 239, 243, 244, and 253 by Robin Layton; page 240 courtesy of Tynan Hutchins; page 241 (top) courtesy of Kevin Mazur/WireImage; page 241 (bottom) courtesy of Michael Caulfield/WireImage; page 248 by Robert Erdmann/Icon International. All other photographs courtesy of Dave Navarro.

A hardcover edition of this book was published in 2004 by HarperCollins Publishers.

don't try this at home

FIRST IT BOOKS PAPERBACK PUBLISHED 2005.
Reprinted in 2011.
Designed by Bau-Da Design Lab, Inc.

The Library of Congress has catalogued the hardcover edition as follows:
Navarro, Dave
Don't try this at home / Dave Navarro and Neil Strauss
p. cm.
ISBN 978-0-06-039368-7
1. Navarro, Dave 2. Rock musicians—United States—Biography. I. Strauss, Neil
II. Title.
ML419.N28 A3 2001
787.87'166'092—dc21
[B]

In memory of
Jen Syme and D'Arcy West

1. According to

A. If life could become a party, then life is worth living.
B. Too many questions can make life not worth living.
C. Fortune and fame alone make life worth living.
D. The unexamined life is not worth living.

contents

june

july

august

september

october

november

december

january

february

march

april

may

june 2000

postscript: june 2004

don't try this at home

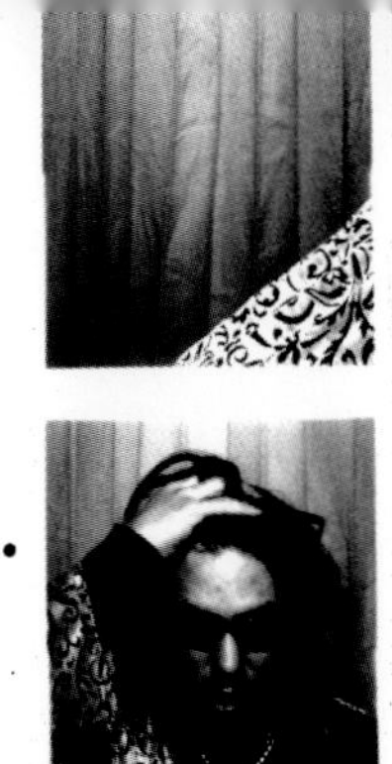

june

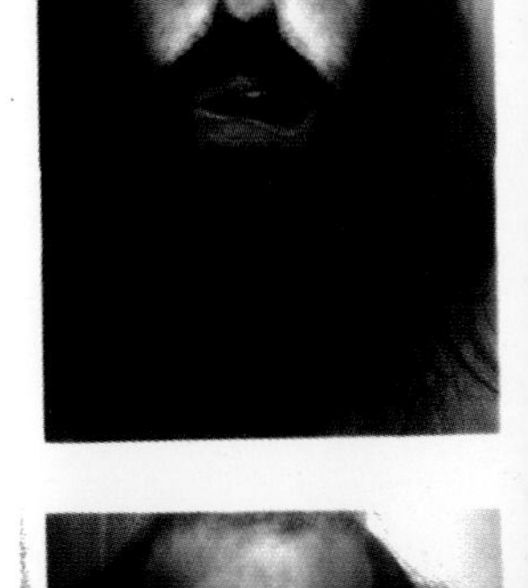

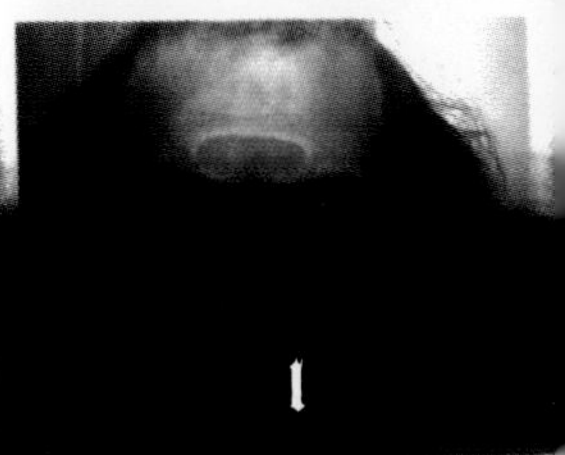

part I THE CONCEPT

"Do you know what to do when somebody shoots up too much?"

That's the first question Dave Navarro asked as we began this collaboration on June 1, 1998, making it clear that I had more than a life story on my hands: I had a life. Not a series of past events filtered through the dirty grate of memory, but a heart that was still beating. To document the beating of that heart was the goal, and if the past was relevant at all, it was only as the blood that coursed through that heart and gave it a reason to beat. Or to not beat. Because at times, that heart didn't want to beat.

That night, Navarro showed me what he called his *Spread* movie. It began with a phone call to a rehab center. Navarro told the operator that he was in trouble and needed help badly; the operator said she'd call back later. The rest of the movie was a series of scenes he had filmed to the accompaniment of his music. It centered around three images: a spoon in a bowl of Jell-O, symbolizing the nourishment of his past; a spoon with a rock of cocaine, symbolizing the nourishment of his present; and a picture of his mother, the bond that connected both spoons. In the movie, he shoots up with a picture of his mother in the background, an image all the more disturbing if you consider that Navarro's mother was murdered by an ex-boyfriend, a man Navarro had grown to trust. Occasionally, the camera would pan to a computer screen, which displayed the phone number of his lawyer and directions on how to find a certain song in his CD changer.

The movie seemed disgusting not because

of the images, but because of Navarro's eagerness to exploit a tragedy for the sake of a self-aggrandizing art film. At least, that's what I thought until Navarro said it wasn't an art film. It was his will. The song in the CD changer, which he wanted played over and over at his funeral, was "This Is How We Do It" by Montell Jordan.

"That was my checkout movie," he said. "It was supposed to be a note of explanation before I ended it. I was going to take a bunch of pills afterward, because I thought it wouldn't be as ugly as being found with a needle in my arm and blood all over the place. I got the idea from *Final Exit,* which I always considered a how-to manual. But when I started editing the video, somehow it showed me there was something to live for, there was something *else* I could do creatively. I realized that because I was getting picky about certain scenes and wanted to reshoot parts. I guess I cared."

Navarro stood up and rolled thick black curtains across his picture window overlooking L.A. ("I bought a house with a picture window so I could imagine myself pissing on L.A."), as if that would keep the sun from rising. And it did, at least for us and Mary, a statuesque, raven-haired drug dealer who sat mutely on the floor with her arms wrapped around her knees. A beautiful South Dakota girl too smart for her hometown, she moved to Los Angeles seeking a new life and somehow wound up selling drugs to people like Navarro, Leif Garrett, and Marilyn Manson. Sitting limply at her feet was her ladybug backpack and a needle dragon, a felt animal-shaped zipper bag containing syringes instead of the pencils for which it was intended.

All does not seem well at Navarro's Hollywood Hills home. But at the same time, things have never been better. Since a messy split with the Red Hot Chili Peppers and the suitably named Jane's Addiction Relapse tour, Navarro has been in a strange transition. In the months leading up to June, everything changed for him. His career as a guitarist in two famous rock bands ended; he had a messy parting with the label that was going to release his solo project; he turned his back on the friends and relatives closest to him; he suffered a rough breakup with his girlfriend, Adria; he started shooting up coke and heroin again; and he bought a photo booth.

Socially, artistically, and chemically, Navarro restructured his entire life—or had it restructured for him—with the photo booth serving as a way of systematizing the friends, dealers, prostitutes, and strangers passing in and out of it. By the end of this yearlong book project, a process piece chronicling twelve months of his life in photo-booth strips, essays, and conversations, the outcome of these changes will become clear. This is a story that will either have a happy ending or a tragic one: there is no in-between.

"Maybe I'll die and make the book a bestseller for you," Navarro said that first night. It would have been easy to laugh off the comment or think of it as a self-pitying plea designed to make the listener feel uncomfortable, but it was not a joke or a test. As he spoke, he tied off his left arm with an RCA cable and plunged a syringe into his arm, tapping the plunger as the phone rang. He picked it up, needle dangling from his skin like a cigarette from someone's lips, and put the caller, Marilyn Manson's drug-addled bassist Twiggy Ramirez, on speakerphone. Twiggy had just snorted a fingernail-size line of Ketamine, a cat tranquilizer, and was freaking out. His walls and *Star Wars* toys were closing in on him, the red wine wasn't bringing him down, and he wanted to come over.

One of the biggest changes Navarro made in his life this month was in transforming his Hollywood Hills house into a cross between a crack den, an after-hours club, a halfway house, and Andy Warhol's Factory. It became a fucked-up focal point for wretched freaks and glamorous stars to gather and discover that inside, the freaks feel like stars and the stars like freaks. The house is best summarized by the road sign perched one hundred feet uphill: DEAD END: NO TURNAROUND.

"I used to feel like life was such a fucking chore that all I ever really looked forward to was going home and turning myself off in an environment that was somewhat of a sanctuary," Navarro, shirtless with Calvin Kleins creeping out of his jeans, said about the house's past. "It had to be immaculately clean and free of responsibility. I was living my life very much in a regimented fashion, following the strict way of health and sanity. I was drug-free and I was so fucking strict about the wrong things, like what I ate and put into my body and how I looked, that I was miserable. I could never leave a dish in a sink because that meant I was focusing on all the outside stuff. There was something to do, and I couldn't relax as a result of it."

But when Navarro decided that on an emotional level he didn't feel any better, he relapsed—returning to the drug habit he thought he had kicked five years earlier. It was a conscious decision, he always says, not a matter of circumstances. At the same time, he started making his checkout movie, and in order to get more footage he opened his house to other people for the first time.

"I decided to give in and just live moment-to-moment how I wanted to, and see if that would do away with the emotional weight that I was carrying. I always felt uncomfortable because I was constantly thinking about what I should be doing and what was coming up. So I decided to say, 'Fucking hell with it.' I decided to see what it was like to be less uptight. Since the option of death was always available, I had nothing to lose. If somebody came over and spilled a glass of wine on the couch, I could always kill myself."

Then came the photo booth, a triumph in

cynicism, mistrust, and fear of abandonment. Though the project of documenting everyone who steps in the house (minimum one photo strip per person per month) over the course of one year is so many things, at its core it is an experiment to prove or disprove Navarro Hypothesis #1: The only people who stay in your life are the ones you pay. Your friends and family will disappear, but the cleaning lady, the pizza delivery man, and the drug dealer are forever.

So who do we have in June? Eight rock stars, seven television crew members, six music executives, five sycophants who were either kicked out or barred from the house by their visit's end, four actors, three drug dealers, two prostitutes, one cleaning lady, and a dog.

The photos tell one story; the house tells another. The month had its share of tales that would be whispered about at Hollywood bars: Leif Garrett coming over at 6:30 A.M. to fix a curtain rod in exchange for drugs; Rose McGowan picking up what she thought was a stack of poker chips only to be told by fiancé Marilyn Manson that it was a masturbation sleeve a prostitute had given Navarro; the entire crew of a television show waiting outside for forty-five minutes as the producer futilely tried to wake a partied-out Navarro, checking his pulse to make sure he was alive; Navarro jotting down his phone number on a syringe wrapper for a horrified music executive; and Navarro briefly dating an über-groupie in order to put his hands where Jimmy Page's hands had been.

Then there's the night Manson and Dave spent two hours computer-manipulating a photograph of a scantily clad Courtney Love lying sprawled outside Trent Reznor's hotel room so that they could first transcribe the psychotic rant she had written in lipstick on his door and then blow up a picture of her vagina to use as an album cover for Dave's demos.

But perhaps the best tales that the month

Then came the photo booth, a triumph in cynicism, mistrust, and fear of abandonment.

NAVARRO HYPOTHESIS **#1:**

The only people who stay in your life are the ones you pay. Your friends and family will ***disappear,*** *but the cleaning lady, the pizza delivery man, and the drug dealer* ***are forever.***

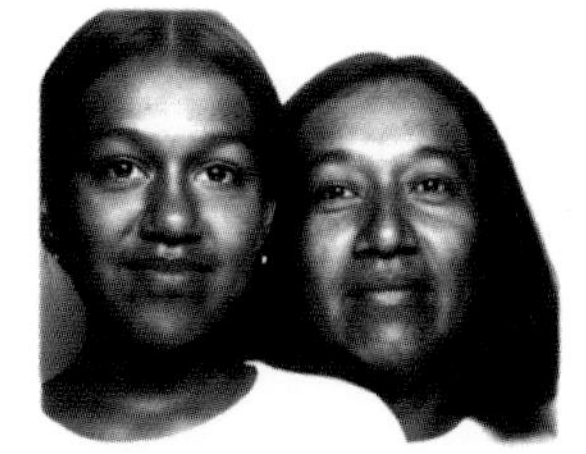

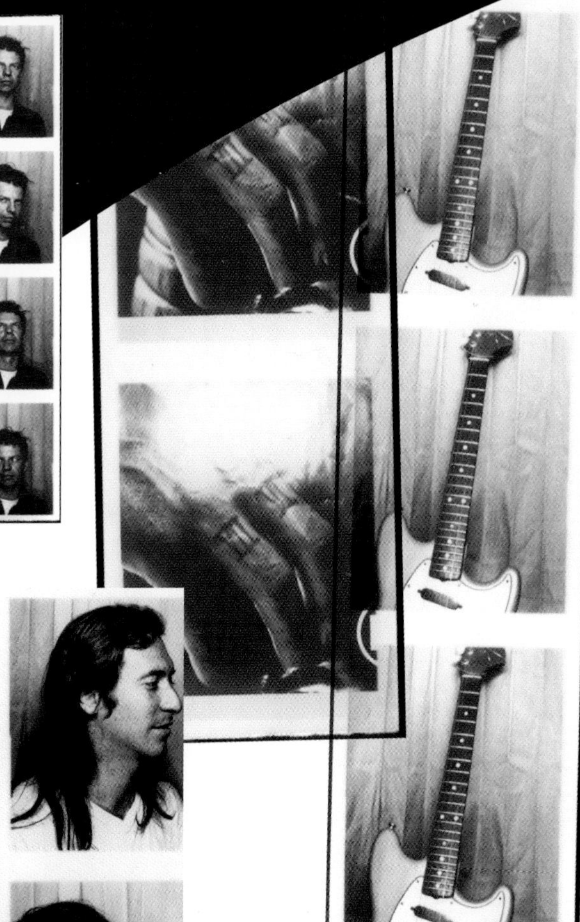

HIDE

produced took place on the rare nights when Navarro actually left his dwelling place and social laboratory, a feat in itself considering the strong magnetic pull the house has come to have over him. And each time, his destination was a party at the Playboy Mansion (that is, with the exception of a two-minute appearance at his own birthday party at the club Barfly on June 7, which Hugh Hefner actually attended with the three blondes he was concurrently dating in tow).

For the first of two Playboy parties in June, Dave and Twiggy rented a limousine to bring them to the mansion. But as the car arrived to pick them up, Navarro turned to answer the door and knocked one of his small glass unicorns off a shelf. Picking it up, he noticed that its horn had broken off. He searched the floor, but the tiny horn was nowhere to be found. The limo driver honked impatiently.

"Let's go, let's go," Twiggy urged, jumping around with his usual childlike energy.

"Dude, I can't," Dave said darkly, crawling around the floor on all fours. "I have to get that horn. I feel like bad things are going to happen to me if I can't find it."

Obsessed, Navarro spent the next hour using a lamp with the shade removed as a substitute flashlight, searching for the horn whose loss he considered a symbolic disaster. This logic was either drug-addled obsessive-compulsive behavior, or an excuse to keep from going out. Eventually, he found the unicorn fragment, which had been kicked underneath the rug, and made it to the party, where—with the lucky horn in his pocket—he picked up a Playmate and a Penthouse Pet. The Playmate was an argumentative model who quickly earned herself the nickname The Pooper as she constantly tried to manipulate the events of the night in the direction of gas stations, diners, and bars where she could take foul-smelling shits in private. The drop-dead gorgeous Pet, renamed Where's My Purse after misplacing her handbag eight times that night, went on to earn herself the honor of being quite possibly the stupidest woman ever to sleep with Twiggy. And that says a lot. In later visits to Dave's in June, Where's My Purse would get lost as many as twenty times trying to find the house, calling for new directions with each wrong turn.

Dave's next visit to the Playboy Mansion would be his last; not by choice but by necessity. His companion this time was Melissa, a petite brunette with a large wound on her back as a result of recent friction with the carpet in Dave's studio, which still bears the corresponding bloodstain. Melissa had been excited about the party for months, spending three hours that evening getting ready. When she finally showed up at Dave's, dressed in new clothes from Fred Segal, she found him sleeping. She was so upset that she burst out crying as she shook him awake.

After she finally coaxed Dave into the shower, the doorbell rang. Melissa, tears of dashed expectations still in her eyes, answered the door to find a very dolled-up prostitute with stiletto heels and a garter belt hanging from the bottom of her skirt. The woman, a former Heidi Fleiss escort, held a bag full of hooker clothes in one hand and doggie biscuits in the other. Melissa stood there speechless.

Dave walked upstairs in his underwear, looked at her, and—much to Melissa's disappointment—knew her name. "Sara!" he exclaimed. "It's not cool for you to just do a drop-by without calling."

"Well," she said, "I'm dropping these clothes and dog biscuits off for Sylvia," another prostitute. Then she proceeded to sit on the couch, pull a crack pipe out of her purse, and light it with a small silver torch.

Dave asked her to leave and then ran downstairs. "What the fuck?" Melissa yelled after him. "We're late for the party. Enough of this drama. Let's go already!"

But instead, Dave called Sylvia, who came by

for her belongings. He then proceeded to sit on the couch and carry on a long conversation with Sylvia about how it wasn't cool for the other prostitute to do a drop-by. As Sylvia's dog ran laps around the house, Melissa sat isolated in a desk chair, smoke practically rising from her salon-styled hair, repeating to herself, "This is not happening, this is not happening."

While Dave and Sylvia continued to chat away, Melissa called a limo, which took an hour and a half to arrive. By the time the two of them finally arrived at the Playboy Mansion, the party was well into its fifth hour of revelry.

Wandering through the estate's tacky game room, they noticed a girl following them. And when Navarro walked into the bathroom, the girl slipped inside with him. "Oh my God, Dave Navarro!" she gushed. "I fucking love you."

Afterward, she trailed behind Dave and Melissa until they all found themselves in the larger of the game room's orgy chambers, with mood music playing, a spongy floor, adjustable soft lighting, and boxes of tissues around the room. Dave's interest in entering the room was purely in getting his drugs in his system, but as the group walked in, a third girl Dave knew appeared.

As Dave sat down to pull out his supplies, he suddenly found three naked women using the orgy room as it was intended. "It was like something out of a movie—and it was all happening as I pulled out a syringe and got high, which to me was part of the decadence," he remembers.

In a gesture not unlike the Fiona Apple incident that landed Navarro in trouble (spraying a message to the singer in blood—or, as he puts it, from the bottom of his heart—on her dressing room mirror at a concert), Navarro took out his rig and started writing on the wall of the orgy room in blood. "The mansion has always been somehow holy to me, and I began to feel weird," he says. "All my life I'd wondered what it was like, and here I was at thirty squirting blood on the walls with three naked girls at my feet. So I cleaned it off. But it was too late. They had the whole thing on video. When we left the room, several security guards escorted me out of the mansion and asked me never to return. I wonder what they did with the video."

That was one thing Navarro and Hefner had in common: they were avid documentarians. In months to come, not only would there be a photo booth in Navarro's house, but there would also be a tape recorder under the couch, a recording device hooked up to the phone, surveillance cameras outside the front door, and several fake VCRs and clocks with hidden cameras capturing the alternately mundane and bizarre events taking place at the end of this dead-end street.

It's important to note that for Navarro, like Hefner, the installation of these low-tech devices was not just a product of paranoia. It was life as art, with most of the evidence routinely uploaded onto the elaborate Internet homepage Navarro started this same month and worked on obsessively during his sleepless days and nights.

bebe
bebe

part II THIS IS HOW I DO IT

BY DAVE NAVARRO

One of the ideas that I am attempting to execute on my own is to allow the audience a chance to have a glimpse at what it is that I am actually whining about. Many times, artists have made me say to myself, "Sure, you're sad. But you have a great life, so stop whimpering and trying to sell it to us!!!! How full of shit you are to think that I could ever believe that you are a miserable, suffering, dark, and misunderstood loner when you are 'made up' to appear that way in some video!!!"

Don't get me wrong. I am not invalidating the right of an artist to express his or her pain; I am simply challenging it. I believe and feel that a positive future can come from the expression of a negative past. This part of the healing process, not to mention *any* part, has yet to be shown to me by any of the whimpering babies out there today. As some of you know, I am not a huge follower of contemporary music, so perhaps I am wrong. I suppose that I just haven't heard about them/it/him/her yet. Just know that there is the possibility of a time in one's life when gratitude for the wrongs done to us and those we love is in order.

This is not to say that I am happy I lost a loved one. I have simply come to a place in my life where I can be thankful for the losses and troubled times I have been through, as well as the love-filled and magical times. My experiences with drugs fall into both of these categories. Now of course I would never claim that we should all have our mothers killed to find a future with which we are happy. However, the same concept applies to all misfortunes. We all have different elements of our lives that are the ingredients of who we are as individuals. I have been asked, "Your work is so personal. Do you expect us to relate to all of the mother and loss issues you confront?"

My answer is yes, because everyone has lost something they have loved: a puppy, a girlfriend or boyfriend, a parent, a baseball card, etc. My mother is, for me, a symbol of all things lost and irreplaceable. The creative process of moving through the experience of loss, and learning from such experiences, is where the gratitude for life and all experiences comes from.

This book contains many depictions of graphic and drug-related moments in my life. These moments are included to establish the serious and sometimes life-threatening times in my life. I am not, in any way, promoting and/or encouraging drug use. My intention is to point out and re-reinforce the reality of danger within such actions and life choices. At the same time, I refuse to omit these moments, as they are, in some ways, a factor in the equation of how and why I am where I am today.

My mother is, for me, a symbol of all things

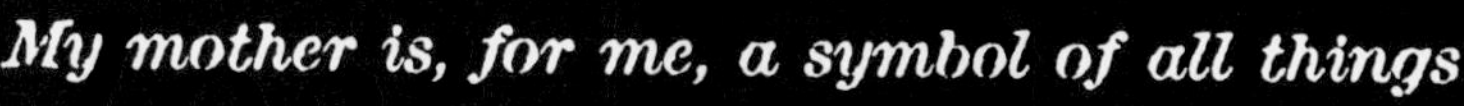

part III HOW THE RECORD INDUSTRY IS LIKE A UNICORN

FRIDAY, JUNE 19, *was not the best night at Navarro's house, nor was it the worst. It was a typical night that produced an atypical tale.*

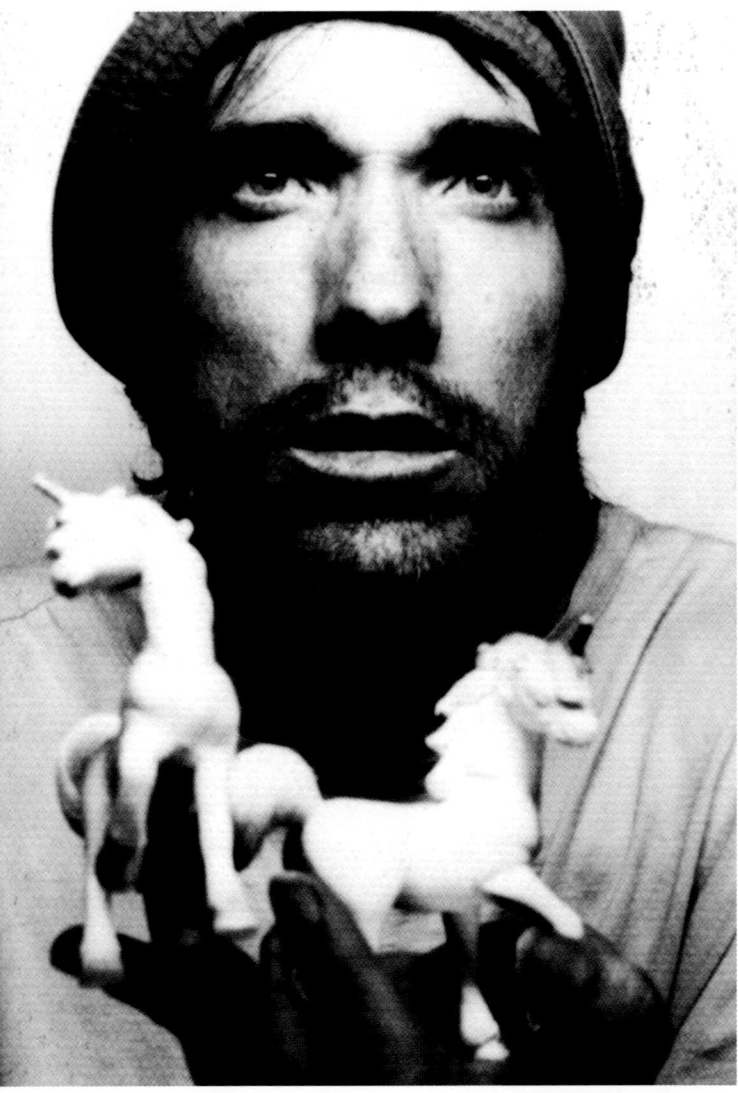

BIJOU PHILLIPS: Dave, have you ever shot heroin into your dick?

DAVE: Come over here. We're recording a story. Like to hear it? Some names and places will be changed to protect the innocent.

When I was seven years old, I was moderately happy. I came from a house in Laurel Canyon and . . .

[*phone rings*]

WOMAN'S VOICE: Hello. May I speak to Mary?

DAVE: She's not in right now. May I take a message?

WOMAN: This is Beth Ann from Triple A.

DAVE: Oh, you want Bijou. Just a moment.

[Phone conversation omitted.]

DAVE: Anyway, I felt that I was not good enough to be commingling with the people that I went to school with. I went to school all the time with this inferiority complex. The school was in Bel-Air, and we had to wear uniforms and every kid was rich and got dropped off in a fancy car. Lisa Marie Presley was two grades under me, and there was a day when Elvis dropped her off with fucking cops on bikes protecting him. I had no idea who Elvis was. All I knew was that I didn't have a police escort.

This was around the time my parents were getting divorced. I remember seeing a commercial about the circus coming to town, and I had a Barnum and Bailey poster in my room that I would always misread and mispronounce, trying to imagine what the poster was supposed to be advertising. I would make up all kinds of things, like it was a ride or a movie or a type of coffee. The only distinct thing about it was that there was a polar bear on it.

So this commercial came on TV saying that the circus has a unicorn—"The world's first and only unicorn in captivity! Come see it! Don't miss it! It's the greatest thing ever!" I was so excited—like, "Wow, a fucking unicorn, this is unbelievable"—and I begged my parents to take me to the circus.

So, anyway, we go to the circus and there are trapeze artists and other circus things and, to add to the atmosphere, I'll say that I had too much to eat, though I can't really remember. The truth is, I was waiting to see the unicorn. That's all I knew. And then the lights went down and there was a drumroll and spotlights cruising around the tent, and the announcer says, "Ladies and gentlemen, the first unicorn! It's incredible." And they wheel out, on a rickety little cart, this baby goat with a fucked-up horn coming out of the side of its head at a forty-five-degree angle. And it's shaking and letting out this terrified *baa*. I was picturing a magical creature, an illustrious, strong, white, muscle-bound horse glistening with freedom and magic, and instead it was this scared little baby goat being pulled around on a decrepit cart by a pack of clowns. I got incredibly sad and felt so bad for the goat.

I looked around the rest of the circus, and everybody was thrilled and excited, taking pictures and going "Wow!" And I kind of felt guilty. I never made the connection until years later, but it was as if because I was so excited to see it, I was one of the people who caused it to be there. It was my doing.

I guess that was my first memory of being flat-out lied to. Those were the years when I learned about lies. I had this pet turtle named Frank, and one day I came home and he was gone. I asked my mother where Frank was, and she said he went to turtle heaven. I was bummed out and I went outside to play. For some reason, I went into the trash cans by the side of the house and I saw Frank lying in the trash. I went back inside and told my mom, "Hey, Mom, remember how you told me that Frank was in turtle heaven?"

And she said, "Yeah."

Then I said, "Well, how come he's outside in the trash?"

And she didn't have an answer for me.

Those years are so important in a child's life—they mold your psyche, and I felt like I was being lied to all the time. When I'd hear yelling in the house at night, I'd wake up and come into my parents' room and they would tell me that the dog was in the house, making a mess. Even at that age, I knew what the truth was: they'd been fighting.

BIJOU: I'm serious, Dave, have you ever shot heroin into your dick?

DAVE: It also seems that in my childhood I equated animals with my first feelings of love. And abandonment, because I kept losing them. There was Frank the turtle, the unicorn, a bird named Tweety that died, and a dog named Dusty that my parents gave away when they got divorced. There was a cat that got hit by a car in front of my house, and I found it lying there in the street with its guts hanging out.

It was just a fucked time in my life, and when my parents finally split up, somehow it was all my fault. I knew that because after they divorced, my mom sent me to see a child psychologist. And my perception was that if I'm going to the doctor, there must be something wrong with me. And since I'm going to the doctor because my parents aren't together anymore, I must have caused that.

BIJOU: That's so sad. But what about shooting up into your dick?

DAVE: Well, not into my dick. But because of my dick.

part IV STALKED

One of the people working on a documentary about the Jane's Addiction reunion tour calls Dave to warn him that he has just given a girl Dave's phone number. Now, this is not a typical girl, brought to Dave's attention because she may be a perfect soulmate, bedmate, or coffeemate. This is a girl who has been stopping by the homes of movie crew members a little too much, almost every day, in fact. She has also been spotted snooping around Jane's Addiction singer Perry Farrell's house and loitering on his doorstep.

The girl has been insisting that Dave is in danger, that his mother has been communicating with her, that his ex-girlfriend Adria is a black witch, and that she needs to talk to him. It's a matter of life and death for him, for her, and for many others, she keeps saying. The guy working on the documentary, for some reason, believes her. Maybe it's because she's blond (dyed), not unattractive (slightly pudgy with smooth, creamy skin), and seems very sane on first impression (even on second or third impression—basically until she starts talking about the magical powers and insights she claims to possess).

Dave, it turns out, has actually met this girl before: two years earlier at a car wash. He remembers only her strange fashion sense, which seemed stuck in a very *Flashdance* period of the eighties, and the fact that she is the kind of person who thinks that when she's staring at you she's being intense and mysterious when all she's really being is annoying.

After several of Dave's other friends call him with strange messages from this girl, he decides to call her back at four A.M. one morning. He is pissed off. "Do I know you?" he says as soon as she picks up the phone. "It's Dave Navarro."

Before the word "Hi" finishes squeaking out of her lips, Dave is off and running. "I want to know what's going on. My friends have been telling me that you're talking to my mother. And that you've been discussing personal, intimate details regarding my life."

She stutters and grows flustered, caught off guard, but finally manages to tap into her inner neurosis. She explains that when he is hurting his body or doing drugs, he is hurting her and she wants to help. "You are on the wrong path," she warns, trying to sound prophetic. "And the end of that path is not a bright reality."

"It doesn't take a fucking genius to tell me that," Dave says. "I've been on the wrong path for years."

"Your relationship with Perry [Farrell] is hurting you, because you are on a separate path from him," she intones.

"I've always been on a separate path from him, and I really don't have any relationship with him right now. So what? My next door neighbor has told me the exact same thing, and he actually knows it."

"You are entering a perilous space," she continues. "And you are in very serious danger of hurting yourself and everyone around you."

Soon it becomes clear that the girl wants what many people in Hollywood want. She wants to get close to a star. Some deal drugs to do that, others find work as entertainment accountants, and others become prostitutes or groupies. She just happens to have become a stalker. "I love you, I need you," she begs as Dave tries to extricate himself from the conversation he started. "Don't go away."

Suddenly it dawns on Dave: she isn't trying to help him at all. She wants him to help her.

"Why do you try to take your own life?" she asks.

"You know what?" Dave says, deciding to lie. "That was all made up in the press to create an image. I've never tried to kill myself. So if your feelings are telling you that I have, then you're misinterpreting the signals and you'd better take another look at this gift you think you have. The problem is not me; the problem is that if you have this gift, you need to learn how to cope with it. I can't help you."

There is silence on the other end. "What is it in your mind that makes you think I can help you?" Dave continues.

"You can love yourself. And that will help me."

"I do love myself. Don't you find what you're doing to me invasive and insensitive?"

"You need to love yourself unselfishly."

"Listen! I believe that in this universe there is some sort of spiritual lesson that will present itself to me and that will allow me to learn to love myself more if I need to. And that will happen when it's time. But I certainly don't believe that you're the person who has been sent to me, because if you have so much insight and you have such a spiritual message for me, it wouldn't have been brought about in a way that's terrifying to me and my friends."

Of course, this kind of exchange doesn't discourage a stalker. It only encourages her because she is now making a connection that is deeper than just fantasy. The man she is obsessed with is actually speaking with her, acknowledging that he is aware of her existence on this planet. Even if the exchange is an angry one, they are feeling emotion for one another. And that constitutes a relationship.

After the conversation, she begins calling Dave's house regularly. Members of Dave's family suddenly start phoning, saying that she has been harassing them. In her phone messages (Dave changes his phone service so that it doesn't accept blocked calls), she tells Dave that she hears voices and that the voices are telling her that there are a lot of people she has to help.

"Well, if there are a lot of people and not just me, then you're really in trouble," he tells her when, one evening, she catches him on the phone. "Because if you think that you can affect my life and change it to ultimately better my future and in turn yours, and then in turn the world, then what you're essentially saying is that you're acting as a god. And I don't believe for a second that you're acting as a god here on this earth. Because to touch my life and change the future is a power that I don't believe you have. And if you do have it, I don't want to know anything about it because I want my path to unfold on its own."

But inside, Dave is worried. When his doorbell rings unexpectedly or he hears footsteps in the house, he thinks it's her. Friends think Dave is overreacting when he says he's scared, but he snaps at them and tells them an obsessed man killed his mother and aunt. So of course he's going to overreact.

However, after the god exchange with Dave, she never calls him or his friends again. But it's too late. She has already gotten to him, and he can't keep from worrying: Where has she gone? And, even worse, what if she is right?

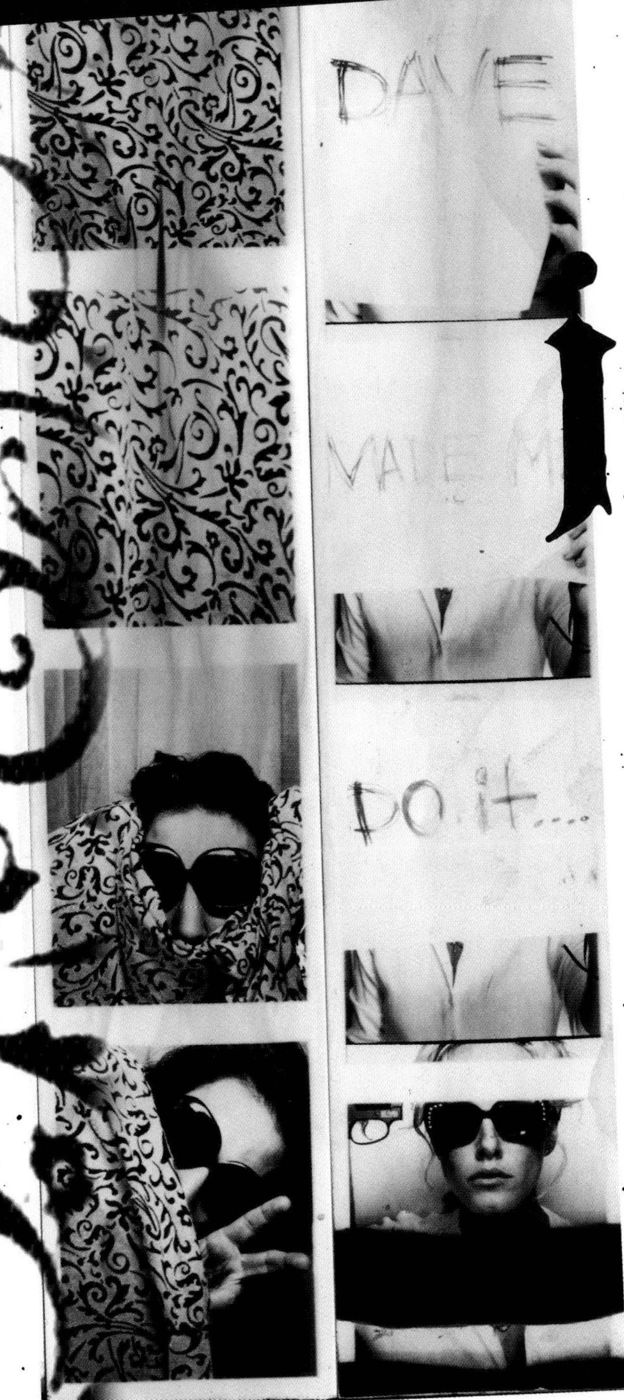

july

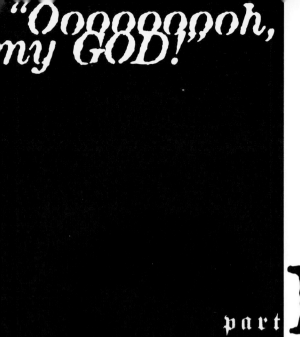

part I THE FIRST PERSON DAVE'S PAID TO COME OVER TO HIS HOUSE WHO HAS ACTUALLY KEPT HER CLOTHES ON

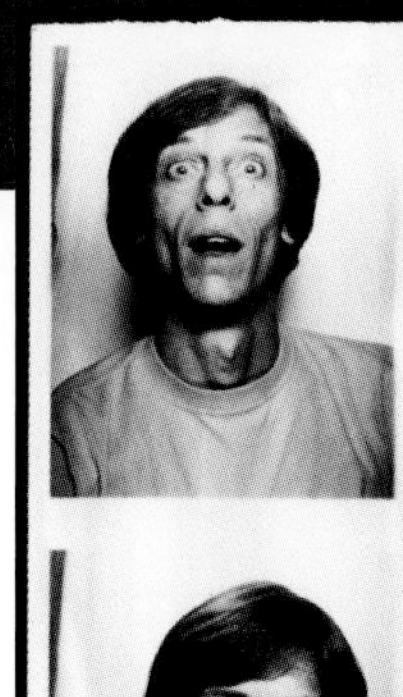
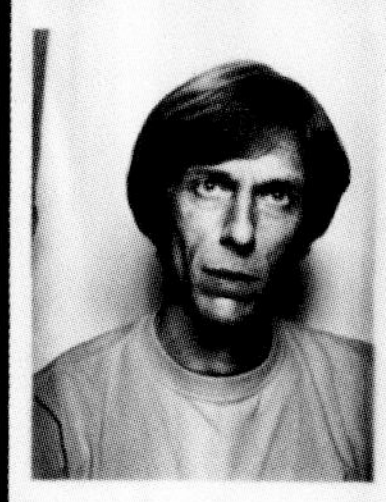
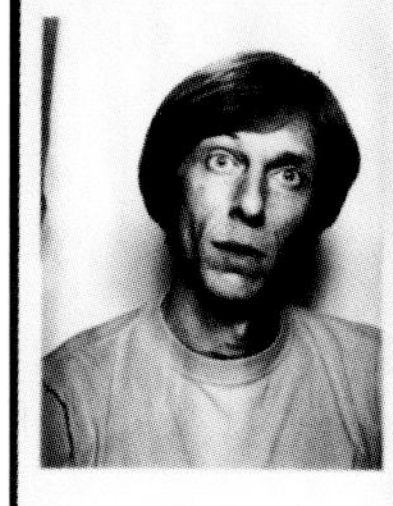
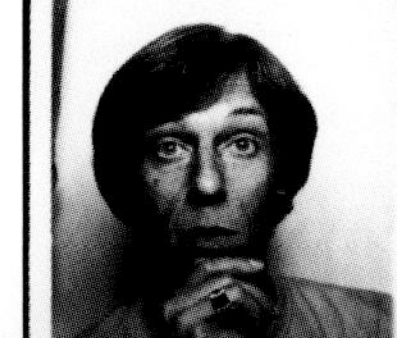
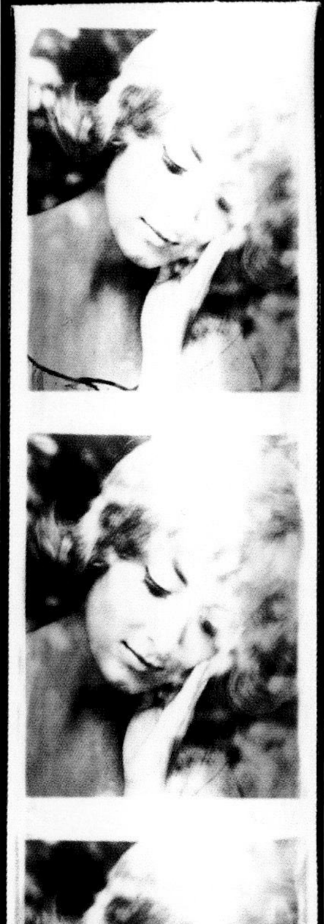

She won't get out of the car. Navarro has waited so long for this day, worked so hard for it, spent so much money (more than a thousand dollars, in fact), and she won't get out of the goddamned car. She's just sitting there outside, talking with her manager, who is standing next to her pink convertible pleading in a hushed whisper. Within an hour, she will feel like one of Navarro's closest friends. But right now she doesn't want to go anywhere near him.

Navarro's obsession with this woman began when all he knew of Hollywood and the Sunset Strip was what he glimpsed from the backseat of his father's car. When he saw billboards of Angelyne—larger, blonder, and bustier than life—the advertisement worked. She sold herself to him as not just a star, but *the* star, the ideal embodiment of the Hollywood holy trinity of glamour, success, and desire. But, like the advertisements for the circus unicorn he had seen as a child, reality did not conform to expectation.

As he grew older and saw her around town, he began to realize that she wasn't a real star or a great beauty. She was a sideshow attraction. He finally met her when he was eighteen and new to the L.A. club world. He was sitting at the bar of the Pyramid Club improvising a sculpture out of glasses, ashtrays, and purses when Zatar, the manager, walked over dressed in his usual jumpsuit. Dave had been banned from the club for the past two weeks because his last sculpture had collapsed and set the bar on fire. Either in order to apologize to Navarro or to impress Angelyne, Zatar brought her over to meet Dave. Young, bashful, and excited, Dave meekly raised his hand to shake hers. She glanced at it, then turned her head in the other direction.

As the Siouxsie and the Banshees song "Spellbound" blasted out of the speakers, Zatar yelled into Angelyne's ear that Dave was from Jane's Addiction. Her attitude suddenly changed. She turned toward Dave, face lit up, and began talking a mile a minute like they were best friends.

Normally, that would have been the final stroke of disillusionment, the end of the fantasy. But, after some time, it became a moment of reillusionment. Because to Dave, with that sensibility, Angelyne became an even more accurate embodiment of Los Angeles.

"To me, she's a human being Andy Warhol would have created," Navarro says, "a pop culture icon out of the Factory. The other thing I find attractive about her is that she has become a mythical creature, like the Loch Ness monster. You have to go to a certain area to look for her, and even then you never know if you will see her or whether she'll look anything like the photographs."

Around 1993, after a tae kwon do class on Santa Monica Boulevard, he ran into Angelyne's manager of ten years, Scott Hennig, whom he recognized from an Angelyne documentary. He begged Scott for a poster and hung it in his garage, where, like the picture of Dorian Gray, it yellowed and wrinkled as Angelyne stayed the same. Soon after the photo booth arrived, Dave took the poster down and taped it to the inside of the booth, and the image of Angelyne became an early photo strip. Now it was time to obtain the real thing.

There are few who truly know where Angelyne came from or what her real name is. There are just the rumors. According to what seems to be Angelyne's most truthful version of her story, she was born in Idaho. Her parents died when she was young and she moved to Hollywood with hopes of becoming a star. She sang in a band—punk rock, she says—and it was while promoting her music that she began plastering her face around town. As the band dissipated, the posters and billboards continued, now promoting nothing more than the living product into which Angelyne was fast turning herself.

"Some people become famous for being in music, films, TV, sports, whatever," she says on her website. "I became famous through billboards. No one had ever done that before or even thought it was possible."

Why billboards? "Billboards are huge," she continues. "I love huge. I am huge."

And thus Navarro's obsession with getting her in the booth. "If she's about huge," he said, "and I am taking the tiniest picture I can take of her, that's amazing."

So Navarro called Angelyne's manager, Scott, and presented his proposal. She has turned down *Playboy* covers, major movie roles, modeling jobs, and countless interviews, but, surprisingly, she accepted Dave's offer. First, however, Scott had to come over and inspect Dave's place to make sure it was up to the standards of his client.

He stopped by on a Tuesday, two days before Angelyne's appointment on Thursday. He was tall and skinny, with a deep voice, a slightly backdated midwestern twang (as if at any minute he was going to say "aw, shucks"), and the awkward self-confidence of a genius computer hacker.

"To me, she's a human being ndy Warhol would have created," avarro says, "a pop culture icon out f the Factory. The other thing I find tractive about her is that **she as become a ythical reature, like he Loch Ness onster.** You have o go to a certain area to look for her nd even then you never know if you ill see her or whether she'll look nything like the photographs."

He was like a geek version of Jim Carroll, and, in his mind, Angelyne was the goddess that she portrays herself to be. He seemed to see himself as a chamberpot to the queen: he knew all her dirty secrets and wasn't going to let them out, no matter how much Dave pried.

"How old is she?" Dave asked.

"Young enough to be doing it but old enough to be doing it right," Scott replied.

"Is that the answer you give everybody?"

"I just made it up."

Around one of Scott's belt loops hung a plastic and metal gadget that looked like a cell phone, but clearly wasn't. When he went into the photo booth for his picture, he took it off and very carefully laid it on the oak table nearby. He was afraid to leave it alone in the room while he had the curtain of the photo booth drawn, but at the same time he seemed nervous about bringing it into the photo booth.

"Why don't you just take that in with you?" Dave asked.

"Believe me," he replied, suddenly serious, "there are plenty of better ways to die."

The gadget, he explained after taking his photo strip, was a communicator from the original *Star Trek* television show, used to transmit such lines as "Beam me up, Scotty." It was the holy grail to any *Star Trek* fan, and had cost him three thousand dollars.

"I've got a lot of stuff like my communicator," he explained, "a lot of strange metaphysical items. And Angelyne's very much into that too. That type of magic and power works in Hollywood, because that's what Hollywood's all about."

He piously picked up his communicator. "You can reach anywhere with this," he continued. "I've made a hundred phone calls on it, and it works."

"What do you mean by phone calls?" Dave asked.

"You can communicate with whomever you want, even if they're dead. But you can't say anything about *Star Trek* into it or you'll die."

He held it in his hands and offered it to Dave. "I thought that maybe you could use it to talk with your mother."

"No, that's all right," Dave deferred. But Scott insisted and pleaded, so persistently that he began to seem more eccentric than Angelyne. Eventually Navarro took the prop, stuck it in the photo booth, and took a picture of it alone, which didn't seem to bother Scott. Nobody died, although Navarro did break a fingernail later that day.

Despite not using the communicator to channel the dead, Navarro passed the test, or so it seemed until Angelyne pulled up outside and wouldn't leave her pink Corvette—one in her fleet of four.

Scott stands next to her, lurching over the top, trying to convince her it is okay to come into the house. Inside, Navarro and his assistant, Jen, have been preparing all day—cleaning, hiding drug paraphernalia, and ordering the pizzas and Diet Pepsi Angelyne requested. Now they watch the black-and-white silhouette of Angelyne and her manager in heated discussion on Dave's security camera monitor and try to figure out what they can do to make her feel comfortable.

Finally, Scott comes inside and tells Dave to go out and talk to her. Navarro, blessed with the power to seduce anybody through mere conversation, cautiously approaches the car and leans in. All he has to say is, "Hi, I'm Dave," and within minutes she is posing for photographs in front of the Corvette.

"You can take a picture of my car," she offers magnanimously.

"Get where it says ANGELYNE," Scott suggests proudly, pointing to the license plate. "She's a pro at this." He turns to Angelyne: "Do you want to leave your door open?"

"No, close it," she says in her helium-fed Marilyn Monroe voice, facing the Corvette and arching her back. "Do you like my leg up or down?"

"Up is great," Dave says gently, cautiously. "Now, let's try down. Thank you so much. No one will believe this."

She wears a very short leopard-print dress with three large pink vinyl hearts up the front, matching gloves, big white glasses, and gold high heels. Her hair billows blond, rolling over her shoulders and framing her impressive cleavage. She has always claimed to be in her early thirties with a completely natural figure, and Dave plays along.

Dave shows her around his house. Through it all, Angelyne coos and oohs and squeals and chirps, as if she is a forties starlet too famous to age. She loves his Basquiat drawing with the words "Tin Tar Lead" drawn in marker, early Warhol print of a shoe, and guitar that used to belong to Kurt Cobain.

"You know, I couldn't get rid of his ghost for the longest time," she says.

"What do you mean?"

"His ghost would follow me everywhere." She is talking about Kurt Cobain.

"Oh, honey, I remember that," Scott agrees.

She turns the corner into the next room and bumps into the wall. "That must be his ghost again," she says. No one knows whether they are supposed to laugh.

Jen, wearing a T-shirt with 22 emblazoned on the back, sits at the computer, which has Angelyne's website on display.

"Twenty-two," Angelyne squeaks. "That's the best number in the zodiac! That's my most benefic, magnificent number. If something happens to you on a twenty-two it stays with you forever. Twenty-two was the first day I put up my billboards—and it hasn't stopped since."

"That's right, honey, it hasn't."

Angelyne fiddles with the straps on the back of her dress, where a pair of safety pins completes the illusion of voluptuousness, and looks at the picture that hangs over Dave's computer. It is a painting of a mother unicorn cuddling her son underneath a rainbow on a riverbank. Dave found the painting on the Internet and obtained it from the artist, Tim Jacobus. He has been considering using it as the cover of his solo album because it represents everything he never had in his life.

"I'm into gods and fairies," Angelyne says as she surveys the painting. It is clear that Dave isn't giving her a tour of his house anymore; she is giving the tour to him.

"I was once where the rainbow hit," she continues. "I was in the rainbow. I was in the orange. Each ring had a different color and you could move through each ring. It was amazing."

"I've never seen that in my life," Navarro says, with either genuine or theatrical admiration.

"No one ever has," she responds matter-of-factly.

On Dave's table—a coffin with the lid closed and crumbs from past drug use still in plain view—there are two copies of *Final Exit.*

"I read that," Angelyne gasps, raising her voice with each word.

"I think of it as a how-to book," Dave says. "I look to it for ideas, I guess."

If Angelyne understands what he is saying, it doesn't register. "Did you read a book called *How We Die*? It's really fascinating."

As she speaks, her manager wanders onto Navarro's balcony, surveying the Sunset Strip below for a billboard site visible from the Hollywood Hills. "Between Crescent Heights going into the curve of Beverly Hills is the most expensive strip of billboard advertising in the United States," he explains. "It can run you ten thousand dollars a month plus."

He surveys the land like a developer, examining each sign along the Strip. "Sometimes we'll go up to Griffith Park and use telescopes and things like that to see what area has the most visibility. You know, we turn down seventy percent of the offers we get because we've accomplished what we set out to do just with billboards. She doesn't have to do anything else unless she wants to. Most people are so crazy for their next job, but she's the exact opposite. She's reached her goal. And plus there's the factor that the minute you tell someone no, they want it three times as bad."

Angelyne marches outside and interrupts him, sending him to the car to get her Polaroid camera. She walks to the photo booth with Dave, side-by-side, almost intimately. It is working; they seem comfortable together.

"What kind of name is that, *Navarro*?" she asks.

"It's Spanish. It goes back to my grandfather, who's from the Basque country. There's a whole region called Navarre that serves as the buffer zone between Spain and France. In the old days, everyone there had a name that was a variation of *Navarre*. Do you know the actor Ramon Novarro? My grandfather's the one who gave Ramon Novarro his name. His real last name was Samaniegos, and he and my grandfather Gabriel were friends. He didn't like his last name so he borrowed my grandfather's, but a secretary at the studio spelled it wrong."

Angelyne steps into the booth and takes a series of pictures alone, signing the release form and sealing it with an immense pink kiss. Pink, she explains, became her favorite color after she received a vision involving the Great Pyramids of Egypt.

Meanwhile, at the computer table, the telephone has never left Jen's ear. Bijou Phillips has called three times. The first was to say that her dog had barfed in the car and she had driven to Dave's house to get paper towels. However, she saw Angelyne's car, thought she might get in trouble, and turned around. The second time was to demand that she be introduced to Angelyne.

"Well, I'm really pissed," she pouted to Jen. "Dave promised me." Jen explained that Angelyne was nervous and too many people in the house might scare her. Bijou hung up on her midsentence.

Bijou's third call comes moments later: "I don't care if she's uncomfortable or not! I don't care if she fucking dies! You guys are treating her like she's the President of the United States!" [*Click.*]

Angelyne, unaware of the commotion, takes a slice of pizza off the computer table and lifts it over her head, letting the bottom corner droop tantalizingly over her lip. She raises her right leg until her shoe is parallel to her rear end and, at the same time, tilts her head back and slowly lowers the pizza into her mouth. She snaps cutely at it, looking around to make sure we see her, then giggles.

"So why do you have this whole *Final Exit* book?" she asks Dave.

"I was in Japan traveling with my girlfriend, Evelyn, and I had nothing to read. It seemed like an interesting, fascinating read."

"Have you ever had any out-of-body experiences?"

"Several times."

"So have I. I came out of my body. Did you ever?"

"I've had overdose experiences, and they were really serious."

Outside, a car horn blares, followed by her manager walking back into the house with photos and posters for Navarro. "That was the official horn sounding your arrival," he says, apologizing for leaning against the steering wheel.

Angelyne ignores him. "Your experiences were scary? Mine were won-DER-ful."

"It was scary because I wasn't supposed to be where I was. And I had the feeling that my mom was angry at the fact that I was there. She was angry that I had put myself there so soon. It wasn't time. So mine wasn't a natural, wonderful thing. It was more like I did something bad to myself."

"Ooooooooh, my GOD!"

Standing opposite each other—Angelyne in pink, Navarro in black; Angelyne in leopard-

skin gloves, Navarro in leopard-skin hat—they look like a self-made angel and a self-made devil struggling to find the little common ground they share. Angelyne suggests Dave come to a burning with her. He agrees, more to make her feel at ease than out of genuine interest.

"In my experiences I'm in control," she explains. "Once I went straight into the light and I became only light, spread out. It was warm and sensual and wonderful and just . . ."

"Did you feel like you had the choice to stay or go?"

"No," Angelyne says. "I wanted to stay, but I had to go. One time, I was doing a burning with a friend who was totally into gothic stuff. It was very windy, and the wind kept blowing one of the candles out. And whenever it went out I saw a pierced . . ." She pauses and deliberates on how to explain the complexity of her vision. "If you think of the universe as a bubble, like a salt shaker, you can come out of the tiny little holes at the top. You're not in a flesh body anymore, you're just free. And you can fly."

"So what exactly is outside this salt shaker?"

"None of the laws that apply here," she answers radiantly. "It is anything you want. Here everything is black and white. You're limited. You have pain and pleasure. There's none of that over there, it's all gray. Here, the good is tainted with the bad. But out there, the extremes are all together. It's all just e-NER-gy."

"She does astral projection," Scott elaborates. "I do that quite a bit myself. But it's not anything I can control. I've gotten to the point where I can recognize when I'm doing it. If you're astral projecting, it's hard to move your physical body. You'll be lying there and if you want to lift a finger, it's like five hundred pounds. A lot of times you get out and you can put your hand through a car and go, 'Wow!' It's like being stoned or something.

"I'm trying to do more with it than just floating around and enjoying the sensation. But I haven't astral projected for about six months. Whenever it does happen, the wind is out, it's really warm, and the leaves are blowing. That's like a flash going in my mind, saying, 'This is astral projection.' But I also keep thinking, 'I can't be wasting this much time here. I need to get back to work.' I'm thinking logically, you know?"

"Ooooh, these are splendid," Angelyne suddenly coos. Her photos have dropped into the tray of the machine, and she is admiring them, picking out her favorites. Although she obsesses over the strips, examining every detail of her pose and image, she is not as vain as many of the models who have been in the booth and insisted on cutting what they thought were the bad pictures out of each strip. Angelyne lets Dave pick the photos he wants to use, discovering something different to love about herself in each one. That is, until Jen makes the mistake of saying, "It looks so old."

"What?!" she asks, alarmed.

"I mean, the picture looks like it was taken a long time ago. You look like a classic Hollywood star from the forties."

"Oh, it looks ancient," she agrees. Her quirks—the oohs, aahs, and purrs—seem to be fading as she relaxes. "They say that the better-looking you are, the greater your chances are of having a bad picture taken," she continues. "And it's true. I've had the worst pictures taken of me."

Angelyne steps back into the photo booth with Navarro, and they take a few strips together, making for a strange set of photos because they look as if they are the same size. Angelyne—a sum of hair, breasts, makeup, boutique clothing, and personality that is greater than the whole of those parts—is supposed to be so much bigger than Dave. But at the house she has been humanized, shrunk to the normal stature of a sweet, slightly neurotic, good-hearted, and spiritually inclined lady.

After the photo session ends, Angelyne

SLOW
COMM

makes no motion to leave. She seems to be enjoying herself. She pulls a cassette out of her pocket and asks Dave to play it. The tape is filled with songs she has been working on. Dave mentions that he used to play in the Red Hot Chili Peppers—she shows no sign of recognition—and Jane's Addiction, whose name rings a bell. She doesn't remember meeting Dave before and he doesn't remind her.

The first song on Angelyne's tape is accidentally amazing, with the pink lady singing in a bubblegum voice—"Can you feel me . . . in your dreams"—over a spaced-out groove. It is like trip-hop, and with a good producer it could have the potential to stand alongside Portishead or Björk.

"I can sing in two octaves at the same time," Angelyne lets everyone know. "But it burns my voice out."

"This is so cool," Dave tells her, humming the harmonies that he would add to the song. "I would put this out if I could."

"We have a psychedelic song too," she says, turning to her manager. "Did you bring it?"

Scott apologizes for leaving it behind. "Do you have my other documentary?" she asks. "I'll have to bring it next time. It's in color. Do you have a T-shirt for Dave?"

"It's in the office. I'll bring one up later," Scott promises.

"Do you have anything you want to play for me?" she suddenly, magnanimously, asks Dave.

Within ten minutes, after playing her a Janet Jackson song he remixed, Dave has Angelyne excited about the idea of him remixing her music. Then he plays her "Jane Says."

"I know this," she says. "It's a classic. Do you have an extra copy I can borrow and bring back?"

"It's my last one."

"Never give away your last thing!"

Angelyne is comfortable, so comfortable in fact that she begins to worry. "I have an acute case of claustrophobia," she blurts as soon as "Jane Says" ends. "So I need to leave soon. I don't want to go down the hill in the dark. But I can come back another time."

"I understand. I'm scared of some things too," Dave says, reassuring.

"I can tell," she says, reassured.

"I'm a little agoraphobic," Dave tells her.

"Does that mean people?"

"I don't like being out."

"Well, I'm going to come up here again if you invite me." She smiles and gets up to leave before dusk falls. "Once I get used to driving up here, I'll be cool with it. I know where you live now. I can come over in the daytime."

And so a friendship is formed or, more accurately, bought. Dave has managed to win over the most inaccessible, enigmatic icon in Los Angeles. He won't have to pay Angelyne to come up to his house again.

But she never does come again. Although Angelyne and her manager call Dave repeatedly from that day on—he even receives a call from Angelyne's record producer—he blows them off. Is winning enough for him? Is he intimidated? Is he over his obsession? I could never figure it out.

I ask Dave much later. He says none of these reasons is correct. In fact, he says that it is my fault: "I'm still obsessed," he says. "The reason she hasn't been back is because the guy who promised he'd be there with me never brought it up again. Would you have her up there alone?"

part

LOVE IN L.A.: CHRISTMAS FOR GROWN-UPS?

BY DAVE NAVARRO

LOCATION: *Animal Farm, a pet store in West Hollywood, C.A. Conrad, a Hollywood Dreamchaser, and I have been drawn inside the shop to see the puppies behind glass . . .*

"There was this girl who lived in the apartment next to mine. I almost thought that she was 'the one,'" explained Conrad, a thirty-four-year-old Variety *magazine contributor. [Insert the image of Timothy Hutton's character in* Ordinary People.*] "We were in love . . . At least I was, but I knew in my heart that I wasn't ready for what she wanted. Marriage. I mean, it'd only been like three months since we'd met! Plus, I had just moved here [L.A.] like two weeks before and I didn't even know the name of the street I lived on!"*

The One. Will you ever meet The One, Dave? The answer is, probably not. As long as I live in L.A., I will never meet The One. Why even contemplate such a fantastic notion? Los Angeles is a town that literally feeds on itself as it does its inhabitants. This is the city wherein the weak and fearful become the strong and attractive, and unknowingly prey on the hunted.

A chain of irreversible events begins to take place. A broken heart manufactures steel plates to protect itself from an unavoidable and impending danger. Unbeknownst to the manufacturer, this plate carries with it an internal magnet. The magnet identifies itself as "ambivalence." When drawn into the magnetic field, an opposing, neutral force is itself magnetized. (In other words, once a person

becomes callous and uncaring—a heartbreaker—it seems to me that they become more attractive, especially to pure hearts that self-destructively seek to be broken.) These events are so horrible that a trail of scattered carcasses are periodically left to decay on the city street corners. Some step over the bodies, as if they were globs of chewing gum melting in the hot So Cal sun. These very select few are known as "the enlightened." I view myself as one of them.

There are two things of which I am certain about life in L.A.:

1. THE BERMUDA TRIANGLE OF L.A., FAIRFAX BETWEEN BEVERLY AND SANTA MONICA, IS ACTUALLY A SMALL TOWN IN ISRAEL AND CAN'T TECHNICALLY BE CONSIDERED PART OF L.A.

2. LOVE DOES EXIST; HOWEVER, ONLY MOMENT TO MOMENT AND NEVER FOR A LIFETIME . . . LOVE FADES.

Contrary to expectation, I have met several fascinating subjects who still view love in L.A., or the idea of love, with an almost endearing yet ignorant optimism. These sorry and somewhat pitiful creatures are, in most cases, transplants from another city or state and have a fairly healthy idea of what love is and/or could be. They seem to be unaware of the Love/Christmas Theory and appear to believe that love is eternal, everlasting, and harmonious. However, when I ask, "Have you witnessed a love between two people work out?" a sudden silence falls.

I have lived in L.A. all my life and I learned about love at a very early age. I suppose that I will always value the lessons my mother and father inadvertently taught me. Throughout my upbringing, I met a number of strangers and watched in confusion as they waltzed in and out of our homes and lives. "Meet Mom's new boyfriend" . . . "Here's Dad's new girlfriend" . . . "No, honey, this is Mommy's new boyfriend" . . . "Hey, Dave, meet Daddy's new girlfriend. You two know each other, don't you take math together?" My head used to spin trying to keep track of all the names and faces, let alone the sporting events. "What is this," I'd think to myself, "*The Story of O*-lympics?" (I used to love it when my mother read that to me before I went to bed.)

LOCATION: *Exterior, Animal Farm. Conrad and I decide to enjoy a stroll down the street while discussing love, life, and coffee . . .*

Conrad continues, "We fuckin' broke up 'cause of the marriage thing . . . I dunno . . . I still loved her deeply. Seeing her go out for the paper and stuff like that was tough . . . It was the hardest part of the day for a while. Work took me to Japan for a week and I couldn't stop thinking about her. When I got back I decided to see her and try to work it out. I went next door to her apartment."

L.A. resident and ex-girlfriend Sarah asked, "Why won't men stay the night?"

I replied: Well for me, if I go home with a chick that I just met, I pretty much assume that caution has been long thrown to the wind and we are following a mere short-term impulse, nothing more. A night like that can be a fantasy come true, given the right set of circumstances. It can fully backfire, though: imagine waking up or "coming to" the next day with some cat-thing crawling over your face, mascara clogged in the corners of eyes, breath and body emitting an unpleasant stench, putting on the "night before" clothes, realizing the fact that there is a picture on the dresser of one of my friends (or even of me for that matter, although the most horrific and terrifying possibility would be if the picture were of Anthony Kiedis), finding a scowling roommate in the hall, having nothing to say to each other, seeing the "cute" little things we played with still out on the living room floor (anything from photo albums to Ouija boards—this can be made worse if the two of you make eye contact right after noticing them), and listening to her laugh extra hard on the phone with her agent to show me how much of a real life she has, while grasping for some kind of lousy excuse like, "Oh my God!!! Is that clock right?"

All this plus that halfhearted attempt at avoiding the "Let-Me-Out-of-Here-Future-Plans" thing. This can, to say the least, destroy any fantasy we may have had. (By the way, if you're some girl whom I might think is pretty, the above does not apply to you; we would, of course, spend an evening filled with tenderness, sensitivity, romance, nurturing, leather, spit, and a little laughter at a picturesque five-star hotel built for two. I would treat you like a flower, and open you up petal by petal until the morning sun shone on our bodies, blissfully entwined in the pool of our love. Make sure to bring extra towels, ladies.)

I think that this feeling is shared among more guys than girls, although, trust me, guys, they feel like this too—only for them, multiply this feeling by a hundred. Let's face it, how would *you* like to wake up for the first time at *your* place?

What are the "Let-Me-Out-of-Here-Future-Plans," you ask? You see, when we men are in a bind such as the one I have just described, for some reason we think that a promise of a future meeting will get us off the hook. It is kind of like this: [*thinking to ourselves*] "She'll feel used and taken advantage of if I split now, I mean . . . she's not drunk anymore . . . What an asshole I am . . . Yeah . . . I know . . . I'll tell her I gotta go, but that I would love to see her later. Surely I can get out of that. No problem. Plus, she'll think I like her and respect her and all that. If she only knew that I don't even respect myself." Then we usually make the mistake of saying, "What are you doing later?"

I know that there might be a few women

d the

erenc

it fo

afte

no girls

to the other

car to

something e

morning I we

and the ticke

with enorm

her for a p

meant to sa

D.W. +
J.L. =
T.L.F

D.W.
m.
T.L

he other

says, "Yeah,

, Im j whore.

D.W. +
B.L. =
T.L.

This morning

pass the butt

hat do you say to a
rl with no arms and
no legs?
ice tits.

SHUT UP YOU

YOU'RE RUIN

D.W. +
D.F. =
T.L.A.

D.W.+S.V.
=
T.L.A.

T.L.F.

he difference between a girl and a whore? N

D.W.+

DW+Y.Y.

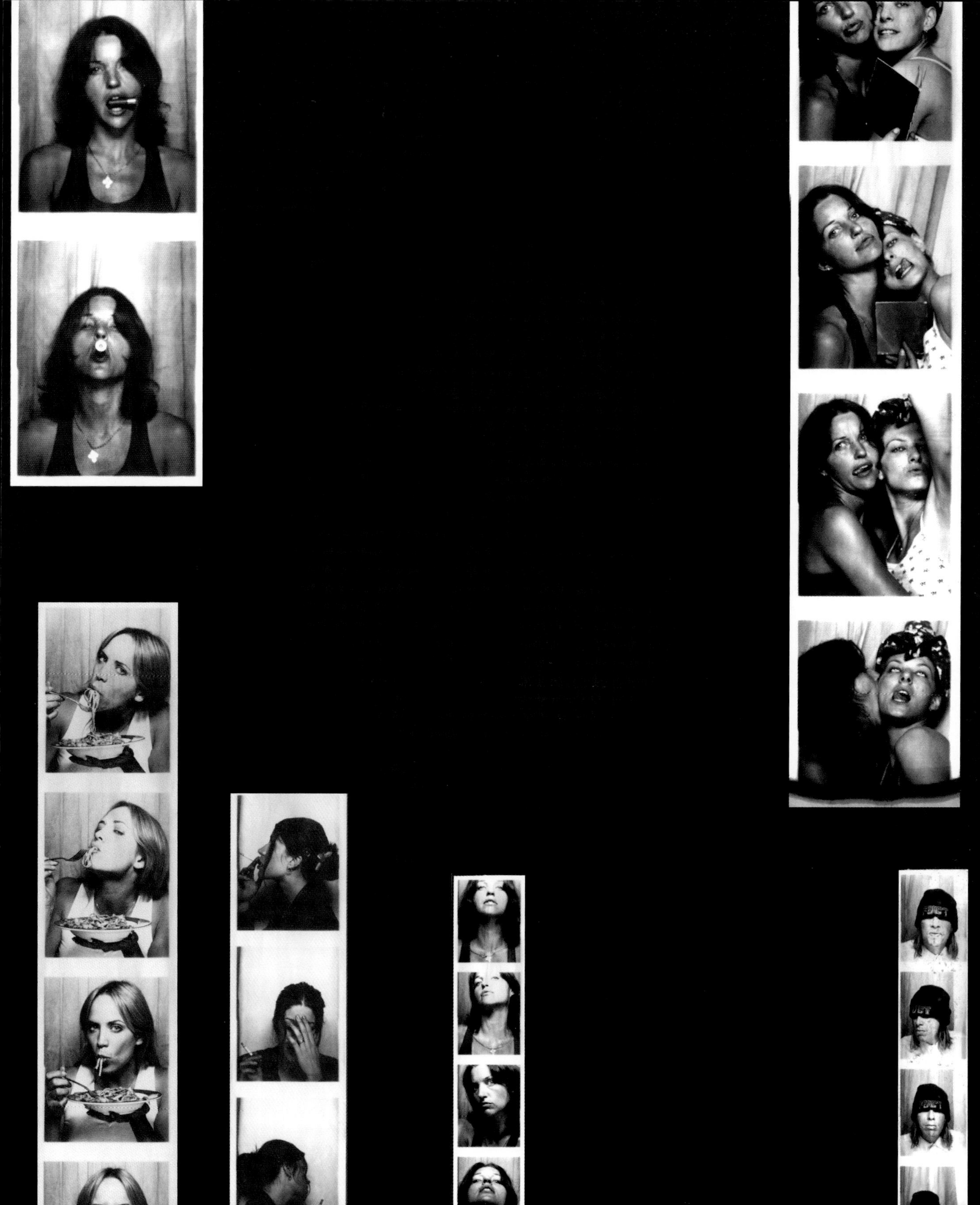

out there who are reading this right now thinking, "What a fuckin' asshole this Navarro guy is!" Before you judge, please hear me out. This phenomenon is just as common among men as the "One Hand" story is among women. Does this sound familiar?

"I can count all the men that I have slept with on one hand." (More on that next column . . . if I am forgiven for this one.)

Conrad sits at a bus stop with his face in his hands. His pain is visible and although I am patiently waiting with him for the bus to come and take him home, he appears very alone. (Perhaps this is because we both know damn well that I have a very nice, plush, and expensive car and I could very easily give Con a ride home if I wished. After all, he does live next door to me . . . In fact, that's how I met the guy. Ahhh, fuck it . . . I'm too codependent and I need my space!)

"I knock on the door and who answers? My supposed best friend! Sherm! I couldn't fuckin' believe it! I tell ya, Dave, it's no mistake that the word friend *ends in* e-n-d! *He claims that he was only tryin' to be supportive 'cause she was all sad and shit when I left and one thing led to a . . . blah, blah, blah . . . So I'm like standin' there like freakin', right? She comes to the door and she's got on this black lacy 'fuck-me' thing . . . She never wore that stuff before. I was so crushed. I thought I was gonna die right there. Turns out that now she wants to* 'claim her body' *or some fuckin' bullshit like that . . . and now she don't want no marriage!!!!!*

"So, Dave . . ."

I was horrified. Conrad was about to puncture my heart and release all of my deepest fears . . . Women, especially in L.A., are exactly like men!!!!

To myself: (Y'know, Dave, you haven't really lived anywhere else. You have always been a Los Angeles resident. What's the real common denominator here, eh, Slick?)

Oh no! Then the Love/Christmas Theory must be true! The decorations and the anticipation of exciting events such as Christmas or even a marriage are what everyone raves about. The actual thing itself, the event, simply sucks . . . Nobody, really . . . knows it for . . . sure? I turn into Roger Daltrey's Tommy at the most fucked-up times! (This self-realizing and potentially spiritually healing human growth moment was, for me, one of those times.)

"Davey, my boy, for the next year or so I'd go to bed, alone, as the woman I loved and my best friend screwed the living daylights out of each other right next door to me. I could fuckin' hear them! It tore my heart out every damn night until I became so numb I ended up jerkin' off to it . . . The funny thing is that ever since then, women always seem to throw themselves at me . . . and you know what? I couldn't care less!"

No surprise.

"Anyway, there's my bus, dude . . . I gotta jam . . . Can I stop by when I get home in a few hours?"

[To be continued . . .]

part II SHE'S SUCH A GREAT . . .

Jason, a music-industry friend of Dave's, has an ex-girlfriend who has been spending the week with him. She is actually more than an ex-girlfriend. She is the person he felt he was supposed to marry. After years of going out (he'd successfully managed to block out the exact number because it scared him), they decided they either had to break up or get married. They broke up.

Since then, they've both had a lot of relationships. And while she's been staying with him, Jason has been trying to convince himself to resent her presence because it supposedly interferes with his work.

So tonight, Jason rushes over, excited to explain that he just had some kind of breakthrough. For the first time in years (he blocked out the exact number here too), he actually felt something for another human being. He felt the rusty hinges of his heart open and experienced a rush so long-repressed that it felt new. Then his head took over, and he got scared and slammed the doors to his heart shut.

As he says this, it becomes clear why Dave has started writing a column on love called "Love in L.A." for *Bikini* magazine this month. It is his head denying his heart, trying to impose some kind of order and rationality on love in order to contain it. That doesn't mean that anyone who writes a column like that on love has forgotten what love feels like; it's that they're scared of feeling it again.

"I've been so fucked up over love and the heart," Dave says that night. "Meeting women, I sometimes try to believe flat-out that they're all whores. I just walk in and think, 'Oh, hey,

God, she's beautiful. She's so nice and smart. She's such a great whore.' That's it—and it's fucked because I don't know if I have the ability at this time, especially in this city, to have a loving relationship. Truthfully, at this stage in my life it's better, because I am so unequipped to give what is required in an equal and loving relationship. I mean me, myself, I don't have it. I'm just like the number one guy without it."

That is Dave's head talking. In his heart, he knows even as he speaks these words that all women aren't whores, that they all won't fuck your friends or abandon you. But some will, and have.

The topic returns to love moments later when Dave's ex-girlfriend Victoria ("Tori") Andaházy calls. Dave met her in 1995 while buying his couch in the furniture store where she worked; they dated for the next year and a half.

As she speaks, Dave puts her on speakerphone. It's his way of opening his life—or at least certain parts of it—to people around him, to let them know that he has nothing to hide.

For the sake of completeness, and because the conversation helps illuminate some of the topics in the months that follow, the entire conversation has been transcribed here. But it is beginning with the word "relationships" that the discussion begins to reflect Dave's use of his head to deny (or is it protect?) his heart:

TORI: Are you still mad at me?
DAVE: No. Who is this?
TORI: Tori.
DAVE: [*silence*]
TORI: You'll never guess what I just did.
DAVE: What?
TORI: I got a tattoo.
DAVE: Not another *D*. [She has a *D* tattooed on her ass.]
TORI: It was a Chinese symbol.
DAVE: Where is it?
TORI: On my wrist.
DAVE: Why didn't you put it in your ass?
TORI: 'Cause I didn't want to.
DAVE: I'd do it for you.
TORI: Why are you being like this?
DAVE: I've been real upset.
TORI: I would never hurt you. I just felt like you were picking on me all day. Sometimes you just want to argue with me and pick on me.
DAVE: I get the same feeling with you.
TORI: What do you mean?
DAVE: We're arguable. We argue a lot.
TORI: No we don't.
DAVE: Yes we do.
TORI: No we don't.
DAVE: We're arguing right now.
TORI: No we aren't. I don't feel like we are right now.
DAVE: Do you want to know why you hurt my feelings?
TORI: Yes, I have no idea.
DAVE: You said that I was wasting all my time on the Internet.
TORI: No I wasn't. I'm so proud of you for what you've done. I was not trying to insult you at all.
DAVE: You basically said there's no reason for anyone to go to my homepage. I don't want to get into it. I'm over it.
TORI: I can't hear you but, yeah.
DAVE: Maybe you're just not the kind of person who likes to surf the Internet.
TORI: What I was trying to say was . . . Am I on speaker right now?

[*Dave picks the phone up, gets Tori's permission to debate in front of an audience, and returns the phone to speaker mode.*]

DAVE: I'm totally cynical and self-centered. I don't care about burning children in Africa. I care about how my hair looks.
TORI: That's true about David: he's very narcissistic.
DAVE: It definitely comes from an insecurity. But if there is a mythological character I identify with, it wouldn't be Narcissus. It would be Zeus. That's an old Woody Allen line. I didn't steal it. It's homage.

TORI: I don't think you're aware of your capabilities.

DAVE: That's why I didn't kill myself. I saw what I was capable of. I'm becoming more aware of that and what I can do.

TORI: I don't think you thought you were capable of starting your own band in the car that one day. You were still in the Peppers and scared about doing something on your own. You didn't think anybody would be interested and you didn't think you had anything to say.

DAVE: It's kind of true.

TORI: What, baby?

DAVE: It's kind of true. No one's listening. All those people who were in my life then aren't in my life now.

TORI: If you made a phone call to Jimmy Boyle, to Heather [Parry], to Rick [Rubin], to any of those people, they'd all be there again.

DAVE: Those friendships I had were everyday friendships until . . .

TORI: You may believe that Chad [Smith, the Red Hot Chili Peppers drummer and Dave's original collaborator on his solo album] deserted you, but I still really believe that you and Chad will come around at some point because you really do love each other.

DAVE: You've said that about other people before.

TORI: You're like a vampire with relationships. You suck all the blood out.

DAVE: That's what you think, a vampire?

TORI: Well, look at your coffin, baby.

DAVE: I sometimes have a power over people. I don't know what it is.

TORI: I do. It's charm. If there's a bunch of people in the room, you'll make every one feel like they're special. It feeds you. It's total vampire shit. You're a total taker. You only give to those who give back.

DAVE: I think I'm probably one of the most generous people I know. I have so much faith in people. But at the same time, usually it takes people so much work to be my friend.

TORI: Oh my God, it's so much work. He's an amazing guy; there's nothing like being friends with him. He's got an amazing heart. But he doesn't give it away that often.

DAVE: [*silence*]

TORI: Dave also appears to give away a lot. He's an open book. But I believe there are certain things he does hold on to. One would think he's real open and stuff. But there are other places he refuses to go with anybody.

DAVE: Hiding in plain sight.

TORI: He'll be out there and radical and doing all this stuff but it's hiding something. I think the real Dave Navarro has yet to be found.

DAVE: I was asked to interview anybody I wanted for [the online magazine] *Addicted to Noise.* I chose Fiona Apple because of her self-exploitation of her troubles and darkness. The topic I was going to get into with her was how you can use the exposing of your secrets as an incredible mask. The thing is, it's a diversion. It's the same thing with the costumes. Everybody's stunned when they see me all done up in some kind of costume, but they never ask what I'm hiding.

TORI: It's enough to fool everybody.

DAVE: I'm not creating a person I'm not. I'm just amplifying a part of me.

TORI: He gives you so much of that, there's nothing else you can think about. You're drowning. Dave's putting himself out there so big you can't see anything else.

DAVE: If I didn't want you to know I had a tonsillitis problem, I'd cut my hand off. Even in eighth grade, everyone came to me with their troubles. They came to me to repair things and get advice. Somehow people looked at me to fix shit for them. My eighth grade literature teacher, Ms. Dunn, called me Uncle Dave.

TORI: What do all these stories have in common?

DAVE: Fear.

TORI: You're afraid of love.

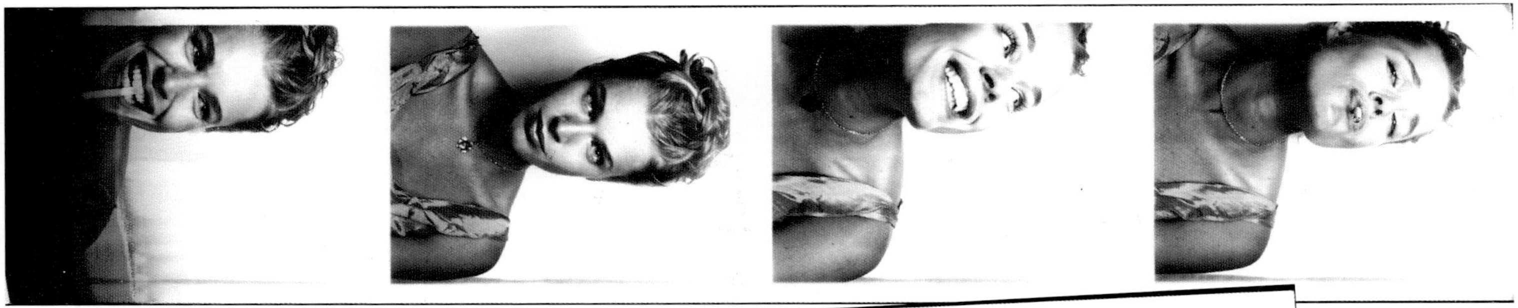

I sometimes
have a power
over people.
I don't know
what it is.

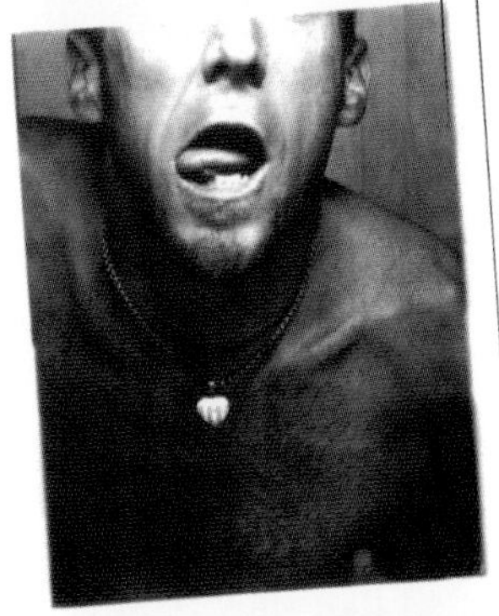

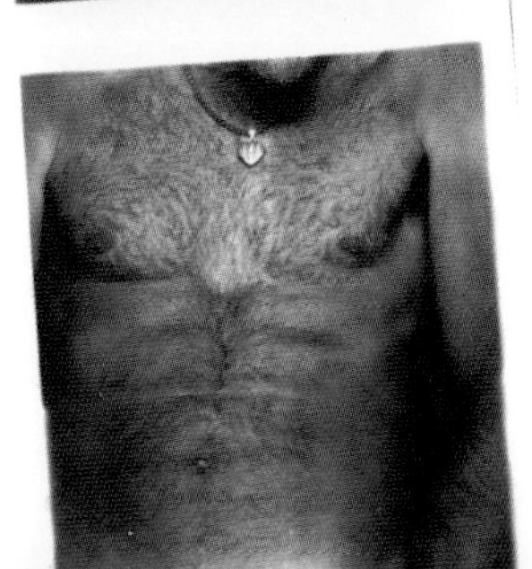

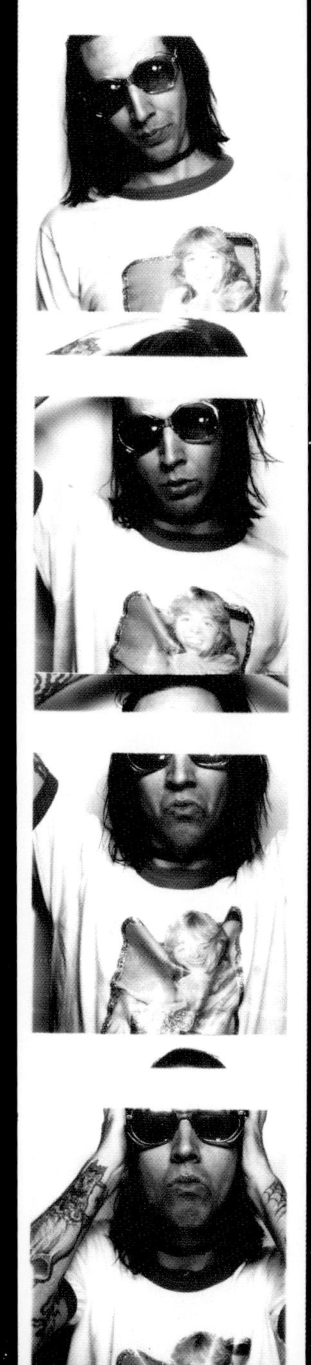

POWELL ELECTRIC

DAVE: I'm afraid of love and afraid of my own capabilities.
TORI: Dave doesn't want to love anybody who doesn't love him back.
DAVE: Love is sacrifice.
TORI: If you're in love you shouldn't have to sacrifice.
DAVE: I know I have an issue with love. I know my mom is gone, and it contributes to how I feel about it. But I don't think there's a man in love who doesn't think of it as a sacrifice. It's certainly a sacrifice because you've been married fifty years and you're fighting, but you stay in it. In society today, one of the main physical expressions of love for someone else is to remain with them. But at the same time, as much as women hate to think this, men are more prone to chase after women because we are ultimately here to spread our seed and increase our offspring. Because we have millions and millions of sperm and women's eggs can only be fertilized one at a time, they aren't inclined to seek out physical action as much as men are. We're putting animal urges and animal instincts into a sociological and intellectual world.
TORI: I believe that men have that drive more than women. But I don't think it's a sacrifice: it's a trade.
DAVE: This debate is about words, then? We're comparing animal instinct and human morality, and they contradict each other. I think love is possible, but I think the general consensus of what society's views on love is—monogamy—is really close to impossible.
RHIAN: [Note that in transcribing this conversation, I accidentally used the name of Dave's ex-wife instead of Tori. Dave requested that the error be left uncorrected.] I agree. Society does confine people.
DAVE: Exactly.
TORI: I think we've come to some kind of consensus.
DAVE: And I think the consensus is that I've won. I think you got thrown off when I said "sacrifice." I think I'm at a stage in life where my bitterness and emotional state of being are defining what I think of love.
TORI: I think it's been that way with Dave up to this point.
DAVE: It's been gradual. Do you know how hard I tried to love and succeed?
TORI: That was a tough thing for both of us. But look at how great it came out. Where you are now there's a big piece of it there.
DAVE: You didn't answer the question. I was trying as hard as I could and, given my age and experience, I was really open to it and trying to compromise with you on things that would ultimately in my mind benefit the relationship as a whole. And I think I'm way more bitter about it now.
TORI: I agree. I do agree.
DAVE: And I don't think our relationship ending is a contributor to that. We were pretty fucking lucky.
TORI: It blows my mind sometimes when I really think about it.
DAVE: This is the only woman I've stayed friends with.
TORI: [*silence*]
DAVE: Navarro, three. Andaházy, zero.

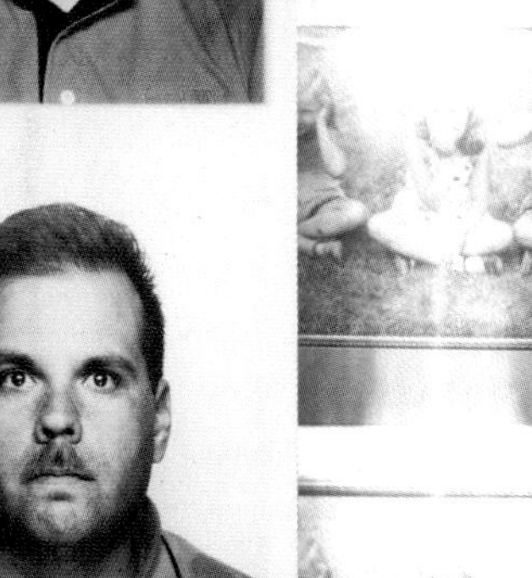

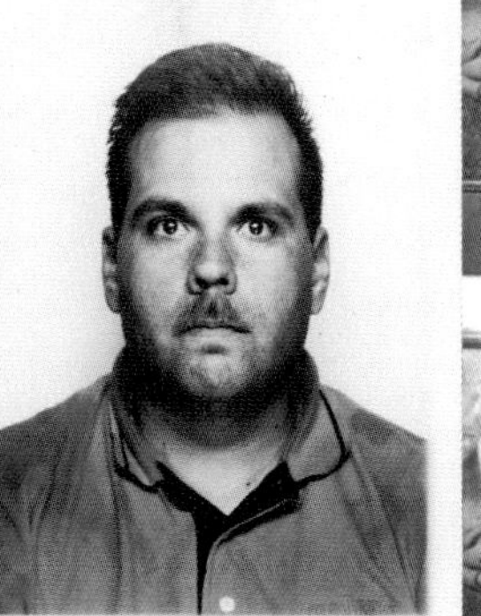
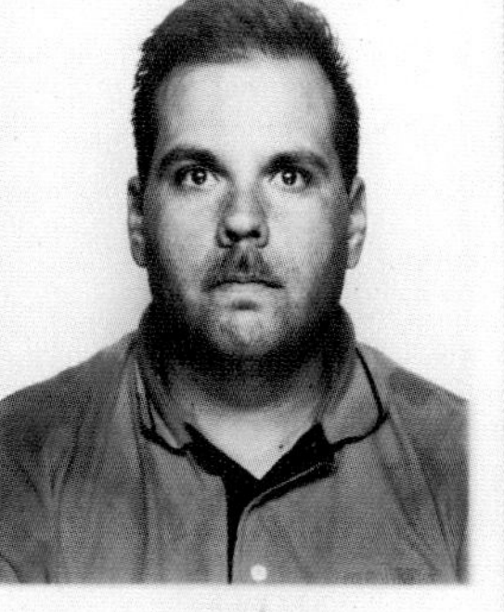

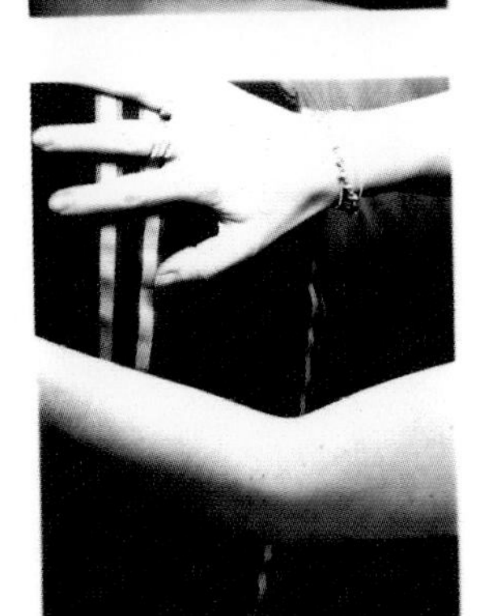

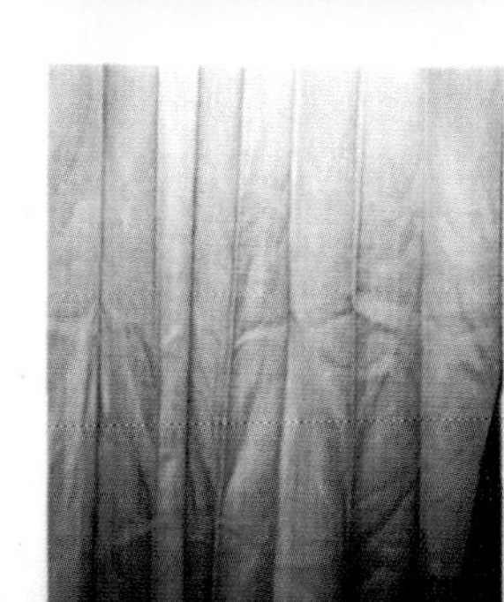

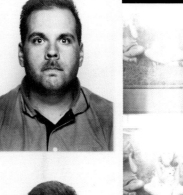

Love is sacrifice.

part

AN IMAGE

Tonight, imagine that the walls of Dave's house are glass. Upstairs, there are three girls—two of them dancers from the Jane's Addiction reunion tour, the other a makeup artist. They are drunk, chasing each other around the house, getting naked in the photo booth, and enacting almost every fantasy known to the male species. Downstairs, Dave sits alone in his bathroom, a glass tube in his hands, smoking ice.

part V SPIRITUAL GUIDANCE

The Ouija board has been trying to kill Dave. Or maybe Dave has been trying to get the Ouija board to kill him. I'm not sure.

Tori had come over and Dave decided the best entertainment would be his Ouija board. We gathered around, fingers on the pointer, waiting for a spirit. After a while, Dave invoked one. It said that it was Dave and Tori's unborn child.

Every time we asked the spirit a question, the pointer shot to the letters *D, A,* and then *V.* Morbidly, Dave asked the spirit if he was going to die. The pointer shot to "Yes." He asked if it would be soon. The pointer shot to "Yes." He asked if it would be because of drugs. The pointer wandered in the direction of "No."

All of a sudden, a switch flipped in Dave's mind. He became obsessed, fixated, tormented. He kept asking it the same type of question over and over—"When will I die?" "Are you trying to say that I'm going to die this week?"—and the confused pointer kept shooting all over the board, contradicting itself and confounding Dave. He was sure he was receiving a warning, although Tori thought he was badgering the poor thing, trying to force a fatal prediction. Eventually, we had to stop. All of us—Dave, Tori, me, the unborn child named Dav—were getting too freaked out.

The next day, we decided to call on the ultimate spiritual authority, the arbiter of all matters celestial and terrestrial: Angelyne.

But Angelyne was on her way to the farmer's market, so Dave consulted the next best source—her manager and oracle, Scott Hennig:

SCOTT: Angelyne is in her car right now and she doesn't have the phone on. She's too busy waving at fans and putting on lipstick to be using the phone.

DAVE: Do you use a Ouija board at all?

SCOTT: I have a really old one I got at a garage sale. It was one of the first ones they came out with. It's the same design, but bigger than the wood ones. I've still got the box it came in. It's from the early fifties. Why? What were you doing with yours?

DAVE: Oh, the other night me and my friends were using one, and I got negative responses from it. I've come to understand that they kind of play with you.

SCOTT: Yeah, plus generally speaking it works on a lower level, which the negative forces have easier access to. A lot of them can't get past a certain spiritual plateau, so they'll use the Ouija board as a doorway to just screw around, like you said.

DAVE: I would imagine that there are spirits who are living in harmony and a spiritual state of bliss, and they don't really want to come down and plant shit . . .

SCOTT: I don't know. They still have weird vibes about this place. I know a lot of people that have had contact with spirits like James Dean or Marilyn, and everybody's got weird stories. But some entities—depending on the specifics of their death—still get the willies thinking about Planet Earth, even though they're off in spiritual form somewhere else.

DAVE: Yeah, this one was telling me I was gonna die this month. I know they are prone to scaring you and playing with you, but I can't help being a little freaked out that I'm going to die.

SCOTT: I've had a few close calls myself: I've almost been shot, I've been in car wrecks. But I come out of them without even getting my hair messed up. The fact that you met Angelyne counteracts all that.

DAVE: The bad spirits just go running for the hills when they see her?

SCOTT: She's got a lot of power and energy with what she represents and the visual image. So many people come to Hollywood trying to make it and regardless of whether they fail or succeed, they see those billboards and her image and think, "Here's someone who made it." It's inspirational to a lot of people.

DAVE: That's true, but . . .

SCOTT: What you ought to do is talk with Angelyne about your Ouija board experience. Get together with her and do a burning too. Just hanging out with her is like a "Get Out of Jail Free" card for anything.

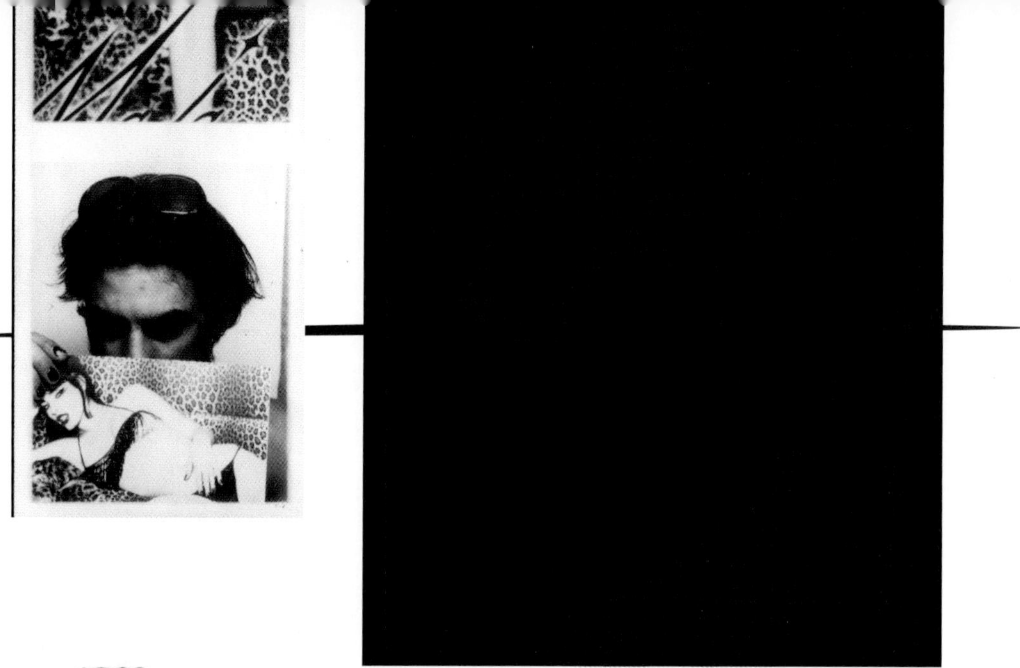

part I THE RHETORIC OF DAVE

Never argue with Dave. You cannot win. He will take your premise and magnify it, mangle it, stomp on it, and set it ablaze until it's so hot and distorted that you don't even want to touch it. Then he'll thrust it back in your face and, mouth burning, you'll beg him to take it away. You'll grovel and apologize. Anything. Just as long as he allows you a retraction.

The easiest way to start an argument with Dave is to insult him. Dave likes to be criticized. If he's done something wrong, he'll be the first to admit it. However, if he's insulted wrongly or blamed for something he hasn't done, he will not take it quietly. He will go to any length to make you realize that you are wrong.

Combine this with the fact that Dave is extremely sensitive and perceptive—he can pick up on your slightest variance in mood in a second—and the window of what is criticism opens a lot wider. He has a radar for the stuff: even if an insult isn't about him directly, he will explore it as something that could be said about him behind his back. And when he doesn't feel he's being treated like an equal—even if he is actually being treated like an equal—he will flip out.

So just you dare to let drop a vaguely insulting or condescending phrase, word, or gesture and, before you even realize what you've said, he'll have picked it up and for the next minute, hour, week, or year you two will be rubbing it red and raw.

Dave is very good with words.

Note: When I read the above paragraphs to Dave, I was scared of insulting him so I changed a few words. From my tone of voice, he picked up on the fact that I had omitted something. Instead of flipping out, though, he suggested adding the phrase "even if he is actually being treated like an equal."

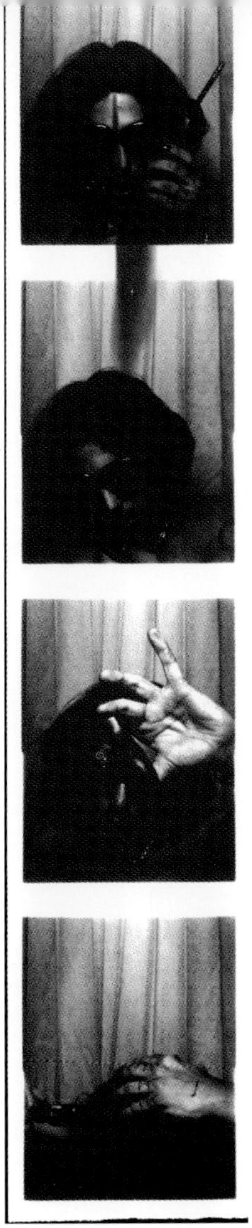

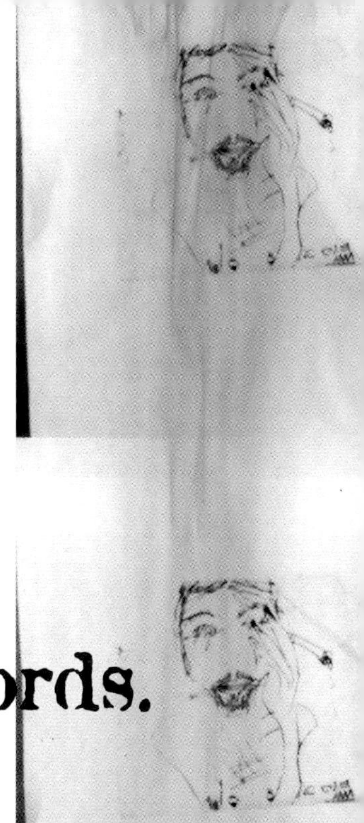

Dave is very good with **words.**

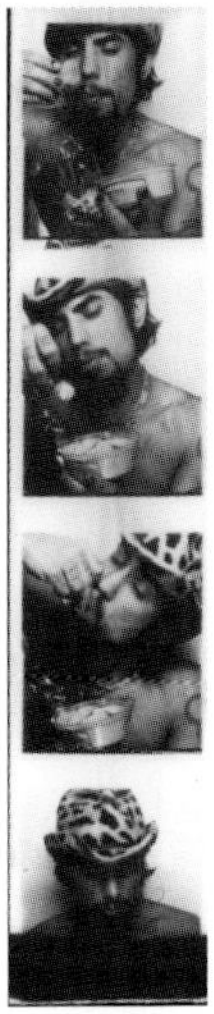

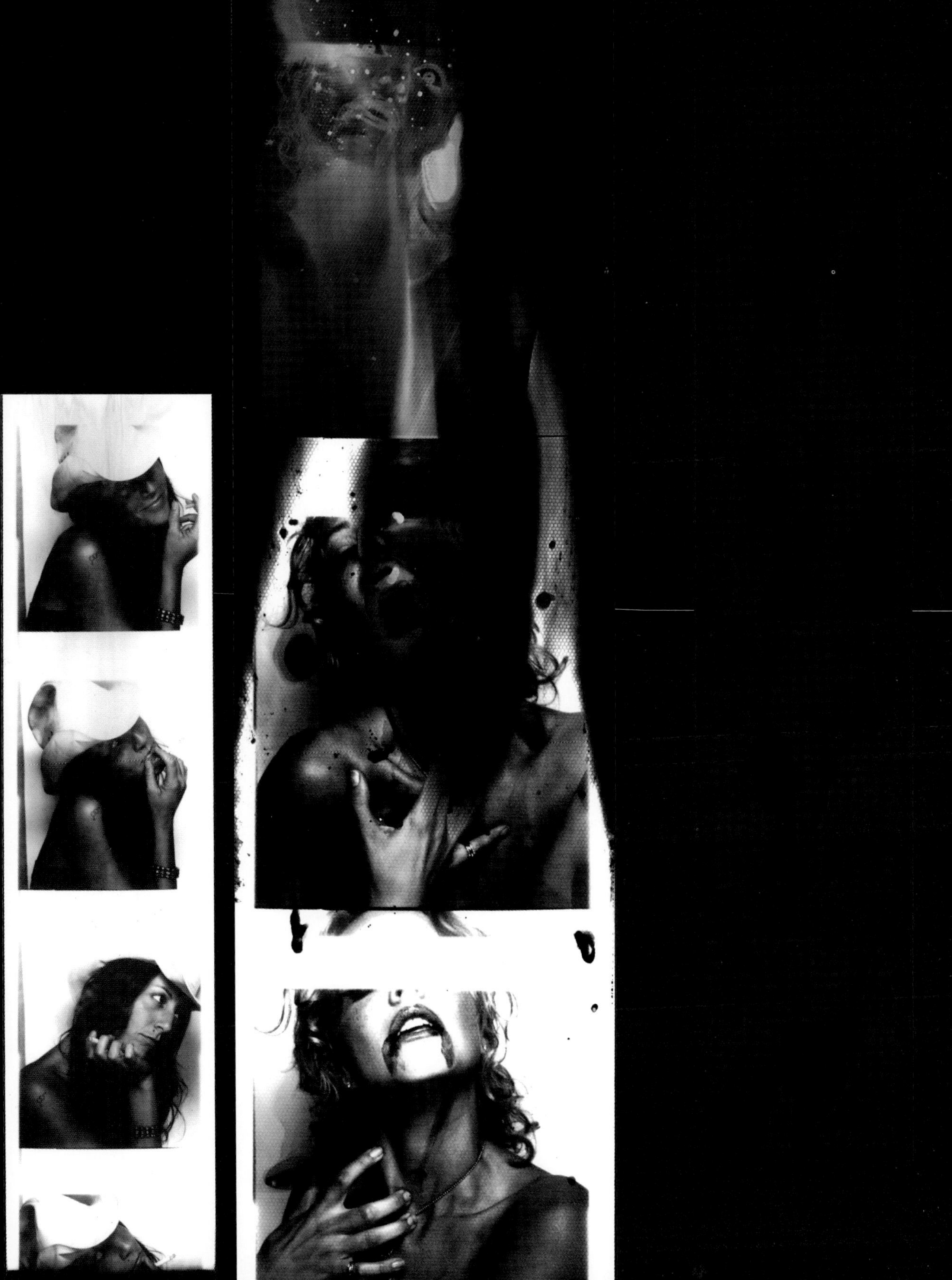

TIN
TAR
LEAD
HIDE

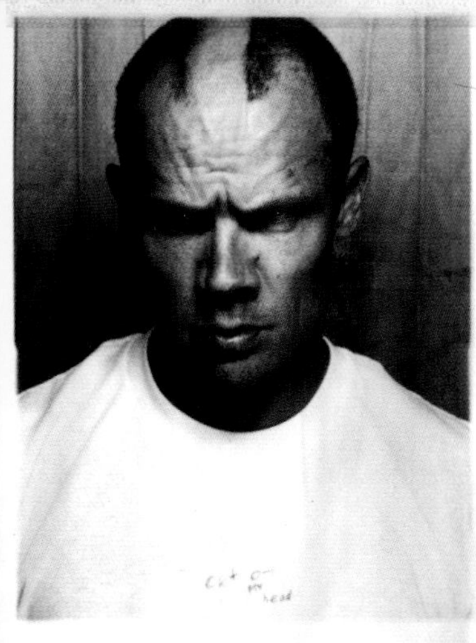

part II THE GREAT CHILI PEPPERS DEBATE: "BRINGING IT ON YOURSELF"*

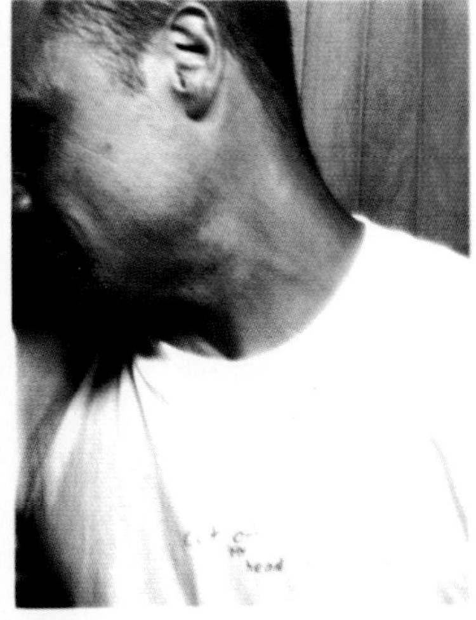

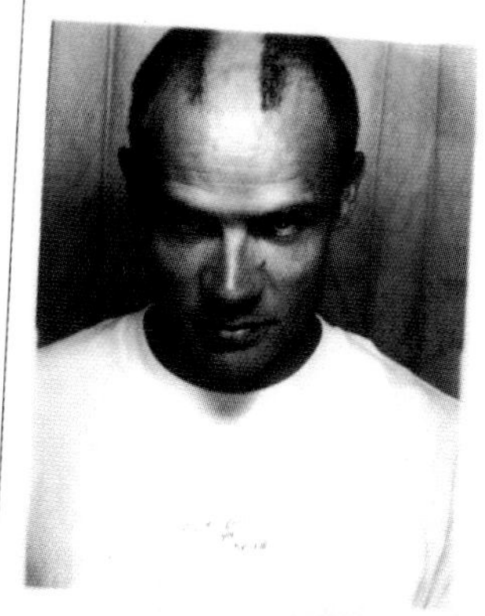

don't try this at home

A NOTE TO THE READER: *As I read this almost two years later, I am struggling with who I am now and who I was when I had this conversation. Today, I have no animosity toward any of the people mentioned here. I am friends with them all. I realize now that my outlook was the very thing that contributed to my downward spiral. Looking back, it's clear how easy it was to point the finger at everybody except myself. I just don't feel like this anymore, or even act like this. I present it in hopes that others will learn from it, because I certainly have.*

—Dave

June 1, 2000

ADAM SCHNEIDER [recently fired and later rehired Jane's Addiction manager]: How much are you going to get into the stuff with the Red Hot Chili Peppers in your book?

DAVE: Oh, we'll get into it.

ADAM: Will you characterize yourself as being asked to leave the band, or will you kind of say that you brought that on yourself?

DAVE: Why did I bring it on myself?

ADAM: By going on MTV and saying, "Well, I don't even know if I'm in the Peppers. I can do stuff on my own."

DAVE: I didn't say that. I just said, "No matter what band I'm in, whether I'm in the Chili Peppers, Jane's Addiction, or neither—and I stress *neither*—I'll be doing something creative." And besides, I wasn't given a reason by those guys other than, "The guys are uncomfortable with some of your life choices."

ADAM: So you're saying that you would have stayed in the Peppers had that not happened?

DAVE: No. I'm saying I didn't bring it on myself. You really think I brought that on?

ADAM: Well, from the outside looking in, to a degree I do think that. I think that's what you wanted to do; I think you wanted to do your own thing. You wanted out of those bands.

DAVE: What I wanted and the way it happened are different things. I wanted out, but how did I bring it on?

ADAM: By wanting out.

DAVE: But I was not verbal to anybody—in

**A week prior to the dialogue that follows, Dave explained his relationship with the Red Hot Chili Peppers thusly:*

I'm going to go over it from the beginning for you. Here's essentially what happened:

When I left Jane's Addiction in 1991, I went through a hard time because I was getting clean. I had been a heroin user. I put together a band with [Jane's bassist] Eric Avery called Deconstruction. It was more of an artistic experiment than anything else. We didn't have songs; some people viewed us as geniuses and others viewed us as fools. And, personally, I could see the rationale behind both points of view very clearly.

In the process of doing this record, I was asked to join the Chili Peppers. I turned them down. Around this time, Axl Rose called me up in the middle of the night and said, "Dude, I had a dream, and you and me were rocking on stage together." He would call me every day and ask me to join his band, and I turned him down too. (The honest truth, though, is that I wanted to take the Guns N' Roses job, but I was afraid of looking foolish and being judged a sellout.)

In the meantime, another kid, Jesse Tobias, joined the Peppers. I caught wind of it when my friend Arty brought me a copy of *Rolling Stone* and said, "Look at this guy, Dave, he just took your job." The headline was ONE RED HOT MOTHER OF A PEPPER or something like that, and the guy seemed handsome. He was pictured sitting there with his guitar, leaning over and looking good. I was bummed when I saw it.

fact, I hadn't seen any of them in months except for Flea.

ADAM: Look, I'm not going to argue with you. But do you wanna hear what I have to say about it?

DAVE: I'm curious as to why . . .

ADAM: On the Jane's tour, the fact that you got back into doing drugs and stuff like that broke down a relationship with Flea [who replaced bassist Eric Avery on the Jane's tour] to a point.

DAVE: Getting back into drugs before I went on the Jane's tour didn't break down any relationships. Maybe it strengthened them. All I did was see everybody and hang out with them more.

ADAM: What about the fact that you got into drugs when Kiedis was coming out of them?

DAVE: I do not see that at all. I did not spend a day of my life fucked up in the Peppers.

ADAM: Well, then, maybe now is the time that is the most controversial for you.

DAVE: That's true, but I'm still asking how I brought it on. I didn't bring it on any more than anyone else in the band brought it on.

ADAM: That's true.

DAVE: I didn't make a choice. And I don't feel like I alienated any relationship with Perry or Stephen [Perkins, Jane's Addiction's drummer] as a result of that MTV show, and that was essentially saying the same thing to them as I said to the Chili Peppers.

ADAM: You yourself said to me so many times that you just weren't into the Peppers . . .

DAVE: But that's not bringing it on, because other people in the band said that at various times too.

ADAM: Well, I just think that when people have a certain belief or a certain kind of attitude that it can permeate their life in a way that has an effect. Like if you say on MTV, "I'm not in the band—"

DAVE: I didn't say that. Let's watch it, I did not say that.

ADAM: Okay, I could be wrong, but the theory is that your heart was not in the Peppers.

Arty looked at me and said, "You should have done this, Dave."

I said, "You know what, I'm going to."

He said, "What are you talking about?"

I answered, "I don't know, but I'm going to be in that band."

He said, "All right, whatever," and kind of rolled his eyes.

Sure enough, a couple days later [Chili Peppers bassist] Flea called and asked me to jam with him. I had a sense of what was going on but I didn't want to get too excited. Ultimately, they kicked Jesse Tobias out and I joined the band. To my knowledge, I never really signed anything with them or with Warner Bros. again either. So to make a long story short, I'm now in the Chili Peppers and I'm in there for four years.

I don't really need to go into all the stuff that happened throughout this time, but let's just say that it was a very different way of working creatively than it was with Jane's Addiction and it made it very difficult for me as a new member. In my mind, making the album was a much longer, slower process than I was used to.

Despite this, we finally finished the record [*One Hot Minute*] and went on tour. Chad Smith became my best friend, and Anthony [Kiedis, singer] took time off toward the end of the tour. So Chad and I were sitting there going, "What

DAVE: Granted. That's not a theory; that's a fact. But I still don't see how I brought on leaving the band.

ADAM: What if I was to ask you how you'd have liked things to have played out with the Peppers?

DAVE: I would have liked to have been able to have a conversation with the band and say, "Look, what are you guys feeling? Here's how I'm feeling. I'm on the fence." Either way I would have liked the same outcome, but (a) I would like to have been friends and (b) I would like to have been respected enough to be involved in the decision making.

ADAM: Absolutely.

DAVE: I don't want to be in a situation where every time I hear the Chili Peppers or think about them, I'm fucking pissed instead of thinking, "Oh, those were fun times."

ADAM: I totally understand that. But looking at it from their insecure point of view, they've got a guy that's a big star . . .

DAVE: Even if that's true, it doesn't mean I brought it on. I can understand their point of view—

ADAM: Well, "brought it on" is the wrong way of putting it, then.

DAVE: I honestly resent the implication that I caused it.

ADAM: Oh, I don't think you caused it—

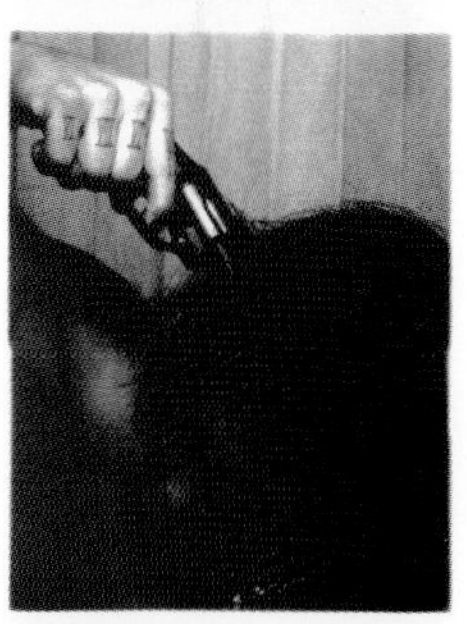

the fuck, man, let's just go make a record." So we wrote and recorded an album in a month and a half, from note one to finished product.

Throughout the process of this album, I became excited about the idea of having so much control. I'd never been able to voice my feelings as a guitar player like that. I had spent twelve years with my mouth shut, having to express myself through the words of other people—occasionally words I didn't believe in.

What ended up happening, I found out later, was that a band employee to whom I had spoken about my excitement over working by myself got off the phone with me and called the rest of the Peppers.

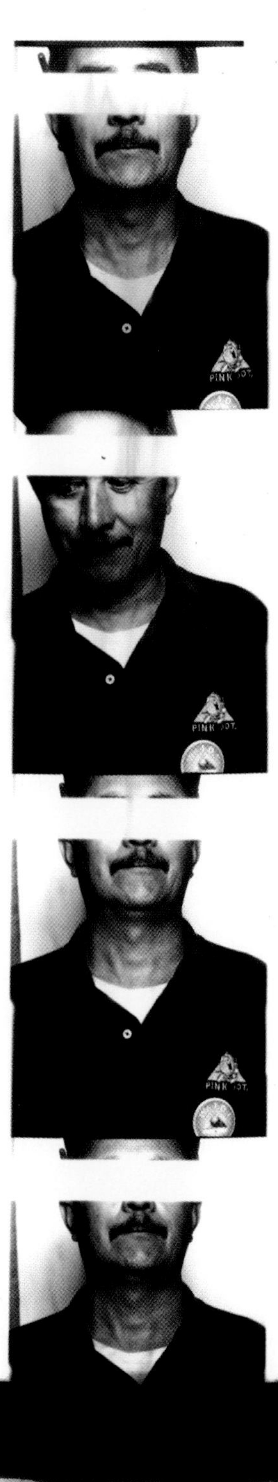

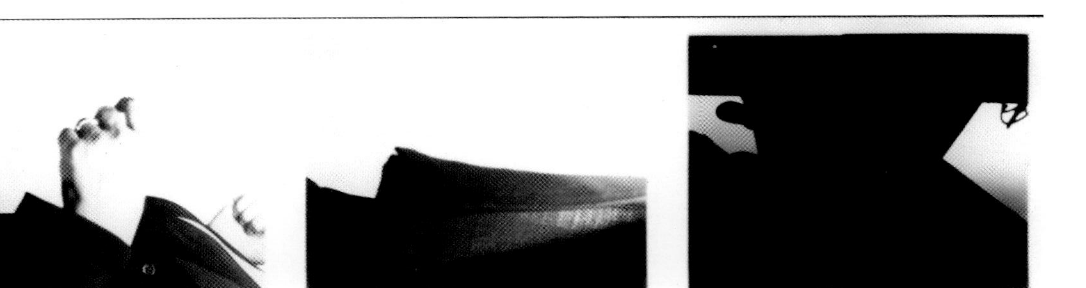

I wanted out

but how did I bring it on?

DAVE: But that's the same thing as bringing it on, don't you think?
ADAM: Do you think your solo thing figured in it at all?
DAVE: Maybe, because I am playing on one record with their drummer, and I'm going on tour with their bass player with Jane's. But you know why I made the record? Because the band took time off and I needed something to do.
ADAM: I understand that. I'm not saying you did anything wrong at all.
DAVE: That's why I did it. I said to Chad, "Let's fucking play something."
ADAM: Maybe what I mean by bringing it on, Dave, is that you do that by being a talented, strong player.
DAVE: That's not bringing it on; that's what they wanted from me.
ADAM: What I meant was that your talent and prestige and direction in the music gave these guys a problem that they couldn't deal with consciously. It happens all the time that bands split up because of ego, and because one guy overshadows another guy and there's a fight for the spotlight. That's never happened before with Perry Farrell.
DAVE: I would never attempt to overshadow anybody anyway—
ADAM: I know you're not trying to do that.
DAVE: I know he [Perry] is just like the raddest, that's why I'm with him. He's the greatest writer. I never questioned him. Even when I was just doing the band, I was like, "I've never seen a better showman or frontman—"
ADAM: You know, I remember that mansion party where Jane's played and Anthony had that exchange with you in the dressing room

Ultimately, I got a call from Flea: "Dave, in order to continue to make music and work in a productive way, we feel like it would be better to do it with another guitar player."

Initially, my reaction was pretty much understanding because I was leaning in that direction anyway. At that point I was relatively okay with it. I asked Flea, "Why? What happened?"

"Well, we all had a meeting." Those were the first words that came out of his mouth. I was floored. If I had been at that meeting, I would have said, "You're right, I have my own thing. Let's be friends."

But under these circumstances, I felt upset and humiliated. And when I asked what their reason was, Flea said, "You know, you've started doing drugs again. We've already lost one guitar player to a drug overdose, and Anthony's had his struggles and is trying to live in a healthy way. And it's not conducive to making music harmoniously."

"So what you're saying is that you're jealous," I replied. At the time, I really thought that was true. There was silence on the other end. I think it was Flea's turn to be floored.

where he said, "You're in the Rock and Roll Hall of Fame now" or something. Basically, he gave it up to you. Do you remember that?

DAVE: Yeah, I do remember that. I remember feeling really emotional about it.

ADAM: I was really impressed that Kiedis seemed to have some humility and was complimenting you on something he was genuinely impressed by. I think this also points to why it's smart that you're doing your own thing too. I think it all points to that in a way . . .

DAVE: Points to that?

ADAM: That you're someone who has enough going on to do it on your own. And maybe you didn't bring it on yourself, but you were prepared for it when it happened, at least artistically speaking. So I understand what you're saying.

DAVE: Do you really?

ADAM: Yes.

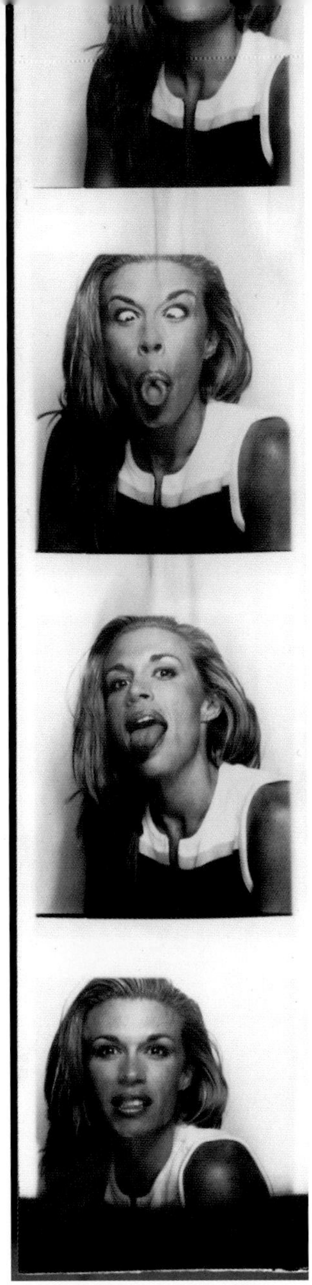

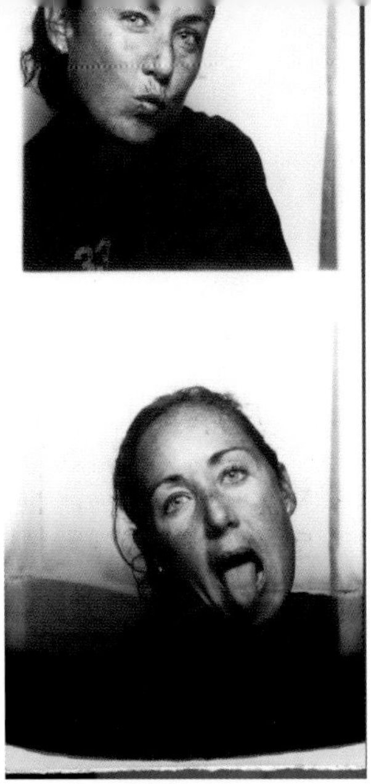

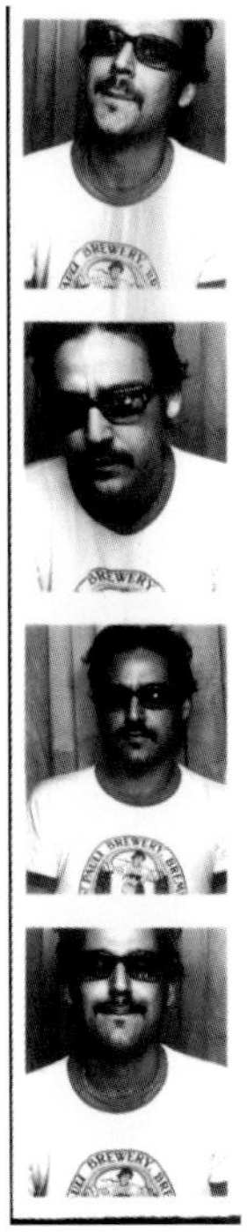

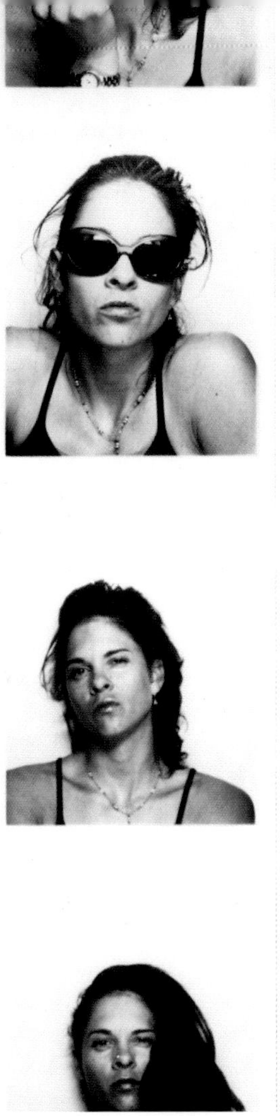

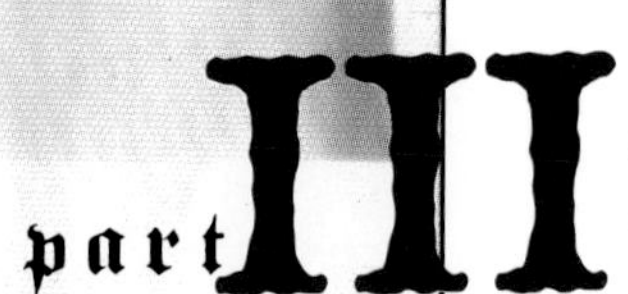

part III THE GREAT STEVE VAI DEBATE: "SPEAK ONLY FOR YOURSELF"

JASON [a record-label employee]: I went to see Les Paul, Slash, Stephen Stills, Steve Vai, and a bunch of other guitarists at the House of Blues last night. It was pretty good, but have you ever seen Steve Vai play before? I don't understand it.

DAVE: How's that?

JASON: It's the way he plays. It's empty. There's nothing behind it. He takes any kind of magic there is in music for you and me, and just . . .

DAVE: Who's saying it's got to make sense to you?

JASON: What I'm saying is that, to him, a guitar is just a piece of wood and six strings. He could just as easily be a carpenter.

DAVE: What do you mean? He's doing what he wants to do; he's playing music. It's his craft, it's joyful. You may not like the way he plays, but you can't say there's nothing behind it.

JASON: Let me put it this way: What Steve Vai plays is not what I seek to get out of music, so I have no interest in it.

DAVE: Okay, that's fair enough; you have no interest in his music. But I'm a guitarist too, and someone may not get the way I express myself.

JASON: But the way he plays the guitar, there's no human element. It doesn't connect in any way.

DAVE: It doesn't connect with you. Seriously,

FLOWER
FLOWER
LOWER
FLOWER

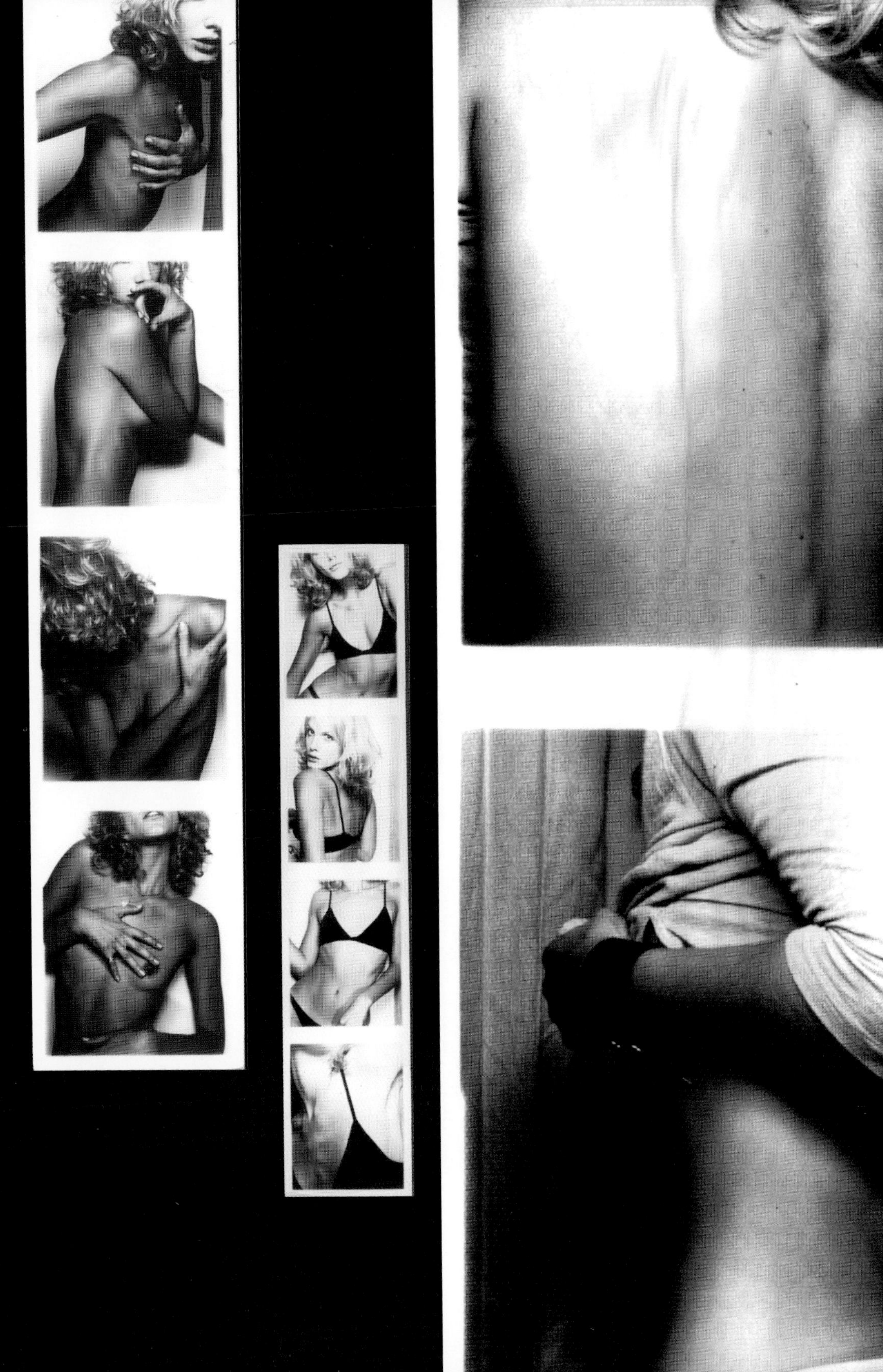

DUB TEAM
WEAK BEATS

But you know what?
I can't see why somebody in China
likes Chinese music.

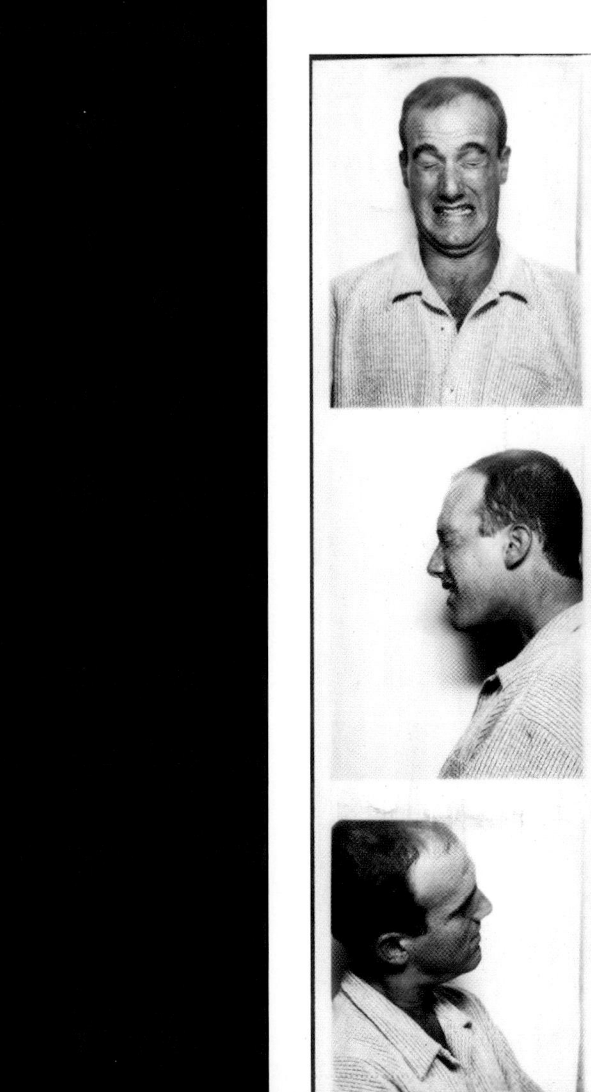

dude, think about it. I don't know how you can say that, because that's really arrogant. Isn't it? Honestly, I don't like him either. I can't stand listening to him play guitar.

JASON: So what's wrong with what I'm saying?

DAVE: You have to add "to me" before that sentence. Because I'll bet you a million dollars there's a listener out there who loves Steve Vai and buys a record and freaks out.

JASON: But they love it for exactly the reasons I don't like it.

DAVE: How do you know what they love it for? Who are you to say what somebody you don't know loves something for? Seriously.

JASON: Yeah, you can bust me every time. But it is possible to listen to something and say, "I may not like that, but I can understand why somebody would like that."

DAVE: But you know what? I can't see why somebody in China likes Chinese music. I don't belong to that culture, I have no idea what it's all about, it's not attractive to me.

JASON: But you can see there's something there, like the high-pitched voices and the way they hold their hands, and there are so many subtleties that you might not understand but you can recognize.

DAVE: There might be a piece of music or a band I would see that with, but not across the board for some type of music. For Steve Vai, though, a concert is how he entertains. And when he comes up with the shit he's coming up with, that's his art.

JASON: All right, let's just say I was disappointed that to him a guitar is just six strings and a piece of wood.

DAVE: Did he say that?

JASON: No, but he played that way.

DAVE: How can you say that?!

JASON: Am I pissing you off or are you just playing devil's advocate?

DAVE: No, I'm just saying that . . .

JASON: Because you're relating this to yourself, and thinking that people have said that about you before or they might say it about your solo album.

DAVE: No, just . . . that's a problem that I'm having with a lot of people. This essentially is the morality issue I have in my mind: One man's perception is not another man's reality. I'm with you, I don't like his playing. It leaves me empty.

JASON: Okay. Then let me correct myself: "To me, it seems like to him it's six strings . . . "

DAVE: *Seems like,* that's the whole point. For him it might not seem that way.

JASON: What if I said, "Listen, man, I love that guy, the way he connects with the guitar, he's fucking amazing"? My perception could be wrong; he may think he's a shitty guitar player. But you wouldn't have busted me on it because I said something positive.

DAVE: Because negativity breeds something more than just an opinion. Negativity breeds arrogance, whereas the positive and complimentary, they tend to be . . .

JASON: Naïveté.

DAVE: I don't think it's naïveté. At the root of it is loving and respect, which this world needs more of. If loving, complimentary actions happen as a result of naïveté and as a result of mistaken perceptions, so what? I don't think that hurts the world and the human race. And I think that's something we need to look out for with people.

JASON: I was joking when I said naïveté, but I see your point. I guess I just didn't like the way he played that night.

Sept

ember

part I HOW TO GET OFF DRUGS WITHOUT REALLY TRYING

It begins like every other month.

"I need some heroin," Navarro says as he holds his lighter under a spoon, watching a white chunk of cocaine dissolve into a small puddle of boiling water.

But it promises to have a different ending.

"I'm going to clean up," he adds, casually.

"What do you mean?"

"I'm going to a place where they clean out your blood in like six hours. They keep you there for just two days."

"Then what?"

"Then I go home."

It sounds too easy. "How do you keep yourself from using drugs afterward?"

"We'll see what happens. I just want to get off the needle."

This is the first time Navarro has ever expressed a desire to clean up, the first time he has admitted that there is something he needs that he can't do for himself.

Whenever the opportunity has arisen in the past, his friends have told him they'd like to see him drug-free. But Navarro's usual response has been one calculated simply to absolve their guilt: to let them know that they've done their part and now no longer have to feel guilty about not saying anything. He is going to decide for himself when enough is enough.

"The fact that you feel guilty," Dave told Adam Schneider one night, "implies that you have power over what I do. You've got to wipe that out of your head. Don't guilt yourself out over something that's actually an egotistical way of thinking." Dave paused, reflecting on the logic of his comment. "Not to be mean about it, but that's a good way to rid yourself of the guilt."

Then there was the time Perry Farrell called and said that he felt responsible for Dave's addiction because Dave was somehow emulating him. Perry explained that he had a dream in which he saw coke spirits who told him to phone.

So what has led Dave to, all of a sudden, decide that the time has come to clean himself up?

"Because it's been almost half a year and I want to start showing up on time to work on my record," he replies. (He has just made a deal this month to release a solo album.)

"It doesn't make sense to have worked this hard to fuck it up," Dave continues. "As long as I can get clean and strong, I'll be okay. I don't care about being high. I don't have a bad life. I'm not a depressed guy. I just want to be able to perform well—and look good doing it."

The doorbell rings and, as if on cue, his drug dealer, Mary, arrives with coke, heroin, and another present—a small metal torch designed for cooking up drugs. Compared to Dave's other dealers—mostly unshaven, friendless males—Mary always looks like she could have other prospects. She is tall, beautiful, and seems intelligent, though she talks so

’t make sense to
ed this hard
it up”

seldom that it's hard to tell. What happened?

"It's a lot more fun to not find something in L.A. than to not find something in South Dakota," Dave offers.

Dave tells her about his plan to clean up, and she doesn't seem disappointed at the prospect of losing a customer. She is actually supportive.

"They have this thing called rapid detox," Dave explains the process. "They put you under and in six hours they artificially induce withdrawal by pumping your body full of a certain kind of hormone and a drug called Narcon. It detaches the opiates from your body's receptors and makes the body reject everything that's impure. So if someone uses heroin, it wouldn't take effect because the receptors are blocked. It's pretty gnarly. I keep asking myself if I'm ready to put my body through worse punishment than shooting coke all day long."

Dave has already met with one doctor for a physical and needs to get in touch with another for post-treatment care. "I'm trying not to do heroin," he tells his dealer. "I've only done two shots of it in the past two days, which is phenomenal for me. And I'm not sick, like I expected to be. They want me to be off coke for five days before the heroin detox, but if I went off coke, I'd be at death's door. It's hard for me to kill the cycle of waking up, calling you, and shooting up. I want to spend a couple days at a place where I can't."

The longer Dave talks, the less convincing he sounds. "In no way am I suggesting that I'll be clean and pure forever," he finally says. "I'll be an addict for the rest of my life."

He constantly checks a new security camera he installed to patrol the front of his house, a sign of either the paranoia that stems from too much coke or the obsessive nature that led to the addiction in the first place. In addition, a trip to the Spy Tech Agency has resulted in hidden cameras in every room—VCRs and clocks with concealed lenses, positioned more for documentation than actual security.

Moments after Mary leaves, a small, somewhat chunky girl appears on the security monitor. Dave lets her in. She has dyed metallic auburn hair and is wearing all black, except for the fur trim of her jacket. She calls herself Hope and is attractive, but only because she is making an extreme effort to look that way. Her breasts are pushed up so that they peek over the top of her lacy dress like two thumbs pressed together.

She first talked to Dave when her friend—who she says is a stripper and Dave says is a prostitute—was living temporarily at the house of a speed freak named Taylor. The stripper/prostitute gave her a phone number and said it was Taylor's, but it turned out to be Dave's. And since Dave could charm his way into anyone's pants, heart, or pocketbook . . .

"Me and my friend called Dave's house and asked if Taylor was there," Hope explains.

"I don't even know anyone named Taylor," Dave says. "She must have gotten my number from another hooker."

"Anyway, Dave kept talking and asking for my phone number. I said, 'You could be a psychopath murderer.' And he told me, 'I'm not a murderer because my mom was murdered.' I thought he was fucking with me because my mom died. She committed suicide two years ago. I thought he knew me and was being an asshole. He gave us the address of his website. But we didn't know who he was yet. Two days later, we went on the site and saw who it was. So we sent him a poem."

"I deleted it," Dave says. "I hate poems."

"He kept deleting them," Hope sighs. "So I called him."

Hope says she moved to Los Angeles to get into porn films. But she just filmed a couple and quit.

SONY

"I don't trust anybody."

"She was probably a prostitute," Dave whispers when she goes to the bathroom, "judging by all the madams she knows."

We gather around the television on the lower floor of Dave's two-story house, and Dave puts in a documentary-in-progress about Jane's Addiction's Relapse tour that he is coproducing. She watches it while he sits at the computer, loading images into his website. The final scene is a beautifully filmed shot of Dave leaning over Perry Farrell and joining mouths with him in a passionate French kiss.

"I should be using this video instead," Hope says as she watches it.

"What's the video you normally use?" I ask, wondering if she is alluding to what I think she is alluding to.

"Some Red Hot Chili Peppers video."

"And when you say *use* . . ."

"Yeah, you know what I mean," she says, blushing.

Now on the prowl, Hope turns to Dave: "You don't have a girlfriend, do you?"

"Why?"

"I can't imagine you spending all that time on the computer," she replies. "I'd throw it out the window."

She probably made this comment to regain the power she lost by confessing to Dave that she was attracted to him, but instead she only succeeded in pushing a button—the exact same one Tori had pressed in July.

"Well, I don't think I'd want you as my girlfriend," Dave responds.

"Why?"

"I don't think I'd want a girlfriend who did films."

"Why? I did bondage films. All girl-girl."

"When I say that, I'm not putting down films. I'm not emotionally strong enough to separate sex on film from reality. I don't trust anybody."

"Neither do I," Hope says, trying to cut her losses and return to common ground.

"After my mother and aunt were murdered, I realized that anybody is capable of anything."

"So what happened with your mother?" Hope asks, crossing her pale, pudgy legs on the floor. "Who found her?"

"My dad," Dave says. "I was supposed to stay with her that night but at the last minute I went to my dad's. If I had been there, he would have killed me too." He pauses. "It was so hard on us. She was a model when she was young, on *The Price Is Right* and in a bunch of commercials. She also did set design for commercials when I was a teen. I would cry when they came on. So eventually I turned to drugs and music. That's when I seriously got into music. Those were the two things that made me not feel it. Whenever I had a good time, I'd beat myself up for it, which is so unfair to do to yourself."

"I can't figure out which is worse," Hope says, her eyes reddening, "for a parent to be murdered or for a parent to commit suicide. I don't just feel angry, I blame myself. I hate my mother for what she did and the pain she caused, and that she didn't leave me a note. She lied to me. She had problems like this for most of her life. She called me and kept saying she was going to kill herself and how she was going to do it. I broke down and said, 'You can't keep doing this to me.' And she promised she wouldn't, unless she was really seriously considering it. So she flat-out lied to me. I found receipts from where she had bought a gun. She'd been very carefully planning it for a long time. And she flat-out lied to me."

"I feel guilty because before the guy killed my mother, he broke into my house at gunpoint and held me up, and he made me promise not to tell anybody," Dave says. "And I didn't. And a week later he killed my mother, so I've always felt like I could have prevented it. He was free for ten years. They caught him on *America's Most Wanted.* I remember hearing her name on television, and then watching a dramatization of it with an actor playing me. I had to actually sit there and face him in court last year. I had to take the stand as a witness, and to the left of me were pictures from the scene on a fucking board that they didn't even cover up. I had to ask for them to be covered."

"I had a premonition since I was a little girl," Hope blurts after an awkward silence. "My biggest fear was that my mother would commit suicide. I couldn't imagine anything worse. But even if you know that, how do you prepare for it? After my mom died, a porn star whose makeup I did killed herself, then a friend jumped off a bridge in New York, and an ex-boyfriend overdosed intentionally. Another guy I'd known since I was a kid also overdosed, but it was accidental. He never did drugs, but I kept telling him how much he and my boyfriend had in common. Eventually, I introduced them, and my boyfriend got him hooked on heroin. So I feel guilt there also."

"I had premonitions too," Dave says. "I kept having them for a whole month. I knew things were shit in the house."

"Do you still have your father to talk to?" Hope asks.

"I'm in a fight right now with my dad," Dave answers, wistfully. "I'm not even sure what it's about. But I know how important he is to me. I said something scary to my friend Tori the other day. I said, 'When my dad checks out, there's no more being careful.' It's the same way for him too; if anything happened to me, it would destroy him."

"At least there's correspondence between you and your dad," Hope says, uncrossing her legs and stroking them with her hands. "I met my dad once, and never saw any photos of him. I knew nothing about him. One day when I was a teenager I was waiting for a bus, and this guy standing a few feet away started approaching me. Even though I had no idea what my father looked like, I knew it was him. He walked right up to me and said my name and said he was my father. I said, 'No, you're not. I don't have a father.' The only thing I remember him saying are seven words: 'Fuck you, you're just like your mother.' And then he walked away.

"I know his history now," Hope continues. "He tried to kill my mother when she was pregnant with me. He kept kicking her in the stomach. She was smaller than me, and my dad was 6'2". My dad kicked her in the stomach while she was pregnant, threw her down a flight of stairs, and pushed her out of a car. And she still didn't have a miscarriage. All this stuff he did to her because he didn't want to have a kid. My mother had to leave town to give birth to me, and to retaliate my dad beat up her brother, who was in the process of becoming a cop. So he got back at my dad, broke his ribs and everything. My dad, who came from a prominent family, pressed charges, so my uncle never got to be a cop. He was finished.

"He never contacted me, even after my mother killed herself. For my high school graduation he sent a friend to give me an envelope filled with three hundred dollars as a present. I just ripped it up and threw it in his face."

"That is why I don't want to have a kid," Dave says. "I don't want to be that guy."

Dave walks into the bathroom to shoot up, then returns and tells Hope he has work to do. She walks upstairs to the photo booth to document her visit and then hesitantly approaches the front door, as if there is something she has forgotten to do. As Dave hugs Hope goodbye, she wraps her arms around his head and tries to navigate his lips toward hers. He turns his head to the side and holds the door open for her.

part II TEN WAYS TO TIE OFF

1. **A GUITAR CABLE OR STRAP.** ("You leave the guitar plugged in, of course.")
2. **ELECTRICAL CORDS FROM KITCHEN APPLIANCES.** ("Going to the kitchen creates the illusion that you're not hiding, especially if you've already gone to the bathroom twice that night. If you leave the fridge open and tie off with a nearby electrical cord, it just looks like you're trying to get a drink.")
3. **IN PARTICULAR, CORDS FROM TOASTERS.** ("The toaster weighs the cord down perfectly around your arm so you don't have to use two hands.")
4. **THE CORD CONNECTING A TELEPHONE HANDSET TO THE RECEIVER.** ("You can be paging your dealer while doing your last hit.")
5. **THE SLEEVE OF A SHIRT OR THE LEG OF A PAIR OF PANTS.** ("Usually I'm wearing the shirt or pants. I'll just take off one leg or arm.")
6. **TWIGGY RAMIREZ'S DREADLOCKS.** ("That's the only live animal I've ever used.")
7. **THE SASH ON A ROBE.** ("It's the breakfast of champions.")
8. **A COMPUTER MOUSE CORD.** ("You can always email 911 if there's a problem.")
9. **A CONDOM.** ("Just make sure it's not lubricated, it's not your last one, and you take it off your arm before going back in the room or restaurant.")
10. **CAR SAFETY BELTS.** ("I've actually gone so far as to reach in the back of the car, grab an empty Coke can, rip it in half, turn it upside down so the little indentation on the bottom becomes its own spoon, and cook the heroin in it. Then I suck it up with a syringe and tie myself off with my shoulder strap, all while driving. I've even gotten my cousin, who's a terrible shot, off while driving.")

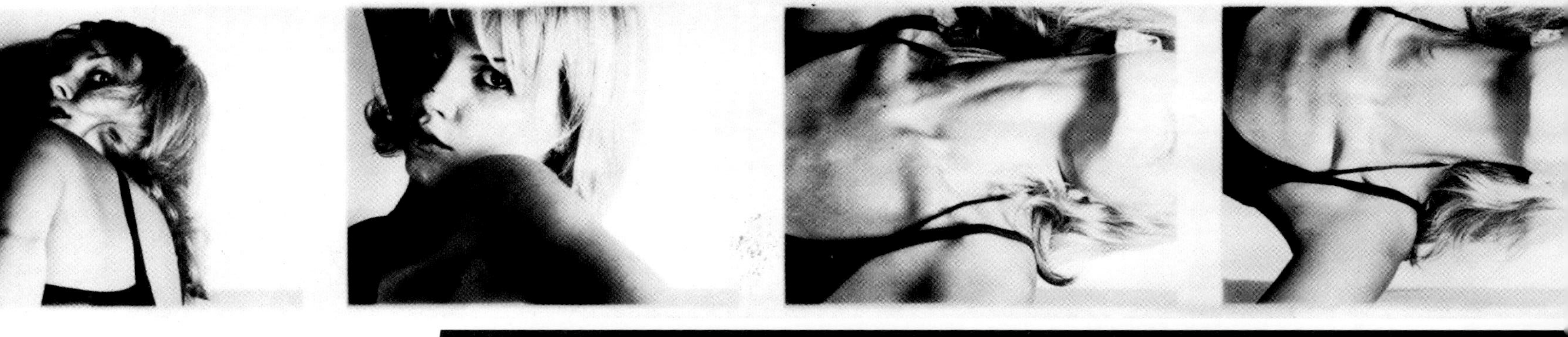

“If I’m insane right now, I don’t want to be restored to sanity.”

III ON DAVE'S DICK

The phone rings. It is Bobbie Brown, known for her appearances in art films like the Warrant "Cherry Pie" video, an episode of *Married with Children* in which she plays a sexy supermarket dweller, and a CD infomercial that features her talking about the rock stars she's met backstage.

"I'm at Jack in the Box," she says.

"So?" Dave asks.

"I'm with two blond friends."

"Do you want to come over?" Dave suddenly changes his mind. "Just for a little while. A very little while."

One friend is Kelly, a tan blond with shoulder-length hair, a soft figure, and a sweet, almost childish face. She seems like just another one of the many women who come to Los Angeles because in the small towns in which they grew up, everyone told them that they were so beautiful and popular they should move to Hollywood to become a star. But they arrive in Los Angeles only to discover that there are thousands of other special small-town girls just like them, all competing for the exact same jobs, all getting seduced by the same rich, older men, and all convinced that anytime they want to they can quit taking the drugs they are fed night after night.

This month, Kelly is going out with a guy named Richard. "He's on Studio A and I'm on Studio B," she explains.

"On what?"

"Oh, a little show called *Baywatch*." The funny thing is that no one who has ever seen Kelly's photo can recognize her from *Baywatch*. Even Pamela Anderson has never heard her name before. Maybe she plays the role of Sunbather #6. "When I met Richard, I loved the way he moved. And when we talked, it was real. We were just two people who felt real."

She keeps saying real, as if without each other Kelly and Richard would discover their true fakeness. Their relationship seems to be built less on love and more on being a good conversation piece. Many people in (or trying to be in) the entertainment business in Hollywood have a very narcissistic view of friendships and relationships: a true friend or lover, they say, is someone who makes them feel good about themselves, someone who helps them in their fight to hold on to the self-esteem that every day is being chipped and frayed in the competitive, status-seeking world around them. Other human beings are simply ornaments to their own vanity.

Kelly, Dave, and Bobbie pile into the photo booth. Dave suggests a committed three-way relationship.

After Kelly walks out of the photo booth, the other blond, a tall, collagen-lipped woman who, through the miracle of modern surgery appears to be in her late twenties, steps in with Dave. She has remained in the background all evening, not speaking a word or displaying any evidence of a personality, but evidently she has other talents: as the camera snaps away, she performs caricatures of famous rock duos—Page and Plant, Lennon and McCartney, Anthony and Flea—with her breasts. Despite the impressive variety show, which also includes her requesting a black sock to use as a Van Dyke for a Dave and Perry imitation, Bobbie is soon snoring away on the couch. Dave disappears downstairs immediately afterward, mumbling something about taking care of business.

Kelly, in the meantime, can't stand the loss of attention. She keeps knocking on the door downstairs, whining that she is ready to go home, complaining that her friend is never going to leave because she is tweaked out on glass (a killer amphetamine that cuts your nose to shreds on the way up). Between lamentations, she vamps in the photo booth, removing her clothing one item at a time and asking with each disrobing how she looks naked.

I walk downstairs to find Dave with his dick in his hand, masturbating. It is a pose I'm familiar with because a picture of it is on his website. He's very happy with the penis God gave him. "I'll be upstairs in two minutes," he says, not bothering to stop.

Meanwhile, upstairs, the breast puppeteer is getting restless. "I have to bring my daughter to school," she says, still running on glass, "then I'll be back over."

By the time Dave returns to the room, the women are gone. "You should have seen how much I came," Dave tells me. "I came all over myself."

Dave walks to the photo booth and removes Kelly's strips from the tray. There are more than a dozen of them, and they are fantastic. In black and white, she is the hottest, most eye-catching woman who has ever set foot in Dave's house. She made love to the photo-booth lens like no one before her (perhaps because it *was* a lover, in the sense of being an ornament to her vanity). Dave reconsiders her hotness and begins to devise strategies of getting her back to the house without offending Bobbie or her blond friend. Maybe he could include her on the jacket of this book as a pretext for calling her.

Dave brings the photos to his computer and starts scanning the month's strips into his hard drive. As the night progresses, he begins to fade. He is moving slower, thinking slower, responding slower. But he refuses to stop working. Finally he calls some hookers (classed under the heading PELICANS along with drug dealers in his address book, which probably has more pelicans than the entire Florida coast).

"Just one girl, real quick." He leaves two messages, then passes out on the couch with one hand on the phone, the other down his pants.

ber

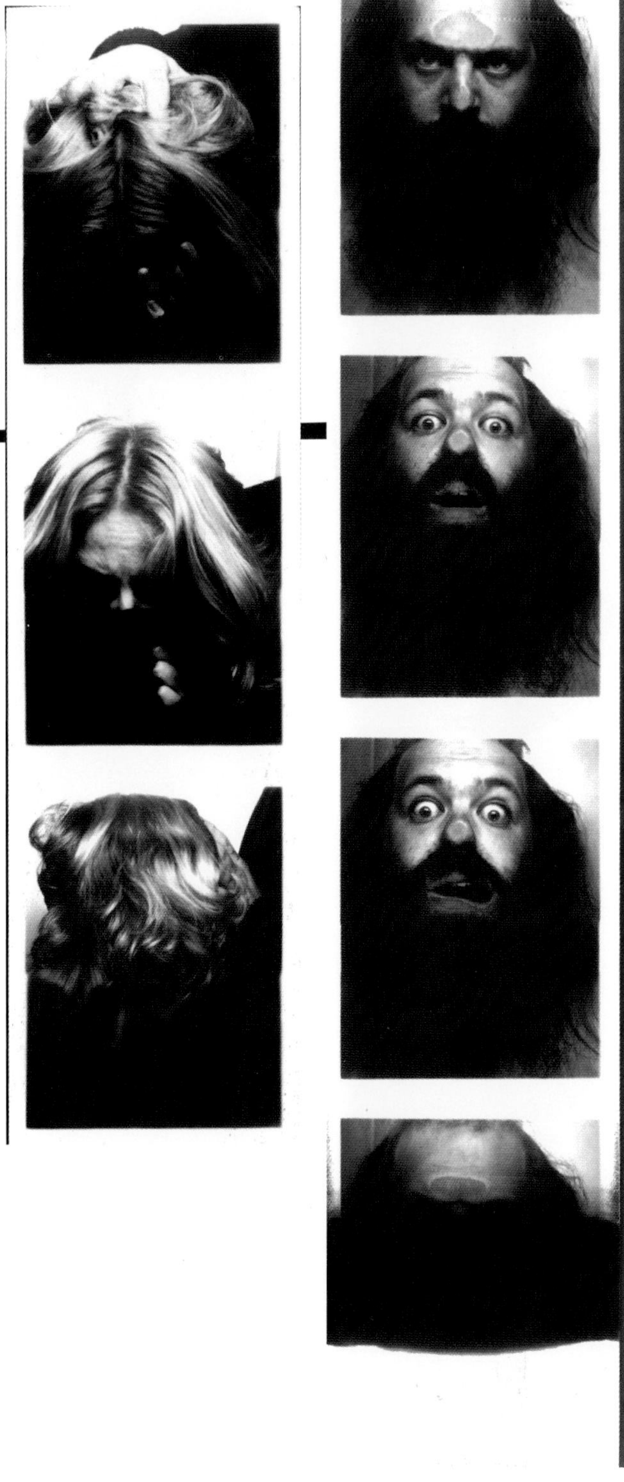

part I DEAR DIARY

BY ADRIA TRUE

July 17, 1996

You will never believe what happened to me yesterday. Stacy, Isobel, Tim, Howie, and I went to go see KISS yesterday at Irvine. They were playing in full makeup for the first time in like fifteen years. Okay, get to the point. Isobel and I flirted with security and got backstage, and who was the first person I ran into? None other than Mr. Dave Navarro in the flesh. And do I even need to mention that, out of all my friends, I'm the only one who has not met him, stalked him, or been crazy infatuated with him?

What happened was Isobel and I were going to the bathroom and we saw a bunch of guys hanging out, so I glanced over and almost fainted when I saw Dave staring directly in our direction. He shot all this energy at me with those big, sensitive eyes. Isobel looked at me, because she picked up on it too. At first I thought, *uh-uh,* but when I turned toward the bathroom (I had to go bad), he came up to me. Then I thought, *uh-oh.*

DAVE: Excuse me, have I met you before? Actually, I'm lying. We haven't met before. But I did see you at a Peppers show we played at Moguls a couple months ago, didn't I? You were wearing big sunglasses, and an orange shirt, sitting on top of the speakers, right?
ME: Doink . . . [I couldn't get my lips to work.]
DAVE: Hi, I'm Dave. [Like I didn't know!]
ME: I think I saw you at Perry's last weekend. [Duh. . .]
DAVE: Well, if you saw me, why didn't you say hi or introduce yourself? [Ouch.]

We walked together and I swear that every girl we passed gave me the evil eye. Anthony Kiedis even gave me his number! But I only had eyes for Dave. He picked up my stinky, filthy feet and gave me a foot massage under the table. Wish I'd gotten that pedicure! Isobel was watching it all, totally jealous, which is fine because she deserves it after sleeping with Todd. Dave asked me to go home with him. I said that I wanted to, but I wasn't that kind of girl, though I really wanted to be that kind of girl. He hugged me good-bye and pressed his phone number into my sweaty palm.

At two A.M. I was knocking on Dave's door. Silly me. I had to take a plane to Paris for a fashion show the next day. And he was about to go on tour. So I thought we'd just talk and then never see each other again. I promised myself I wouldn't do anything with him. But I've never felt lips like his before in my life. (Yeah, some life!)

In a velvet room lit like a church, this gentle Pan seduced me with his pipes. He took my hand and said, "I can't say I won't kiss you." (So sure of himself.) And he leaned over and our mouths locked and our tongues intertwined and every fiber of his being poured into me. I felt like I'd been there before. With his fingers, he stroked my hair from front to back, and a soft wave of chills shook through my body. I bit into his lip. "You can bite me as hard as you want," he whispered. I already knew that.

We walked downstairs, and I found myself naked in a dark room with a mirrored wall. I wondered how many women that mirror had seen. I watched my reflection as Dave scooped me up and laid me down on the plush lavender of his bed. He placed a hand on either side of my head, and pulled it back gently but firmly. He sunk his teeth into my neck—still gently—and entered me slowly—still firmly. I opened and took him in all the way, and a feeling that I've never had before rushed over me and we melted into each other. When he caught me watching him watching me in the mirror, he turned his head and spit into my mouth. I wanted to freeze that moment, so that I'd never have to leave it my whole life.

He snored. It didn't bother me, so long as he kept holding on to me. I held on to him holding on to me. In the morning, he woke me up with the most beautiful music on the piano and brought me coffee in bed. Then his driver had to come and take him to San Francisco. He grabbed me again in the doorway and kissed me passionately for all the neighbors to see. I took my grandmother's ring off my finger and slipped it on his. I hope it makes him think about me every day. I hope it keeps him awake thinking about how very clever I am. I hope my absence makes his heart grow even fonder.

My horoscope: "Leave your past behind and make a fresh start. A new opportunity, friend, or love interest enters your life now. There is nothing to be afraid of." (Yeah, right.)

July 18

My first day here was okay. I had to break down and get ice cream. I felt it on the runway and at the photo shoot. All day I couldn't stop thinking about Dave. I want to call him *so* much, but I don't want to scare him. Why does this stuff always happen when you least expect it or want it? I don't want to give this guy power over my mind and heart, but he already has it and I don't want to be hurt. Can something really be so intense after one day? Do you think he really remembered me sitting on the speaker at his show? What the fuck is going on? Help . . .

July 20

I told you. Now I'm pissed. The very first girl I talked to in Paris said she'd dated Dave or fucked Dave or something. And she was a trashy whore. She told me he was married a bunch of times. I saw his mother in my hotel mirror yesterday. She was a beautiful person, inside and out. She was trying to communicate with me. She saw me and she talked with me. I asked her to protect us, and she told me that I could help Dave.

July 22

Dave and I finally talked. Yay! "Is this the light of my life on the phone?" he asked. He was so sweet, but how many women did he say that to today? Even if I am the only one, I can *not* let another self-centered, egomaniacal rock star suck me into his fucked-up world.

He said he'd buy me plane tickets to come visit him in Prague tomorrow. I *so* badly wanted to say yes, but I can't just abandon my work over some guy I've seen once. So I said no and now I hate myself. What if he flies someone else to Prague? What if he's found a new light of his life by the time I get back? He promised that would never happen. Then we both admitted that no one had ever dumped us before. So basically what we're looking at here are two totally self-confident, narcissistic, and egomaniacal people. This is not going to be easy. But that's okay: we have his mother's spirit to guide us. And I'm a Taurus. I can handle it.

HIDE

part II ABOUT A GIRL

This is the girl who broke Dave's heart, one of the reasons why he remade his life into a world of parties, prostitutes, painkillers, and photo strips. And last month, she came back into that world. In her first photo strip, Adria, a willowy top-heavy brunette, can be seen flipping the bird to the camera in all four frames, as if to say that she is back in Dave's life against her will. She was reluctant then, although the very fact that she expressed her reluctance through her participation in his photo project was a sign that these defenses would soon break down. Perhaps it served her own documentary needs: proof that she had maintained her pride as she willingly reentangled herself in a relationship she swore was behind her.

Though we'll never know the true story, because memory provides far less reliable reproductions than photographs, Dave remembers the courtship a little differently than Adria's diary tells it. "At first I tried to avoid her," he says. "I assumed she wasn't girlfriend material because I met her at that show and she went home with me that night. Then I went on tour and she went to work in Paris, and she would call me once in a while. But she was too pretty for me to like and she was only about nineteen. When I came home from the tour, I was tired and burnt out and months had gone by since I had met her. But that night she stopped by without calling, and I hate that. I hid inside with the lights off until she drove away. For weeks afterward, she called me and I wouldn't call her back. Every now and then she'd catch me unaware: she'd walk her dog near Starbucks, where she knew I went to get coffee every morning after the gym. I felt like I was being stalked.

"We did get together a few times, but I'd always try to keep her at arm's length—meeting in hotel rooms instead of at my house. I didn't want her in my house and getting involved with my life. I tried everything I could to stay away from her."

With love, you can take all the precautions you want to protect yourself, but no armor is thick enough to keep it out. Once Dave let her in his house, they left the terrestrial plane and entered their own bubble world. But they built a vacuum so tight that, after a while, the bubble began to collapse under the pressure. During a New York trip, she broke up with Dave after he took ecstasy with a model friend of hers at a Halloween party. They began dating again a few weeks later (the first breakup in a relationship is never a fatal bullet—only a warning shot), but this time it was a fragile, tempestuous alliance that lasted until Adria flew to Las Vegas during the Jane's Addiction reunion tour and broke up with Dave again, accelerating his downward spiral.

"Adria called me, and asked if I wanted to

get together, which I'd been dying to do because I missed her so bad," Dave said about her reappearance in his life. "I've always loved her and probably always will. And I knew that the only thing that kept us apart was pride. She didn't call me, I didn't call her. So I wasn't with the woman I love for almost a year because I was being proud and she was being proud. And it breaks my heart to think that."

So Adria is back, and Dave's house is beginning to change. There are fewer people over, as reflected in the decrease in photo strips. Often, he will spend the night in his living room, working on the computer until dawn while Adria sleeps downstairs. Although the drugs remain ("Adria has me smoking pot again," Dave says one night, "and frankly I'm afraid it will lead to harder things"), the circus is dying down.

Only when Adria is away do the clowns start to stream in again, running around in painted faces and high-heeled shoes. The prostitutes invite themselves over, again just to hang out, with no sex or money involved. And this is not kept from Adria: the photo strips now serve the additional purpose of enabling her to monitor the goings-on at the house when she is not there.

The changes in Dave's life are mirrored physically in his living space. As he grows more stable, so too does his house. He buys a new refrigerator, gets his kitchen redone in a *2001* space-age style, installs recessed lighting in his living room, buys a washer and dryer, hooks up digital satellite television, and gets a new car—a Mercedes-Benz 500SL convertible. As in everything else Dave does, he goes overboard, pouring money into his home.

"That's pretty conscious," he explains. "Part of letting myself go is letting my house go. As I get it together, the house gets more put together and there are less people in the book. The girlfriend is in place. The only thing to go now is the drug use. I really think I learned a lot this time about myself, and what the things in life that truly bring me joy are. And what the illusions that bring me joy are."

He pauses and paces across the carpet. The tone of the documentation is beginning to change as well. The story is no longer about the party house, the new Factory. It is now about a relationship. Adria is a very mystical person: she believes in voodoo and magic and special powers, not unlike his stalker from June. ("If you're attractive, you can talk to my dead mom all day," Dave jokes when the comparison is made.) Suddenly Dave is documenting coincidences in their lives that have to do with ladybugs, and trying to figure out whether a colorfully wrapped totem found under his couch is a voodoo spell of bewitchment that Adria has cast on him.

"I'm learning that human contact has brought me more joy than I'd like to admit," Dave continues. "I never wanted to be dependent on others because I've been hurt so much. I was an only child. I didn't want to have to be around other human beings to feel whole. But this entire experience has taught me that there is a happy medium within reach. My plan is not only to clean my house and my life up, but to search for that medium, that middle ground. I'd love to live less insanely."

It is a strange statement considering that just a month ago, Dave said, "If you threw a woman into this equation right now, I'd be a mad fucking mess." When asked to describe Adria then, he compared her to the movie *Snow White*—not to the protagonist but to the evil queen asking, "Mirror, mirror on the wall / Who's the fairest of them all?"

Although Dave was married before, it was not as serious a relationship. It was to a woman, Rhian, whom he had met at the rock club the Whisky-A-Go-Go. After two intense weeks together, a combination of escapism and obsession led them to Las Vegas to get married by an Elvis Presley impersonator. The

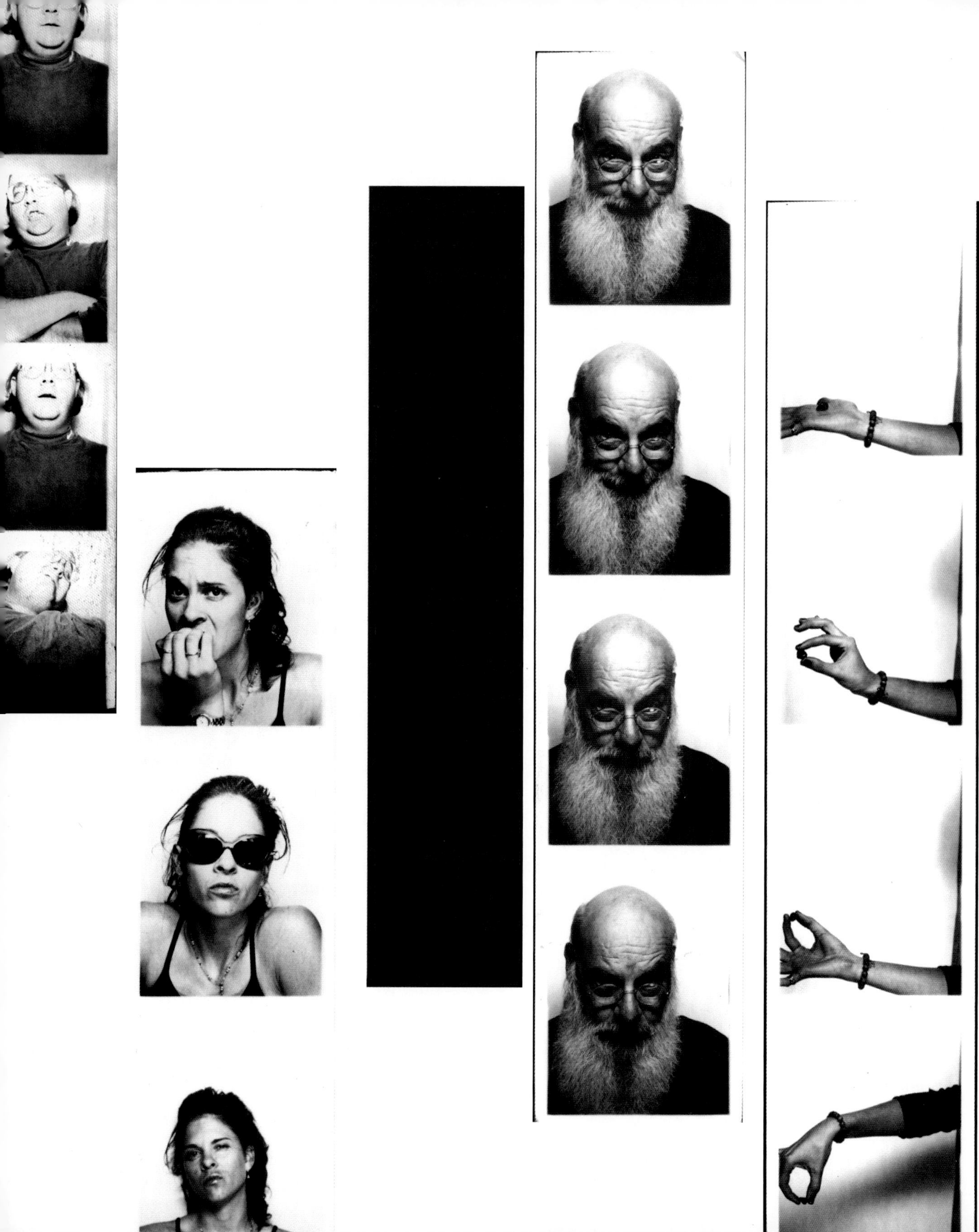

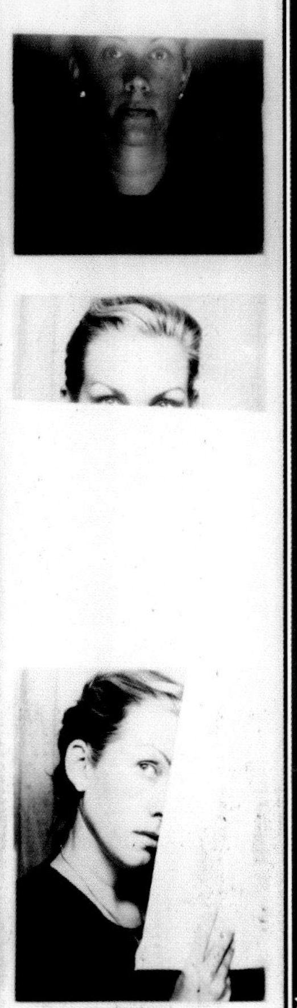

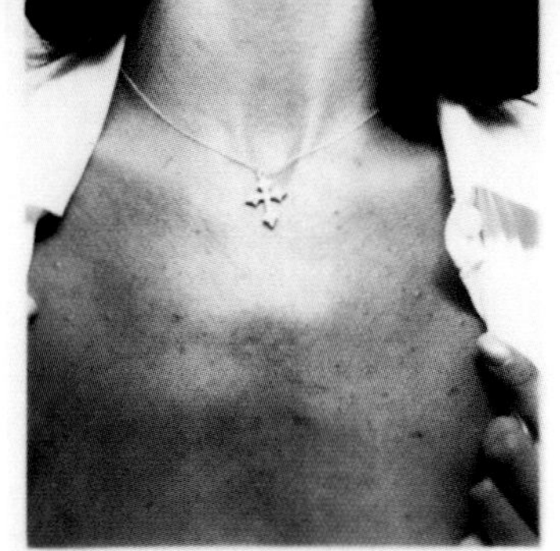

. . . the clowns start to stream in again,
running around
in painted faces
and high-heeled shoes.

marriage was annulled after a month.

Dave picks up his guitar, puts Jimi Hendrix's "Are You Experienced" on his stereo, and starts playing along, weaving in and out of Hendrix's solos. He often does this to practice. When he fumbles over a riff, he pauses and says he has just thought of the most egotistical thing a guitarist could ever do: release a record in which he or she plays along with Hendrix in order to "fix" everything that's wrong with the original recordings.

"I remember riding a skateboard in a skate park and hearing 'Purple Haze,'" Dave recalls. "And that moment, I knew that playing guitar was what I was going to do.

"Since then, almost every dream I've ever had has been handed to me, even my new dreams," he continues. "In retrospect I've gone further than I ever intended to—as an artist, as an icon, as a personality, and financially. So what am I so sad about all the time?"

Half an hour later, the answer comes to him: "Because what I was looking for the whole time was human compassion, a relationship."

I've ever had
has been handed to me,
even my new dreams."

part III CRYSTAL KOALAS, PET ROCKS, AND THE TENNIS MOM THEORY

The following was transcribed from a tape left running during Navarro's first session with a therapist since the commencement of this project. The date was October 3 at four P.M.

YOU MAY BE AFRAID OF ABANDONMENT, AND THAT MAY BE REFLECTED IN YOUR CHOICE OF PARTNERS.

That's true. I essentially always pick out the same type of woman, which is somebody who is pretty codependent and pretty suffocating. If you put a hundred women in a room and said, "Pick the one of your choice—you have that power today," I would somehow pick the one who is the most unstable.

They say that you look for the woman who is your mother, and you try to make her correct the wrongs your mother did. And I'm certainly looking for a mother figure. That's probably why I have this Rene Russo fascination, probably why I was interested in Pamela Des Barres, probably why I always go for totally put-together rich older women. I have a phrase called "the tennis mom." I'm totally into tennis moms, like a friend's rad blond mother who plays tennis because she really has nothing else to do. And she's had every surgery known to man, and she's rich, and her husband doesn't hang around because he's off fucking some younger blond. My dream was to be a paid boy toy for one of these women. But at the same time, the true love of my life, who I'm starting to date again now, is eight years younger than me. And she is just as unstable as me: I have mother issues, she has father issues.

WHAT KIND OF RELATIONSHIP DID YOUR PARENTS HAVE?

My parents had a rough divorce. I can't judge them for that but at the same time it was hard to see both of my parents go through so many boyfriends and girlfriends. My dad is so suave: tall, dark, and handsome, like a James Bond type. He could just pull women. He had this saying, "twenty-four and out the door," meaning that when his girlfriend turned twenty-four, that was it. And he kind of stuck to it. I couldn't believe it. Imagine walking around the house with these women around all the time. So maybe that's where the older-woman thing comes from. I don't know what it is, but I always feel inferior when I'm with them. But at the same time, I enjoy feeling that way. I'm so in love the woman can do anything she wants to me.

But then check with me six months down the line and I'm a different person. I'll get furious at the smallest thing. I remember coming home one time and my girlfriend was on the computer. I wanted to sign on to America Online, and she was sitting there downloading pictures of fairies. I told her, "There's nothing bothering me" when she asked what was wrong. But inside I wanted to die. I broke up with her soon after that.

I also get insanely jealous. Not at first, but after a few months I'll get paranoid that she's into other guys. I will start imagining shit, and getting pictures in my head which are really bad to get, and then it just becomes a sickness. And in her head she's already dealt with the fact that she thinks that I've been with ten zillion girls on the road. They deal with that shit right away when they're deciding if they want to be with you. I have a theory about jealousy: nine times out of ten we're wrong, and if it's the tenth time and we're right, there's nothing we can do. So it's useless to say or do anything about it.

TELL ME ABOUT THE FIRST TIME YOU FELT BETRAYED OR MISLED BY A GIRLFRIEND. I SUSPECT IT WAS AT A VERY EARLY AGE.

It was when I was thirteen and with my first girlfriend, whose name was Jillian. She was older than me, and was the most incredibly rad chick that anybody had ever seen in my age range. She was very developed and mature. She could look like a woman if she wanted, but she had this harelip. I never noticed it, though, because I was too busy looking at her breasts. I was so excited that I had a real girlfriend and we were going to have sex that the harelip didn't exist for me.

When we finally did have sex, I came right away. Then she asked me to leave. She was really upset or ashamed, I think. We never talked about it. And of course I was bummed, but I was also so excited. I walked home just thinking, "I fucked a girl! I fucked a girl!" I basically fell in love for the first time. We were on and off for a long time, and I was the envy of all my friends because she was the prettiest girl any of us had ever seen, maturity-wise.

But I was so blind. A friend of mine named Ian used to ask, "Dude, what would you do if Jillian hooked up with another guy?" And I'd laugh and say that it would never happen. I even wrote a song about her, using words that began with each letter in her name to make the sentences in the chorus. It was really sappy. We used to take acid for weeks at a time and go to the park, tripping all day. Finally, Ian and Stephen Perkins (who I went on to play in Jane's Addiction with) told me that she had slept with a friend of mine who we went to school with. I was so destroyed. I had never felt that kind of pain before.

It was the same year that my mom died, a year when I was losing all the females in my life. And it just annihilated me. While we were going out, I had collected everything: movie tickets, pictures of us, rocks we found, so much stuff that my room was almost a shrine to her. So instead of yelling at her or freaking out, I put everything in my room in a big bag and took it over to her mom's house. I knocked on the door and asked if she'd come out. We sat on the grass and I went through each thing, one by one, and showed it to her and said things like, "What a great time that was . . . Remember this? . . . Oh God, what about these bears? . . . Remember when we were on acid and found this rock?"

I spent two hours going through everything. We broke into a nursery school once and stole these tiny chairs, and we used to pretend that they were going to be for our kids. I even brought those over. And basically I just left everything on the lawn, spread out around her, and said, "Good-bye." I turned around to walk to my car, and when I looked back at her, she was sitting in the grass, a sea full of shit around her, crying her eyes out. And I just left. It was one of the first times I felt like vindictiveness and rage and revenge could work. That no matter what anyone says, you can win. And I did it by reinforcing that I was a great guy who loved her.

THAT'S A DANGEROUS WAY OF THINKING.

I know. I realized the day I left Jillian crying that I'd never trust anybody again. And then I began to act like the most untrustworthy guy in the world. I fucked the girlfriend of a close friend. And when I was on Lollapalooza, my girlfriend and I were hanging out in our room with Siouxsie Sioux, her husband, and Richie [Richard Patrick] from Filter. I had started this thing where I'd make out with all the guys on the tour. Me and Richie were making out, and finally it turned into the guys making out with the girls. And then it came down to pretty much just me kissing Siouxsie, who's another older woman I've always had a crush on. And she looked at me and said, "I don't want to kiss you." I said, "Why not?" And she goes, "I just don't want to."

I told her that maybe she was afraid to kiss me, and she said, "Maybe." Then, literally the next thing I remember is lifting my head up and realizing that we were going at it next to my girlfriend, who left and slammed the door shut. I chose an unhealthy, dishonest relationship over a more healthy one. That developed into a strange affair, because I was doing a lot of drugs at the time. I would wake up naked in hotel lobbies.

I HOPE YOU'VE BEEN MAKING AN EFFORT TO HAVE HEALTHIER RELATIONSHIPS NOW.
Now I have my guard up more. There was a girl over at my house last month that I was thinking of sleeping with. But at one point, she was crawling across my floor when suddenly she went, "Oh my God, there's a fucking bug. Kill it!" And she just completely snapped and fist-punched this bug with all her might. A completely different person came out, just rage and fury. That was fucking frightening. I was like, "Dave, whatever you do, don't touch this girl!"

MAYBE THAT'S WHY YOU SEE PROSTITUTES, BECAUSE YOU DON'T NEED TO HAVE YOUR GUARD UP LIKE THAT. THERE IS NO WAY THEY CAN HURT YOU, NO WAY TO GET EMOTIONALLY INVOLVED.
That's exactly it. There are no complications, no baggage. It is just sex, which is a lot more honest to me than leading somebody on emotionally just because you want to have sex with them. When I was on tour once in Australia, I met this hooker and ended up seeing her for two nights. I guess she took a liking to me the first night, because on the second night I came out of the bathroom and on the table was a little crystal koala that wasn't there before. I asked her what it was, and she got all quiet. It was a little gift she had bought for me. She liked me. And I told her, "Wait a minute, you're not supposed to be human. You're not supposed to have feelings. This isn't about feelings." And I couldn't have sex with her after that. It just destroyed it. So I had her leave.

But on the way home from Australia, I started thinking about her. She was really cute, and looked kind of like Anne Archer. And I thought that maybe at the agency she worked for there were stacks and stacks of crystal koalas for the hookers to give to their clients on the second date, as a technique of making the guys think that they're special. Maybe she didn't give a shit about me.

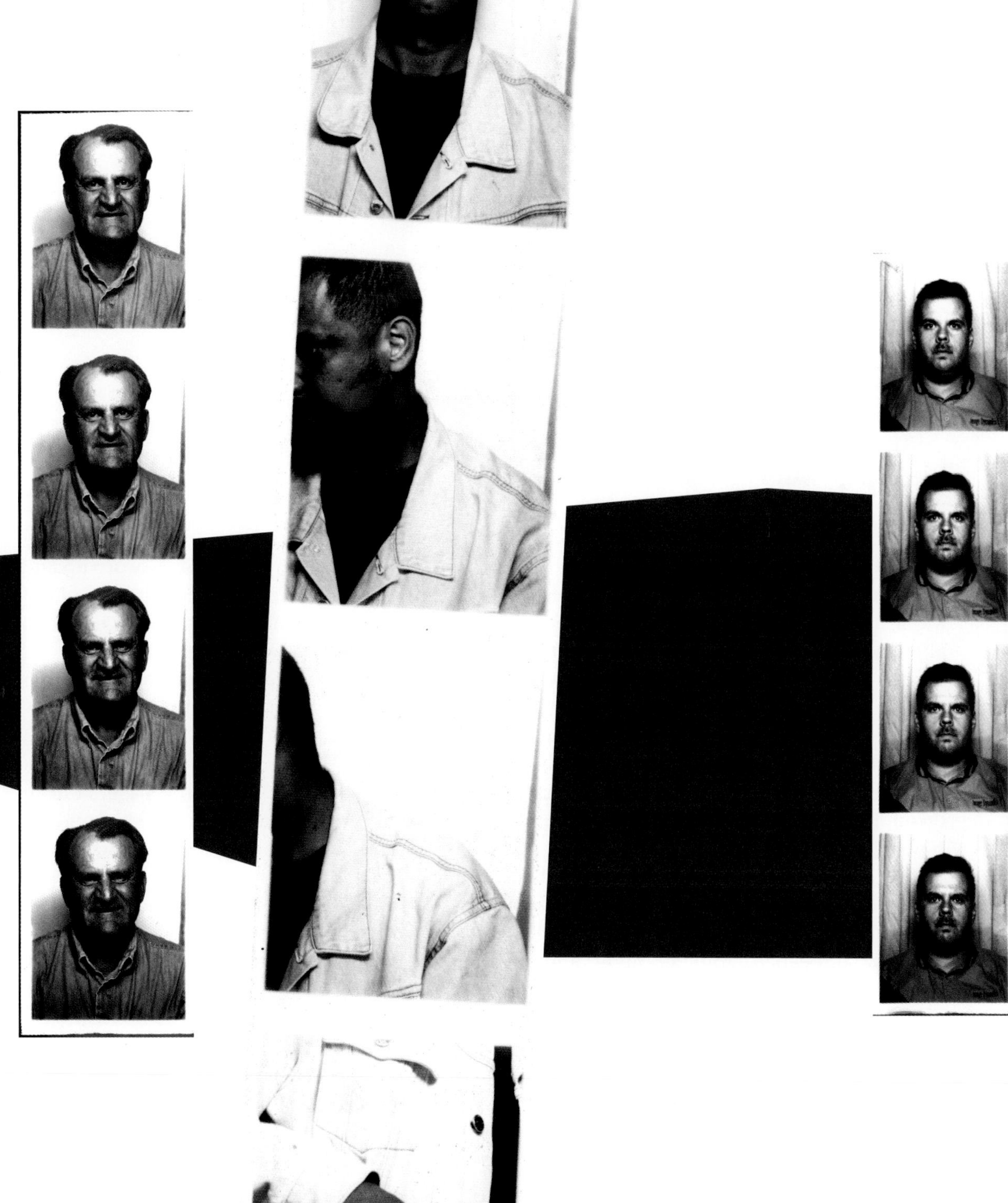

part IV THE MYSTERY OF MR. YOUNG

It was a dark and stormy night. Dave had just woken up and walked upstairs for a Dr Pepper when he noticed an unfamiliar object on his kitchen counter. It was black, with a belt clip and a narrow, rectangular screen. It was a Motorola pager.

Rain streaked down the kitchen window and a bolt of lightning flashed in the hills beyond. Two seconds later, thunder pealed through the air, followed by a steady beeping. It was the Motorola pager.

The area code flickered with the numbers 3-1-2. Moments later it beeped again, this time with another area code: 404. All night and all morning it beeped. And all night and all morning it spit out different area codes. Since no one had called to report a missing pager, Dave, our amateur sleuth, decided to take an empirical approach to determining who it belonged to. He began to cautiously, tentatively, return the calls. Each time, a different woman answered. And each time, when Dave asked if they had just paged someone, they denied it, as innocent as children caught with fudge on their faces. They swore up and down that they had no idea what he was talking about. It didn't matter that he had their number on the Motorola pager.

Finally, Dave decided to go undercover, to pretend as if he were the owner of the pager. It beeped moments later with a 212 area code. "Mr. Young?" a woman's voice asked when Dave returned the page. "I'm up here on One-hundredth Street. My daughter works for you." She talked for a while, allowing Dave to ascertain that Mr. Young was a pimp who conducted his business on a Motorola pager.

He spent the next few days trying to piece together Mr. Young's life and career. But there was one mystery his formidable deductive powers could never solve: What exactly was Mr. Young doing at his house? Had Dave become so oblivious to everyone except Adria that he hadn't even noticed the presence of the nation's greatest pimp, standing right there in his kitchen, conducting illicit business with his Motorola pager?

part

INVADED AT HOME

It is directly after Anthony Michael Hall confesses, "I've never bagged a babe" in *Sixteen Candles* that Dave and Adria hear loud noises coming from directly outside the house. The time is three A.M. Paranoid, Navarro creeps to the door and looks out the peephole. Hoping to find Mr. Young returning for his pager with a fur overcoat and a haggard prostitute on each arm, Navarro sees instead two men with orange vests bent over the street in front of his house, working with tools to pry a manhole cover loose.

"Can I help you guys?" Dave asks, shirtless, opening the door. "It's three in the morning and you're in front of my house."

"Oh," one of them responds. "We're from the Department of Water and Power. We got an emergency call from that house next door. Their gauges are broken, and we're here to fix them."

Dave walks back inside and calls his neighbors to confirm the story. It seems a little late for a house call. His neighbors tell him that they haven't phoned anyone.

Dave's heart freezes as he hangs up. He is sure that these men are trying to rob him or worse. He grabs his double-barreled shotgun and pushes the door open, letting the weapon dangle casually but menacingly at his side.

"Listen, man," he tells the so-called workmen. "I just called next door. And you know what? They didn't call you guys."

"Oh, shit," one of the men yells.

"Goddamn," cries the other. "He's got a shotgun. Let's get the fuck out of here!"

Dave watches them race up the street, then returns to *Sixteen Candles* and Adria. But it is impossible to focus on the movie; every time they hear a sound, they panic, worried that the prowlers have returned with firepower. Stoking each other's fears with each passing minute, they soon decide to get out of the house. They hop into Dave's convertible and, top down, drive down the hill to Sunset Boulevard, where they see a Department of Water and Power truck surrounded by six squad cars with whirling blue lights.

Panic flashes in Adria's eyes: "Oh, no. They were for real. And they called the cops."

"And you know they're going to come over to my house," Dave realizes.

Now, one might think that the first thing on Dave's mind would be to clean up his needles and coke dust. But no. This is a man who makes his cleaning lady and her daughter get inside his photo booth every month, who tapes conversations with his therapist, who buys fake VCRs and clocks with hidden cameras. So the first thing Navarro does on returning is set up two covert video cameras in the house to document his impending arrest. Then he cleans up the rooms, stashes the shotgun in his downstairs closet, and sits on his porch, smoking a cigarette and waiting for the police with Adria.

"Oh, no, they're coming," Adria gasps.

"I know," Dave says coolly, almost detached, as if the documentation has made the event no longer real.

The cars wind up the hill in the wrong direction, then double back to a street directly above Dave's house, where they stop and stake him out with binoculars and infrared goggles. The rest of the night is captured on tape:

There is a knock at the door. When Dave responds, he hears: "Police department! Put your hands up! Come on out!"

Adria runs downstairs to hide, worried not just because she might be arrested but because Dave is so calm about it all.

"Is there anybody else in the house?" one of the officers asks, handcuffing Dave's arms behind his back.

"My fiancée is in the house," Dave says, embellishing their relationship to seem like a more responsible adult. "And there is a shotgun in the house."

"Where is it?"

Dave tells him, and two officers march downstairs to retrieve the weapon. And that's when Dave realizes that maybe he is being a little overconfident. Of course, the gun probably won't get him into trouble: he has a license and he never pointed it at the workmen. If the police check their files, they'll see that he's reported several incidents of stalking and vandalism from his house, not to mention a burglary (while he was in the North Pole with the Red Hot Chili Peppers, thieves carried out his entire safe, which contained eight handguns, among other valuables). He is worried because, while downstairs, the officers could snoop around and discover enough needles, heroin, and cocaine to really put him away. And even Dave can't charm his way out of that.

His fears come true when one officer returns with Dave's shotgun and handgun, which is kept in a drawer full of needles, bent spoons, and an orange plastic pillbox full of drugs. To make matters worse, Adria hears the other officer in the bathroom, rattling a wooden container in which she had hidden more paraphernalia.

Neither officer, however, says a word about drugs. And they don't ask to see a permit or sales receipt for the guns. Instead, the police ask the workers from the Department of Water and Power whether they want to press charges. They respond that since Dave didn't point the gun at them there is no need to press charges. Besides, they admit sheepishly, they were working at the wrong address. The people who called them actually live farther up the street. The police relax and uncuff Navarro.

"So you must be some kind of musician?" a thin, stoop-shouldered officer blurts out.

Dave nods his head, and with that gesture, the night begins to take a turn for the bizarre. The officers stay and hang out in the house, as if it were any other night at Dave's.

Dave gives them a tour, the same one he recently gave Kurt Loder when MTV News stopped by to do a piece on the photo booth project. The difference is that Loder understood what he was being shown in artistic terms; the cops can only think financially.

"Look at that. How much did that cost?" they ask as they pass each of Dave's three computers.

"How much did this house cost?" a balding, heavyset officer asks.

"I don't know, roughly five hundred," Navarro replies. "It could have been more. I don't remember exactly."

"Wow," the cop replies. "I just bought a house. But it's nothing like your house. My house is nothing near as nice as this. No, I mean, I wish it looked like this. But it's just . . ."

"Oh, I'm sure it's very nice," Dave says, suddenly the host of a very odd tea party. "My place didn't look like this when I bought it. You have to put into it what you can."

So much of the conversation centers around money that it begins to seem suspicious, as if maybe the cops aren't making small talk at all but actually casing the house for their own purposes. They also seem shocked that Dave knew they were coming. "You guys don't really think that I couldn't see you over there spying on me?" Dave asks them.

"Hey, what band are you in?" asks the officer with the not-nice house.

"Well, I'm doing a solo project, but I used to be in Jane's Addiction." The officers look at him blankly. "I was also in the Red Hot Chili Peppers."

"Aren't those guys gay?" the officer asks.

"Yeah, yeah they are," Dave confirms. "That's one of the reasons why I had to leave the band. I have no problem with sexual orientation, you see. Everyone should have their own choice. But when over and over again I'm being pressured into sexual situations, I have to take a step back. I don't care who you are or how famous you are."

The officers are stunned. "Really?" "Is that what it was like?" "I thought so!"

"No. Of course it wasn't like that. In fact, for the most part I was the guy who brought that reputation on the band. The truth is that in a video I kissed the singer in tribute to my band beforehand, where we had done that. It was pure shock value, because the Red Hot Chili Peppers have always stood for macho guy power bullshit and I thought that the best thing I could do for the band would be something that completely contradicted that reputation."

Again, the cops stare blankly at him, as if he is speaking another language. "You know what," Dave translates, "look at my fiancée. Do you think I'd rather have sex with a guy than her?"

The cops nod and smile, and everything returns to normal. Dave is one of the guys again.

The questions continue fast and furious: "So what's it like playing for all those people?" "Who did this paint job and how much did it cost?" "Your kitchen is great. Who can I call to get that done in my house?" "Hey Skip, look at this. He's got a coffin in his house. How much do you think that sells for?"

And then they see the photo booth. Dave explains the project in an attempt to lure them into the booth. He pulls out a book containing photo strips from July, but accidentally opens it to a page with a picture of him shooting up.

"Ah, you don't want to see that," he mumbles, flipping to another page, which contains a photo of a drug dealer and two prostitutes. "You may recognize some of these people," he says, half-joking.

The officers pile into the booth one by one, each snapping a strip of photos. But instead of signing release forms and handing the strips over, they keep them for their families. "We're with our sergeant," the thin officer explains as they file out of the house, "otherwise we'd leave some photos behind."

"See you soon," the officer with the inferior house waves as the cops speed away, on their way to urgent police business at a nearby diner where the owner lets them eat for free.

part VI THE MARCH OF THE BABY UNICORNS

A strange thing has happened. As the photo strips have decreased in Dave's house, they've increased elsewhere. More than one hundred fans of Dave's webpage began their own project this month. They scoured their hometowns for coin-operated photo booths, took their pictures, and posted the results on a webpage. The fans—age two to forty-two, from America and Europe, employed everywhere from day care centers to adult novelty stores—call themselves "Baby Unicorns."

They wrote to Dave: "You worry that you're on your own now, but know that you have us. You will always have us. We love you, your art, and your music. This site is our present—to you—from us, your Baby Unicorns."

In some ways, the fans have proven themselves to be more loyal than many of Dave's friends. With the parties becoming rare at the house, most of the familiar faces from June and July have disappeared. Instead, there is the strange gray-bearded face of Eugene Berger, the magician; a lawyer with an eyepatch who invented the Mylar balloon; a sweet, gregarious older woman who was actually part of Warhol's Factory scene; and other odd characters whom Dave and Adria met during an attempt to have a normal night out at a middle-aged neighboring couple's dinner party. Instead, they ended up bringing the hosts and their guests back to Dave's house.

Adria sleeps over almost every night now, alone in bed downstairs while Dave stays awake upstairs for days at a time. Things are a little too quiet at Dave's house, too settled. The surface may be calm, but underneath a dark current is raging.

novem

ber

part

IT'S TOO BAD DAVE CAN ONLY DIE ONCE; HE'S GOT SO MANY IDEAS

"Do you know how I wish that I could be found dead? I would like to have my house completely emptied. I'd make a deal with the Salvation Army and have them take everything out of here so that the whole place would be empty. Then I'd paint every wall and surface in the house white—immaculate, beautiful white. I'd leave a note on the door that says, 'Come on in, I'm dead downstairs.' And downstairs I'd be lying naked with a framed picture of Phyllis Diller or Carol Channing or that guy who's got the puppet named Madam. I fantasize about that."

part II SHOW AND HELL

It is nine A.M., and Dave is supposed to be outside his house with the car running. But there's nobody there. I pound on the door. Inside, the phone is ringing. I keep knocking, the phone keeps ringing: neither is answered.

He must be inside, because I have never, since this project began in June, actually seen him outside of the house. Today was to be the first day we left this hideaway dimly lit by computer screens, this former Factory, this current love nest. For the past month, Navarro has been in an on-and-off fight with his father; each feels that the other doesn't respect him. Today is supposed to be a morning of atonement. Dave is scheduled, at nine-thirty A.M., to be a show-and-tell item for his four-year-old half brother Gabe at Sunshine Preschool. His father is counting on him, his stepmother is counting on him, and, most important, Gabe is counting on him. It is Dave's opportunity to step out of his house and his own self-absorption and prevent his younger brother from being scarred by feelings of mistrust and abandonment toward those he loves.

I turn the key in the lock, and step inside. The living room is bathed in dim red light and the blue glow of computer screensavers, to the side of which rests a translucent magenta bong. A leather-clad leg is drooped over the arm of the couch, and a bare arm hangs to the floor. I hope, as others have before me these past months, that he is asleep.

Shake. Push. Prod. Poke. Hit. He stirs, sleepily, and slowly a pale look of drowsy confusion is replaced, inch by inch, coloring his face from bottom to top with a flush of guilt. The phone rings again, and he picks it up, assuring his father that he is on his way. Five minutes later it rings another time, and his father is reassured for another five minutes, until the phone rings again.

Dave dresses and loads his truck with a black bass given to him by Twiggy Ramirez and a guitar with the cover image from the Jane's Addiction *Nothing's Shocking* album on it. As he locks up the house, he points out the photo booth, which has an OUT OF SERVICE sign hanging from it, and explains that he's been using a Polaroid camera for documentation while waiting for a repairman to come over and fix a photo-strip jam. He is fully awake now, and we climb into his car to drive west to the Bel-Air nursery school. In the parking lot, Dave's father and stepmother are waiting, faces clouded with a mixture of anger and relief. His father is an athletic, avuncular man, a young-looking sixty-six. His stepmother, Toby, is a smiling blond woman who seems completely content in her role as perfect homemaker and hostess. In other words, she is the exact opposite of Dave. Dave begs his parents to wait outside, explaining that they make him uncomfortable, but they insist on coming inside to videotape the lesson.

Gabe, a tiny Muppet version of Dave but without a Van Dyke beard, runs and hugs his brother's legs, asking him why he's wearing all black. A blond teacher named Rita, who has been baby-talking her students for so long that she's forgotten how to speak to adults, pats Gabe on the head. "I like guitar music," she tells Dave. "I used to take lessons."

"Sweetie pie," Toby asks Dave, "will you pose for a photograph with Gabe and his teacher?"

Dave, scratching furiously at his left arm, declines: "Can I use the bathroom first?"

This may seem like a bad start. But once Dave emerges, he is the Captain Kangaroo of rock and roll. After Gabe shyly, staring at the carpet, introduces his brother and a special toy that makes music, Dave slowly and surely wins over every little heart in the room, except for that of a little girl named Catherine, who keeps plugging her ears with her middle fingers.

"Criss cross, apple sauce," the teacher says, and the kids drop cross-legged onto the floor, forming a large semicircle around Dave, who is squeezed into a tiny chair in the corner of the room. Dave films everybody with the camera, then flips the monitor around so they can see themselves. Already he is breeding a future generation of self-documentarians.

"Do you know what my name is?" one kid asks.

"Is it Michael?" Dave asks, sweetly.

"No."

"Roger?"

"No."

"Freddy?"

"No."

"I don't know. What is it?"

"My name's Turboman."

"That's nice. Do you see that man standing over there with the camera? That's my dad. This is all his fault."

Dave strikes a C chord on his guitar. Catherine plugs her ears. "What was that?" one boy asks.

"That was my guitar. But, you see, that's not how it always sounds. But when you're talented like me . . ."

The sarcasm is lost on the audience. "Is that a rock guitar?" a boy in a striped shirt asks.

"It depends on whose hands it is in," Dave says. "This is an electric guitar, and the reason it's called an electric guitar is because it's plugged in. It uses electricity so we can hear it. Whereas other guitars are used by—"

"I have a guitar," one boy interrupts. And soon everyone is chiming in: "My brother plays guitar"; "My father has a book with a picture of a guitar in it."

"Well, I can see it's a good thing I came down here today," Dave says with a flicker of impatience only perceptible to those with two-digit ages.

"Coyotes! Pandas!" the teacher says sternly. "Wait. One at a time, one at a time."

"Does anybody here have brothers or sisters who have drums?" Dave asks.

He is answered with a resounding no.

"I didn't think so. But if you ever want to get back at anybody, start playing the drums." Dave noodles on the guitar a little, playing with the tremolo bar. "Gabe said earlier that this is a special kind of toy. And I make a living with this toy. Do you know how your mommies and daddies go off to work every day to provide a house and food for you guys? This is my job. I'm a guitar player in a rock band."

"What are those drawings on your arm?" a girl in a blue-and-white Alice in Wonderland dress asks about Dave's tattoos.

"It's the same thing as that little design you have right there," Dave replies, pointing to a heart sticker on her cheek. "It's something to look at and find pretty. Some people like them, some don't."

"What's that?" Turboman asks, pointing at Dave's other guitar.

"That's called a bass guitar, and we're going to talk about that in a second. It's a much lower-sounding instrument, a little more bottom-end-y. Usually people who are less intelligent play those."

With a sigh, the teacher named Ruth intercedes, "He's joking!"

"Now, this bass guitar was given to me by a special friend, so this is not only a toy but also something I value, and cherish, and collect. Some people collect stamps. Now what else can people collect?"

The kids start screaming: "Toys!" "Rocks!"

"How about snails?" Dave asks. "I used to collect snails."

"I don't like snails," says one boy. "Me neither," says the kid next to him. Soon, the whole room is talking about snails.

"All right, you can stop with the snails," Dave says gently, playing a blues scale on the guitar. "When you hear music on the radio, they make it with one of these. And other instruments. Usually a couple of people get together and play separate instruments together, and that is how music is made."

"David," the teacher interrupts, "can you play them a song?"

"Do you know 'Old McDonald'?" another, older teacher asks.

"Can I play the guitar?" a kid asks.

Dave holds out the instrument, and the kids rush toward him, striking the strings, burying Dave in cotton and pigtails.

"Does anybody have any questions?" Dave asks.

"Why do you have black all over you?" Catherine unplugs her ears to ask.

"It's my favorite color," Dave replies.

"I like *Blue's Clues,*" says one boy, setting off an avalanche of discussion on the subject.

The teacher instructs Dave, "Play a number on it!"

"What?"

"Would you play a number on it?"

"A number? Not really, but I can play a song."

"Oh, Dave," his stepmother, Toby, sighs.

"Boys and girls, sit down. He's going to play. Now listen," the teacher says.

"It doesn't work that way for me," Dave mumbles, racking his brain for a song that they can relate to. "I just don't know what I can do. Everything I play just doesn't work that way, you know what I mean? I don't know if I can explain it to you now."

"Dave," Toby asks. "How about playing them 'Stairway to Heaven'? It's mellow."

"I don't know. I can't play 'Stairway to Heaven.' Um, does anybody have a question?"

"I have a question," the older teacher asks. "Was this your first instrument?"

Gabe is gleefully dancing around his brother, beaming with pride. "I need silence," Dave says. "Um, the first instrument I played was the piano, like that over there."

"And how old were you?" the teacher asks.

"I was about seven years old. And that is where I got all the knowledge that I have now to play any other instrument. Do any of you kids play music?"

As with every question, pandemonium breaks out as the children yell things about themselves and their fathers and *Blue's Clues* and how their grandmother has a piano in the baby's room. One boy starts crying.

"Dad, help me out here!" Dave begs.

When no one comes to his rescue, Dave saves himself: "So I'm going to play a little of this instrument here, and you guys do whatever you want to do."

The teachers smile, relieved that he's going to play a song. "If you feel like dancing or clapping," the older teacher says, "this is a good time to get up and move to the music."

Dave riffs for a while as the kids dance in time on their butts, except for Catherine, who is grimacing, her fingers buried deep in her ears. Afterward, the teacher asks the children to thank Dave. One girl in a plaid dress, with the intelligent face of a twenty-five-year-old, walks up to him and whispers in his ear, asking if he'll be her boyfriend.

Before Dave can respond, a gaggle of boys flock around him, asking to touch his instruments. With much effort, the teachers shoo them outside to play.

"He was very gentle with the kids," the younger teacher tells Dave's parents. "I liked the way he talked with them."

"He's not used to doing this," Toby apologizes. "He was very nervous."

"What do you mean?" asks Dave's father. "He played guitar for like two hundred and fifty thousand people at Woodstock. And he was nervous about this?"

Although Dave wants the videotape, his father won't part with it. Like father like son; each one doesn't trust the other to make him a copy. Dave turns down an invitation to lunch, accepts one to Thanksgiving at their house, then hops in the Benz. "I know them so well," Dave grumbles. "I am never going to see that tape."

He continues after a while, "Toby really does understand things more than you think she does. Last time I was over, everyone thought I was fine—and I was, comparatively. I was just snorting coke. But she says to me, 'You've got to get your stuff together.' I asked her what she was talking about, and she said, 'The coke.' I asked her if I was acting like I was on coke. And she said, 'No, I can smell it on you.'"

Dave's family lives in a beautiful, multimillion-dollar house in a canyon in Brentwood, which they moved into two years ago. "My father grew up poor in the middle of downtown L.A.," Dave says. "He started working when he was nine, and his father died of cancer like two years later. They had no money in the house, so he had to provide. He got into the University of Southern California because he was a gymnast. He was probably going to go to the Olympics, but he broke his back and had to stop. He got a masters in journalism, and ended up doing advertising. Since he was a writer, advertising intrigued him because it's basically using words to convince somebody not just of a way of thinking, like in journalism, but to physically go out and do something. It was a challenge for him, and he worked his way to the top of the corporate ladder until he became vice president of Grey Advertising. By that point, he had already met my mom, who was doing commercials for them."

Dave pulls over on a suburban side street and, top still down on his convertible, shoots up. The rest of the afternoon is dedicated to the vicarious thrill of shooting up in public. At lunch at an outdoor café on Sunset Boulevard, he returns from the bathroom and declares, "Look at this." Underneath his watchband, the plunger of a syringe is sticking out. He slowly, breathlessly, pushes it in, in full view of everyone seated around him. Across the street, he points out a billboard for the movie *A Bug's Life* depicting a ladybug, a symbol of his and Adria's relationship, and then to an ad across the street for the magazine *Jane,* which is meaningful not just because it reminds him of Jane's Addiction but because there is an article on his photo booth written by Pamela Des Barres in that particular issue. Then, while waiting for the light to change, he sinks the plunger again.

part III CLOSE CALLS

An unfamiliar car parks in front of Dave's house, followed by a loud knocking on the door. Adria left his place forty-five minutes earlier, in search of a new apartment to rent because of roommate trouble, and Dave is home alone.

"Who is it?" Dave asks.

"Hey, it's Sven, from Rude Awakenings. I just talked to Adria. She's on her car phone and told me to come right over."

Dave squints at the fuzzy security monitor: the man is burly and heavyset, well over six feet.

"I didn't call you," Dave panics, assuming that Adria has plotted a drug intervention to clean him up. Sven looks like just the type of guy they send to enter addicts' houses, strap them down, and wait until friends, relatives, and counselors come streaming in to coax them into rehab.

Dave's September resolution to check into the rapid detox facility has by now been completely forgotten. He went to his initial doctor meetings, but never checked himself in for treatment. "I'm in the middle of a lot of work right now," Dave tells Sven through the door, trying to drive him away. "I don't know what you're here for."

"What are you talking about?" Sven asks. "Just let me in. Adria called me. It's all right."

Slowly, it dawns on Dave that Rude Awakenings is not a rehab facility, but a pot delivery service. However, Dave is given a rude awakening anyway: Sven walks in, drops off a plastic bag of weed, and tells Dave that a close friend (an actress who danced with Jane's Addiction on the Lollapalooza tour) fatally overdosed. To make matters worse, she had started using heroin on the Lollapalooza tour.

If this is a warning, it goes unheeded. Two nights later, while Adria is out of town for the weekend, Dave overdoses himself. He was arguing with a girl on the phone (as his drug use has increased, so has his sensitivity and tendency to blow up meaningless statements into all-out verbal wars). After he hung up, at about eleven-thirty A.M., he loaded up a needle. "I remember going down and thinking to myself right before I went out that whoever was coming over here would wake me up," Dave recalls the next day.

Who was coming over? "I don't know," Dave shakes his head. "The doors were locked, so there was no way anybody was getting in."

At five P.M., Dave woke up, dazed but alive. He stood up to leave the room and crashed straight into the mirror.

"The scariest thing about it," he says, "wasn't the fact that I was in danger but that I wasn't scared at all."

IV GOOD OMENS/BAD OMENS

DAVE: I'm thinking that if things continue the way they have been, it's not out of the question that Adria and I would live in the same home. I just can't live in this one with her.

THERE ARE TOO MANY GUESTS AND TOO MANY MEMORIES?
Yes, there are too many memories, too many guests and, more important, I just cannot feel alone in any room in this house. There is always somebody else there. I guess I should be happy because my house became what I'd always wanted it to be: a miniature Factory type of place. Not in the sense of great art coming out of here, but in the sense of freaks hanging out and, at the same time, work being done. But lately I've been scared of the energy that's coming around.

WHAT DO YOU MEAN BY "ENERGY"? YOU SEEM TO KEEP PEOPLE YOU LIKE AROUND YOU.
I don't mean it on that level. I feel like there's a really intense thing that's going to happen.

WITH THIS HOUSE?
Yeah, or to me.

SOMETHING GOOD OR BAD?
There's the Ouija board experience, and the overdose, and that fact that I'm doing so much documenting. There's the website, the book, the record. What is all that leading to? What is it supposed to be documenting?

I HOPE YOU'RE NOT USING THE DOCUMENTATION AS AN EXCUSE FOR SELF-DESTRUCTION, TO SOMEHOW RATIONALIZE IT TO MAKE THE PROJECTS INTERESTING.

No, in fact the documentation is doing the opposite. It is making me freak out to the point where I'm seriously considering some major changes.

LIKE MOVING IN WITH ADRIA?
Yes, leaving this environment, trying to clean up somewhere. Not so much because I feel like I need to clean up but because I'm worried there is some bizarre destiny waiting for me if I stay in this realm. I don't know. I get these feelings and sometimes they're right, sometimes they're wrong. I don't know whether by vocalizing this, I'm confirming that it will happen or dismissing it.

WHAT YOU ARE SAYING RIGHT NOW ISN'T GOING TO CHANGE YOUR DESTINY OR YOUR FATE. ONLY ACTING ON IT WILL.
Well, there's nothing to act on except to not be here.

THAT'S ONE WAY OF ACTING.
I think all this is going to lead to us making a great book.

WHAT DO YOU MEAN?
Because it's going to have an angle of foretelling this event.

OH, DAVE, STOP IT. ALL YOU ACCOMPLISH BY SAYING THIS IS THAT YOU JUST MAKE YOURSELF SCARED.
It's going to be a good angle to put into the advertising.

STOP IT. IF YOU REALLY THINK YOU'RE GOING TO DIE OR SOMETHING, YOU SHOULD GET OUT OF HERE AND GET CLEAN.
I know, but then a part of me feels like if I get out of here and go to Palm Springs, I might get killed on the way down there. I don't know if there's a way out.*

THIS IS GETTING OUT OF HAND. STOP THINKING ABOUT IT.
There are two things that I can think of that would lead me to believe that I am not in any danger. One is that—and this is a really dumb one—a psychic foretold the position I'm in right now to Adria before I left on the Jane's tour.

WHAT DID THE PSYCHIC SAY, EXACTLY?
That he's off drugs now, but he's going to get back on them and he's going to get really bad for a long time. But then he's going to get off them and have a better life than he ever knew before. Now what does that mean? It could mean that I am going to have a better life in the eternal gates of heaven, or it could mean that I'm supposed to learn something from this time and apply it. First of all, I'm not sure if I believe in the psychic thing anyway, but at the same time, whatever eases your mind you tend to believe. The other thing is that I just don't believe anymore that what I have to do on the planet's done.

BECAUSE NOW FOR THE FIRST TIME YOU ARE MAKING MUSIC AND ART ALONE, WITHOUT COLLABORATORS.
Right, some people in my life have been hindrances to some of the things I've wanted to do. Even a lot of people who come to my house just try to use me. Like there was a stripper I took home pretty recently and she took a blue coat that Versace had given me and sold it to the Hard Rock Cafe. It makes me so bitter, and I hate being bitter.

---

*A week later, Dave and Adria drive to Palm Springs. Adria is at the wheel of his car, it is raining, and Dave is scared shitless that at any moment they are going to get into an accident. He calls constantly from the road, panicking between bouts of backseat driving. (Some of the worrying can be attributed to the fact that he was run off the road a week earlier while driving down the hill from his house.) "Write this down," Dave says. "It's a great idea for a movie: a guy and girl are driving in a car and rapping. The girl is doing human beatbox. They human beatbox together and get in an accident. And they die." Dave pauses, then adds, "Adria brought me to talk to her therapist yesterday."

BUT YOU WERE USING HER TOO IN YOUR OWN WAY. THAT'S ONE OF THE CONSEQUENCES OF TRADING OFF YOUR FAME TO GET FEMALE ATTENTION.
But she had spent a lot of time with me and pretended like she was my friend. I don't know. I get so disappointed. I really try so hard with people. I don't know if that ultimately may be one of the angles of this story, because you wrote once that I trust no one, and maybe you were joking. But that's really what this whole project is about. The list of people who have fucked me over is unbelievable, and I don't want to make this a "poor me" thing, but I just don't trust anybody. I can count on my hands the people who haven't fucked me over yet. I could say that you haven't fucked me over yet.

BUT I'VE ONLY KNOWN YOU FOR A FEW MONTHS.
Okay. I don't know where we're going with this but I know it's important. Like, I know that something's up with Twiggy, though he's actually being really nice.

ARE YOU GOING TO GO OFF ON TWIGGY?
Yeah.

WHY?
I don't know. I don't have a reason, really.

YOU'RE LIKE A CAT OR SOMETHING. YOU GET UNCOMFORTABLE IF SOMEONE GETS TOO CLOSE; THEN YOU PUSH THEM AWAY.
The long and the short of it is that it appears that I push people away who are close to me, but the truth is that it's the people who are close to me who take advantage. Or they get caught up in a stupid ego thing. Like with Adam Schneider: I posted something on my website saying that I'm "coproducing a film on Jane's Addiction with a guy named Adam Schneider," and he wrote me back a letter saying that he was so offended that I referred to him as "a guy named Adam Schneider." And maybe Twiggy's not as anal as that, but I feel dishonesty from him.

I DON'T KNOW. IT SEEMS LIKE YOUR RELATIONSHIP WITH HIM IS THAT HE'S SOMEONE YOU CALL AND TALK TO AND HANG OUT WITH. I DON'T THINK HE HAS ULTERIOR MOTIVES.
He doesn't, but you can be dishonest in other ways. I'm not a mind reader. I could be wrong. I don't think I know what trust is.

IT IS TRUE THAT A LOT OF PEOPLE IN YOUR LIFE ARE DISAPPEARING: ADAM, YOUR DAD, THE STRIPPER WHO TOOK YOUR VERSACE COAT, THAT GUY WHO MADE YOUR WEBSITE, AND, SINCE ADRIA'S BEEN BACK, TORI HAS BEEN GONE. SO WHO ARE THE FRIENDS LEFT IN YOUR LIFE NOW?
Adria and my old sponsor from rehab who's been a fucking asshole. Somehow my cousin, Johnny, has left my life, which really bums me out because he's one of the only family members I really relate to. And Jen's almost out. I'm going to fire her.

YOUR ASSISTANT?
She gets me so mad. I can never reach her because she's online. So I'm going to fire her through an instant message. That's the only way to get her attention. It will just say "Goodbye," or, "Welcome. You got fired." So along with that stripper and everyone else, there's another person who's going to disappear this year. Looking over all these months of photographs, I'm starting to wonder about something.

WHAT?
Why do we expose all our secrets and vulnerabilities to a girl we want to sleep with for one night but not to the housekeeper who's always in our lives?

BUT AREN'T ALL THESE THINGS JUST CONSEQUENCES OF YOUR OWN BEHAVIOR? AREN'T YOU JUST BRINGING IT ON YOURSELF?

[*silence*]

The long and the short of it is that it appears that I push people away who are close to me.

part V

IT'S TOO BAD DAVE CAN ONLY DIE ONCE . . .

"My next record, if I do one, I want to be like a suicide, with a funeral and everything. Everybody romanticizes what it would be like if they killed themselves. So I want to capture it on a record, and make it a conceptual piece. And hopefully I'll know what it's like, or try to know. The first half will be me whining, and the second half will be someone missing me and telling me what it was like at the funeral: who went and how many minutes the eulogy lasted and what I looked like in my coffin. I just thought of it today. Maybe I should write the first half of the record, then really commit suicide and have somebody else write the second half. But how will I get to hear it? What if I don't like what they've done?"

dec

ember

part I THE FIRST TIME (WITH SOUND EFFECTS)

"I was eleven or twelve when I started getting high. I was with a friend, Bobby Eisenheimer, who used to just lay on a couch in his room all day [*plastic bag crinkling*]. One night, we just looked at each other, and I said, 'Let's get drunk, what's that like?' I had no idea of the chain of events that would be set off by that question. It just came to me, almost like a religious revelation, like a burning bush speaking to me [*lots of chopping sounds*]. So we went into my mom's liquor cabinet and took a sip out of everything we could find. We mixed every bottle and drank so fucking much. I remember calling up the girls in my class and saying all kinds of shit. We laughed so hard that night [*scraping noises*].

"The next thing I remember is my mom coming downstairs. I was laying in a pool of vomit, and both of us were out of our minds. It was horrifying to wake up in that world. I remember that night so well, and I also remember that the next night I wanted to get drunk again. That was the first time [*huge snort*].

"I didn't really touch anything for a long time after that. Except for the first time I did acid, because that was an accident. I was thirteen and it was about eleven o'clock at night [*another huge snort*]. I took two hits and ended up talking to my dad all night, trying to pretend like I wasn't out of my mind.

"I next did drugs with Stephen Perkins in high school. He and I were in the drum section of the marching band, the Tri-Toms. I'd pick him up every day before school and we'd do coke, smoke pot, and split a six pack, all before eight A.M. [*more chopping sounds*]. That's how we started our days. We'd be so fucked up at school, but I somehow managed to get by most of the time, until my mom died. When my mom died it was all over. I had an excuse for everything. I could rationalize all of my behavior, and get away with . . . [*CRASH*] Oh fuck [*scraping noises, from floor*]."

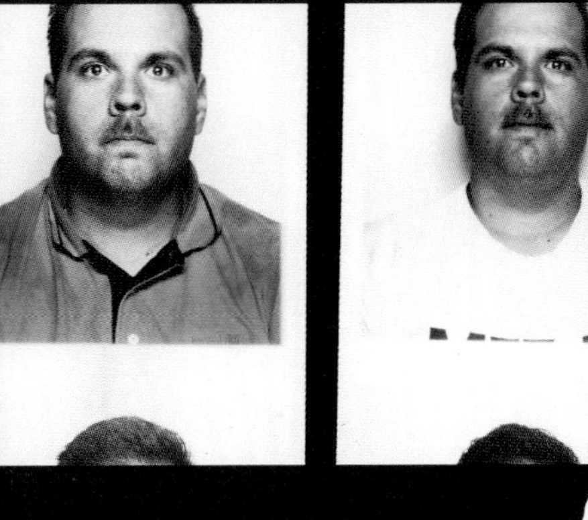

[CRASH]

Oh fuck.

part II CUCKOO OR CUCKOLD?

There are cuckoo clocks everywhere in Dave's house. Sometime in the first few days of the month, he must have slipped out and bought a dozen of them—or, more likely, indulged in his new habit of ordering items from obscure catalogs. There are small plastic cuckoo clocks on the walls over his computer and huge wooden ones in his living room. And all day long, they are continually sounding off, sending cries of "cuckoo, cuckoo, cuckoo" resounding in a dozen different tones, timbres, and sonorities throughout the house. Whatever the reason he decided to buy them, they provide a perfect counterpoint to what's been going on in Dave's life this month.

His face is breaking out in sores—strange, discolored red, purple, and black blotches—and his arms look like a snowy Antarctica wasteland with huge colored pipelines bursting out of the ground. There are fewer and fewer people visiting him, and he is often dejected and uncommunicative. Most of his relationships seem to be unraveling, particularly that with Adria.

Often Dave wakes up to find photo strips of female visitors laid out on his computer or bedside table, as if demanding an explanation. He responds with silence, placing them back in the photo books as if he never saw them. When he comes back from Rexall pharmacy with photo strips of two Goth girls—young teenage fans who happened to be in the store's color photo booth as he walked past—Adria chews him out.

But midmonth, the tables are turned. A call comes in from Dave's accountants at Provident Financial. They have a package from Victoria's Secret sent to Adria and labeled ADRIANA CONTRA NAVARRO. Adria says she has no idea what the package is all about and pulls out a dictionary to look up the words. Dave, suspicious that she is even thinking the words convey a secret message, says not to bother, he has it figured out. The inscription means "Adria against Navarro."

Adria heads downstairs to make a call, and moments later the phone rings again. It is a secretary at the accounting office. "We apologize," she says. "The package wasn't actually for you or Adria. We found the girl it was for."

"What's her name?" Dave asks.

"I don't know," the secretary replies.

"Well, it must be Navarro."

"Then it's Navarro," the secretary replies, flustered, hanging up.

Dave calls back the number on caller ID to discover that it's an unfamiliar extension at his accounting firm. His theory: Someone is having an affair with Adria, sending her presents, and using cute little code words and pet names like "Adriana Contra Navarro." But, by coincidence, this person has an accountant at the same firm as Dave's, and someone in the mailroom mistakenly sent the gift to Dave's accountant instead of his. So when the call came to Dave's house about the package, Adria must have gone downstairs, called the accounting firm, and asked them to pretend like the package was for someone else.

As Dave puts this story together, he suddenly remembers hearing Adria on the phone the previous week, whispering sweet nothings to someone when she thought he was out of earshot. He didn't think anything of it at the time, but suddenly it's all he can think about.

The relationship was already moving on to shaky ground, but now an earthquake has hit. Fights between Adria and Dave break out constantly. Whenever he mentions the package, she gets argumentative and hurls abuse at him until, one day, she leaves the house. Dave assumes he will never see or talk to her again. But two days later she is back.

"She is looking me in the eye and acting normal," Dave says. "Maybe she's not cheating on me physically, but there is at least someone with a crush who's buying her something. I sat her down and told her that I don't believe her and won't ever. But, at the same time, I won't fight with her or talk to her about it because it won't get us anywhere. But I think she'd rather have me yell at her than not talk."

In the meantime, Dave's problems with Adria—not just the mutual accusations of cheating but a fundamental insecurity and distrust that has entered the relationship and is fueling those suspicions—are driving a wedge between him and the outside world. He is depressed and moody, rarely talking to anyone. When he does, he is glum and uncommunicative, often accusing friends of trying to influence him to break up with Adria when they discuss the source of his unhappiness.

When a man returns to a relationship like his, it is usually with the idea that maybe this is the right woman, the one he is supposed to marry. As Navarro wrote in July, "The One. Will you ever meet The One, Dave?"

But now that his best candidate for "The One" is adding more pain to his life than joy, he is confronted with a painful dilemma: his head is saying leave but his heart is saying stay. And both hurt. Then there is the complication of drugs, which are clouding his judgment, and the very difficult situation of being in a relationship in which the insecurity of each person is feeding off the other's, growing into a monster big enough to tear an irreparable rift between them. He seems just steps away from the stage of drug addiction in which he starts seeing CIA agents in trees and ghosts behind the refrigerator

In Adria's first photo-booth strip, she assumed a pose of resistance, contra Navarro. And that pride, that toughness, that stubbornness captured in the strip is tearing them apart right now. What he said just before Adria's return is ringing truer than ever: "If you threw a woman into this equation right now, I'd be a mad fucking mess."

part III LOVE IN L.A. II: THE MYTH OF COUNTING ON ONE HAND

BY DAVE NAVARRO

LOCATION: *Animal Farm, a pet store in West Hollywood, C.A.—Leslie (male) and I have been drawn inside the shop to see the puppies behind glass. (Let's face it, a puppy can help the common man create the illusion of his own innocence . . .)*

Les tried to explain to me the nature of his job. I nearly grasped his theories and marketing concepts, but I suddenly realized that I couldn't care less about what the fuck he did. I interrupted him and moved on to my own selfish, self-centered interests and topics of conversation. We spoke for quite a while about love, loss, exes, friendships, and friendships with exes. We discussed the old First-Love-New-Crush Fire, a romantic, misleading, and infatuating trance. With the power to easily burn in one's heart with an immeasurable and intense fury, this fire can totally destroy one's ability to remember how horrible the quest for love is. I know this fire all too well.

Last week, on one of those twenty-four hour-TV-marathon days, some cable channel ran every episode of *In Search Of* (a late seventies TV series hosted by Leonard Nimoy re: strange phenomena, Bigfoot, U.F.O.s, psychic abilities, etc.). I used to race to the screen and watch the program in complete astonishment as a child, so I figured, "What the hell? I'll check it out!"

An episode that I had never caught before dealt with one of our planet's most bizarre mysteries—a creature that most of us have come face-to-face with at least once in our lives, one that has not only puzzled the finest scientists throughout the age, but that continues to thrive today, surviving on science's complete ignorance of its arrogance. Of course I am talking about Big Fuckin' Asshole. (I think it might be some distant relative of the Sasquatch.) This species of human male always seems to have an endless string of beautiful women at his beck and call. It is almost as if he has somehow taken over Elite or Ford or the Soap Plant. Not only can this hideous creature encourage an entire roster of fashion models to find a new line of work, but he'll also convince this poor, unsuspecting team to remain available at all times for his whimsical spontaneities as well.

He is not attractive. He has no hidden gift or talent. He has tons of money, yet no one can figure out why. (In some cases, it has been proven that the parents of these creatures have cornered the market on some weird thing like lint rollers or those extra-thick eraser things you can stick on top of a pencil that already has an eraser.) So how does he do it? How is it possible to maintain several relationships that are extremely sexual without getting hurt or hurting another? Could it be that this person has maintained friendships with his exes? Is he able to stomach staying in contact with the past lovers he has taken? Does he strike a deal at the end of each relationship?

"We can still meet for a late-night rendezvous once in a while, my darling. No strings. Won't that be dangerous and fun?" he suggests. (It is probably a given that an early Mickey Rourke film is referenced.)

Well, who cares? I can't do that. The show sucked anyway. I will never be one of those guys. I run with a sensitive and intellectual crowd. At least, that's what we tell each other.

"We honestly feel our pain . . . feel our hurt . . . feel our love and lives. We take great pride in our continual inner search for openness and honesty. We have learned how our willingness to share a nurturing relationship with an equally nurturing partner or significant other brings much blessed joy into our lives and the lives of those we come in contact with. We seek not the caretakers in our emotional lives, as we are caregivers. We deserve love and we deserve to let love in, even though Dave has proven many times that there is no such thing."

Goddamnit!!! I am a real human being!!! A human person with feelings and emotions and a heart that beats and loves and hurts!!! I am not gonna let you just use me for your own pleasure and then throw me away like a piece of garbage!!! (I love this stuff—that is, when it's not being screamed directly at me!)

CUT TO: Starbucks—*Les pays a kid to go in and buy a coffee for him, like a fourteen-year-old outside a liquor store. What Les then tells me unravels the inner workings of his insecurities . . .*

A lump in Les's throat instantly swelled. So much, in fact, that I was forced to move my chair back a few feet to keep from getting crushed by it. Tears filled his eyes as he continued.

"Well, there's this place up on Sunset Plaza. This bar place. What's it called? Anyway, I met an amazing girl there, Natasha (God, the name alone could break your heart!), who was just the most wonderful . . . Well, she was working there. The first moment I saw her, I was so in awe. My heart skipped. I had to ask her out and she actually said yes. I got so nervous. I wanted everything to be perfect. I wanted her to be the girl I married. You know how you can just tell? You know? You think you can tell?"

Boy, do I.

"I played it so cool, I didn't even try to kiss her on the first date. Real smooth. I knew I couldn't rush this one. My heart was in heaven."

Uh-oh.

"I was in love. I guess I still am. Anyway, a couple of weeks later I'm eating lunch with this guy Brian I know from the office, and I start rambling on and on about her. I always ended up doing that with everyone. I was so proud. And keep in mind that by this time, Dave, I was so in love with her that I could've married her at any moment! I'd have done it over the phone! I was thinking about how to ask her and all the—I mean, she was a pure angel, driven snow, girlie little, cute little . . . My little baby! Like a dream. So pure, innocent, almost childlike in a way. We redid my whole apartment and shit, ya know? I never felt so amazing and real, free and alive before in my life."

(Thinking to myself) Oh!!! I don't want to hear this. I know I don't!

"So, my old pal, chum, my partner, Big Bri says, 'That chick??!!!! You gotta be joking!!! That sexy Barfly redhead?'

"'Yeah . . . W-w-why do you ask? (Gulp) Ya know her?'

"'Up on Sunset??!!! I know her, all right. I . . . Uhhhh . . . Dude, I hate to be the one to tell you this, but . . .'"

(Warning: The following contains information that could negatively affect the rest of your life.)

"'Kenny and I both fucked her just last night!'"

OUCH!!!

"When I asked her if it was true, she says, 'God, no, baby! I can count all the men I have been with on one hand!'"

[To be continued . . .]

part IV

ONE HOT VISIT

At three A.M. Chad Smith calls. He is in the neighborhood and wants to drop by.

The time is so random and the tone so casual. The truth, however, is that not only have Dave and Chad not seen each other since the summer, when they were in the Red Hot Chili Peppers together and recording demos for Dave's solo album, but Chad's lawyers have been threatening to sue Dave for the songs on which he played drums.

When Chad arrives ten minutes after phoning, he is wearing a baseball cap and a T-shirt. He is either drunk or not very proficient at walking. The first words are strained and awkward.

"Where were you?" Dave asks.

"At Pat's."

"Who's Pat?"

"It's a place to drink. We lost."

"Lost what?"

"Lost the game. My baseball team."

Chad seems sad, lonely, confused. He explains that he is not going to proceed with the lawsuit and just wants to be friends again. Dave urges Chad to enter the photo booth, but Chad won't walk in alone. He insists that they take a photo together. Dave resists, but Chad says there is no way he'll get in the booth alone.

To change the subject, Dave plays a video of a very young Trent Reznor awkwardly but very seriously performing cover songs in a Cleveland club: the Romantics' "Talking in Your Sleep" and After the Fire's "Der Kommissar."

Soon Dave turns the conversation to the Red Hot Chili Peppers. "Do they talk about me much?"

"No, not a lot."

"You mean they don't talk about me at all?"

"Well . . ."

"I'm like a ghost? I'm completely gone."

"You're not like a ghost. Um, when we want to show John [Frusciante] a guitar part, we say,

'This is how Dave used to play it.'"

"But not like that, in other ways."

"Well, um, not really. I think that's it."

"How are you writing songs now?"

"John will come up with a part or Flea will, but most of the time it will come out of jam sessions, like we used to do. But I wish I had more input."

"Yeah, I felt the same way."

"You did?"

"Yeah, I even said that before I left the band."

Chad walks to the bathroom and, though it seems like he's trying to end this uncomfortable conversation and seize the opportunity to sneak out of the house, he returns. Chad seems to be plagued by some sort of sentimentality, perhaps alcohol-induced, but he really seems to miss Dave and the music they made together. He continually refers to the good old days, saying that they were "quite a team together."

Twice this evening, Dave walks into the kitchen to shoot up, assuming that frequent trips to the bathroom will give him away. Each time, he asks Chad to wait outside or to go into the photo booth to take pictures, neither of which Chad does. Instead, he insists on following Dave into the kitchen, as if he's trying to catch Dave in the act.

On the second kitchen visit, Chad gets his evidence, walking in to find Dave with his shirt off and his torso shielding his arm, which is turned toward the wall with a toaster cord wrapped around it.

On the way out of the kitchen, Chad insists again that they take a photo together. He seems really intent on it, as if he needs physical proof that he and Dave are still friends, still a great team. This time Dave relents. They walk in and the machine snaps away. But the developed photos never appear in the tray. The machine is still jammed. Dave tries to fix it, but the photos are destroyed.

Dave takes Chad on a tour of his house and shows him his latest projects: his website and a Christmas ornament that he designed for an auction held by the Sweet Relief charity. Then he plays Chad the latest version of his solo songs. As he listens, Chad snaps straight up in his chair and his eyes widen into alertness, as if he is sobering up on the spot. "That's really, really good," Chad exclaims. "Dude, when this comes out, you're going to look really, really cool."

Unhappy to hear that his drumming has been taken out of the latest recording of "Mourning Son," he warns Dave, "Don't go all electronic!"

They move to the couch in front of the television and watch the latest edit of the Jane's Addiction tour documentary, which has suddenly been filled with scenes of Perry talking with Orthodox Rabbis, reflecting his latest spiritual quest. Chad watches the movie intently, complimenting each performance.

As soon as the documentary ends, Chad grabs his car keys off the table and walks toward the door.

"That's really great—the movie," he mumbles.

"What are you doing?" Dave asks.

"I gotta go home, dude."

Dave walks over and hugs Chad. They part and stand facing each other: Chad in his cap and jersey, Dave bearded and bare-chested. "This," Dave tells him, "is more awkward than when you came in."

Chad nods and walks out without a word. The sun hangs bright in the middle of the sky.

part V DEAR DAD

Dave calls his father on December 13 to wish him a happy birthday. The number 13 has always held a special place in the Navarro family. Dad explains that he, his father, and his grandfather were born on the thirteenth of December. Then Dave was born on June 7, or 6/7, which adds up to 13. And his brother, Gabe, was born at 8:05 in the morning, and those numbers add up to 13. Being a Navarro means believing in destiny, Dad says. And then he explains:

"I'm not sure if you know how our family came to Los Angeles. My father, Gabriel, was left an orphan in the Mexican Civil War. And wherever he went, he always believed that there would be a sign telling him whether it was the right place to make a new life for himself. He was very religious.

"He arrived by train in the old Union Station downtown. He left the station and didn't know where he was, but he started walking anyway, carrying all his possessions and a little money. Pretty soon, he came to a house with a sign that said ROOM FOR RENT in Spanish. Since the sign was in his native language, he felt like the owners would be understanding and let him lease the room, even though he had no job. He knocked on the door and woke up the lady who owned the building. She offered him a room on the second floor.

"Gabriel went to sleep in the west-facing room and woke up late in the day, with the sun setting in the window. He walked to the window and noticed that he was in the corner room of a house on a street corner. Then he looked down at the street signs and read them. He was at the intersection of Gabriel Street and Navarro Street.

"He dropped down to his knees that moment. And he thanked God for letting him know that this was the right place to make a new life for himself."

being a Navarro means
believing in destiny.

part VI PSYCHOBABBLE

DAVE: I just think that I would do it in front of everybody, call him out when he's in the lobby so that everybody could see and . . . Oh, shit!

WHAT?
I just realized what hell would be.

WHAT WOULD YOUR HELL BE?
Trying to stay awake on . . . Do you know what the top of a lightbulb looks like? Imagine being on a mountain that's shaped like that and it's a hundred thousand feet down to the bottom. So if you fall asleep you'll probably slide off it at some point.

YEAH, THAT'S ONE FORM OF HELL.
You'd just slide right off it.

ESPECIALLY IF IT'S AS HOT AS A LIGHTBULB.
No, it's not a lightbulb. It's just a mountain that you're going to fall off of if you fall asleep.

YOU KNOW, WHEN YOU'RE SHOOTING UP, YOU START SAYING THE KINDS OF THINGS PEOPLE SAY RIGHT BEFORE THEY GO TO SLEEP.
Oh, really?

YES, LIKE WHEN YOU'RE ABOUT TO START DREAMING AND YOU'RE JUST STRINGING TOGETHER RANDOM, SURREAL THOUGHTS.
Oh, like the lightbulb and shit?

YEAH.
Stop giving me shit about the lightbulb. It's important to me. You don't understand. To me, it's important. [*Falls asleep.*]

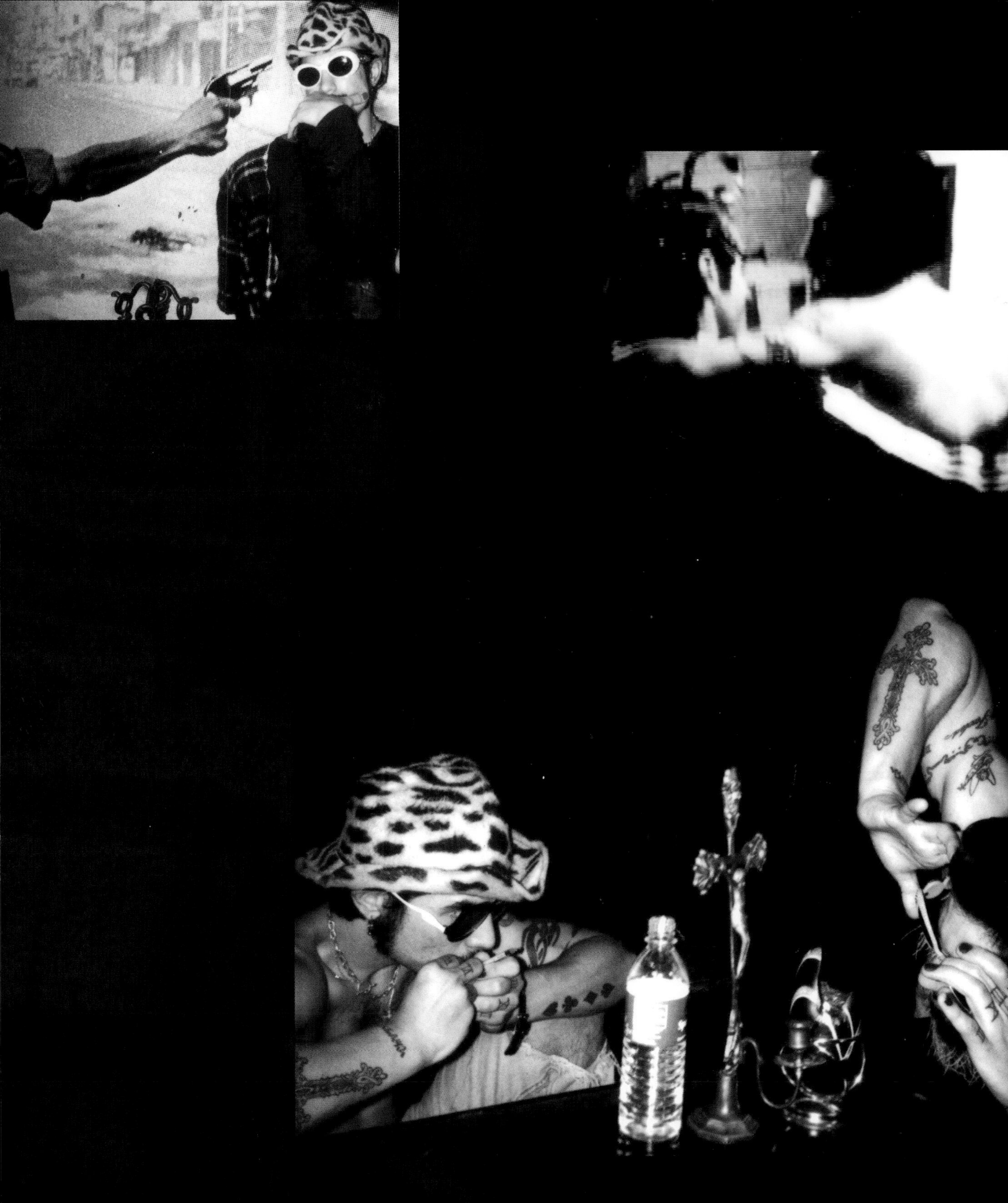

part VII CLOSER CALLS

It is three P.M. on a Tuesday afternoon when the phone call comes. I am on the other line, and tell Dave I will call him right back. But he stops me.

"I just did a really bad shot."

"Shit, what do you want me to do for you?" (I flash back to what Dave asked in June: "Do you know what to do when somebody shoots up too much?" The answer is that I still don't.)

"Just talk to me."

"What did you do?"

"Heroin," comes the reply, muffled, fading.

"Is it the same stuff you did last night?"

"Yes," he says. "You should see my arm. It's so swollen. And my head is swelling. Do you think my brain is swelling?"

"No. But maybe it's cut off some of the oxygen to your brain. You're probably okay. Otherwise you wouldn't have been able to dial my number."

"Twice. I dialed it twice. The line was busy the first time. If I was going to overdose, it probably would have happened right away. Oh, shit, no. My head is starting to hurt again. You should see my arms, dude. I just put them next to each other, and my left arm is so huge. Shit, should I get a camera?"

"You're thinking about documenting it?"

"Yes."

"Then you're definitely okay!"

The next week, Dave leaves town to judge a rock-and-model TV special in Miami. In the Los Angeles International Airport, an undercover officer watches him walk into the bathroom and shoot up. Dave isn't apprehended, however. He makes it to Miami for the first day of the special. But he feels uncomfortable the whole time, worried that in his quest for self-promotion, he is, at the same time, appearing like a sellout to fans for appearing on such a vapid program. "You and me talking fashion at my house is cool," he tells the host, who had paid him a house call to interview him for a different program. "But judging runway models on the beach here, I'm just seen as a dick."

When he loses his dope stash on the set, that seals it. He books the first flight home, growing cold, nauseous, and dope sick in transit. Unaware that he has been followed by airport security the whole time, he is paged to the information desk after leaving the plane to make a connection in Las Vegas. "Are you Dave Navarro?" the woman at the counter asks.

"Yes, that's me."

Suddenly, eight security guards converge on him from the left and right, escorting him into a back room to search for drugs. Fortunately, he was returning home precisely because he ran out of drugs.

Dave is respectful and cooperative the whole time. He tells them that he has no drugs on him, but that they might want to be careful when searching his bag. "I have a needle in there, and I don't want you to poke yourself," he warns.

Possession of needles without a prescription is illegal in Nevada, and it could have serious consequences when combined with the fact that there are security tapes of Dave shooting up in the bathroom. But the officers appreciate his honesty and his attitude, and they let him go without pressing any charges.

"It's a sign," Dave says on returning home.

"I was given a warning. I have a lot of things at my disposal ready to go that could help my future. If I blew it, it would be the most tragic thing that could ever happen after being so close now. And even worse than spending the time in jail would be all the people who doubted me saying, 'I told you so.'"

Once home, he lays off the heroin for several days, shutting himself in alone as he withdraws, growing sicker and sicker. On New Year's Eve, he is supposed to come to Las Vegas to play guitar as part of a Marilyn Manson concert at the Hard Rock Hotel, so I call that morning to see if he's going to make it. When he answers the phone, he is no longer sick, he is high. His reason? He couldn't imagine making it to Las Vegas and performing with Manson while withdrawing. It would be too stressful and traumatic. So he called his dealer for a gram of heroin.

This is the first time that I've ever heard Dave use such a weak excuse to take drugs. Some may say that any excuse for drugs is weak, but this is the first time Dave has said something that even he doesn't really believe.

This is proven true by day's end. Dave's phone rings all afternoon and evening with calls from Manson and others urging him to go to Vegas. He is no longer going through the pain of withdrawal, but now that he's back on heroin his excuse is that he's worried about traveling and getting arrested with drugs on him, especially in light of his recent Las Vegas airport experience.

So he never makes it, and for the first time since I've known him, he has actually let his drug habit keep him from doing something, particularly something that would benefit his career and something that he wanted to do. All of his rationalizations—all his talk that he is stronger than the drugs, that it's an experiment, that he accomplishes more when he's loaded, that he'll get help when he needs it, that he is exorcising his death wish—have just gone to shit. The sores on his face, obsessively itched, have exploded; the clocks are chiming a constant chorus of "cuckoo"; Adria is barely speaking to him; and he is more depressed than I have ever seen him. His worst fear seems to be coming true: the only people still in his life are the ones getting paid—the cleaning lady, the drug dealer, the Pink Dot deliveryman, and me.

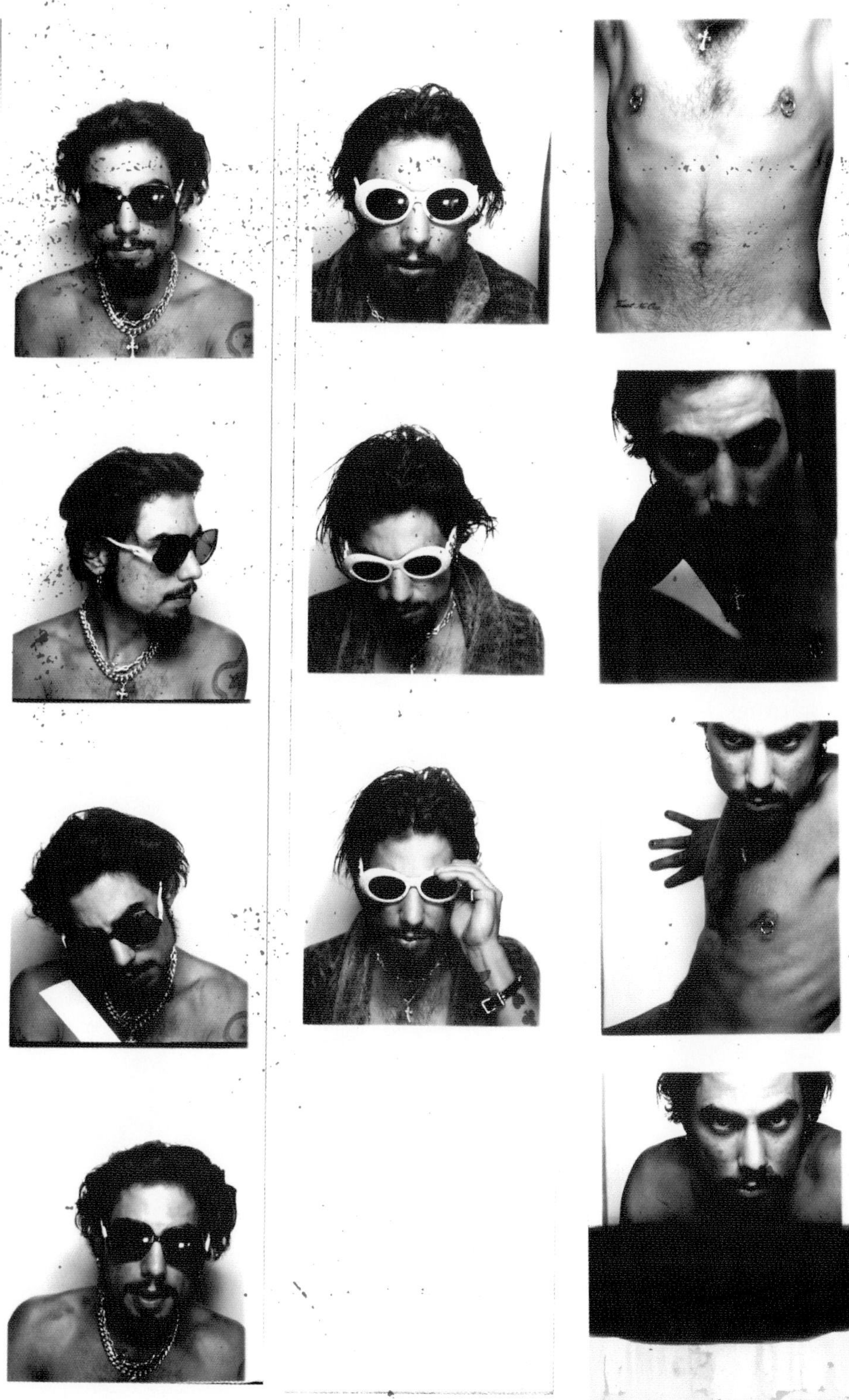

january

part I THE HEISENBERG UNCERTAINTY PRINCIPLE: A WATCHED OBJECT CHANGES ITS COURSE OF MOTION

I DON'T UNDERSTAND WHY YOU'RE SO UPSET.
I haven't criticized you before now. But this is—June, July, August, September, October, November, December, January. This is eight months into it, and now I'm starting to do that.

SO WHAT YOU'RE SAYING IS THAT YOU'RE MAD AT ME.
Where? Let's roll the tape back and find out where I said that.

YOU JUST SAID IT NOW.
No, I didn't.

YOU SAID, "IT'S EIGHT MONTHS INTO IT, AND I'M WAITING UNTIL I GET MAD."
No, I said it's eight months into it and now is when I'm starting to snap at you.

WHICH IS WHY?
Because it's taken me eight months to get to that point.

WHY DID IT TAKE YOU SO LONG?
Because I've been incredibly patient with you.

SO YOU'VE BEEN PATIENT WITH ME IN WHAT WAY? MY ATTITUDE? I'VE HAD A BAD ATTITUDE?
First of all, you're not fucking letting me answer you. Do you hear that you're deciding all these answers for me: how I'm feeling, what I'm thinking, if I'm mad, if I'm frustrated. You're deciding that for me, and then you're reacting as if it were real. It's taken me this long because I've been patient. I'm not mad about the project. I'm upset because it feels like you don't care so much. I'm upset because you've canceled shit on me. I'm upset because when even the slightest hint of coming to one of those topics in conversation happens, you snap at me and you take it out on me. I'm not upset that you can't be here every day for twenty-four hours. I'm upset because my friend is snapping at me. That's it. You know me, dude. If I wanted to be mad, you would know it by now.

SO YOU'RE NOT MAD AT ME?
Dude, I am fucking really mad right now, but it's not the end of the world. And if you could just like take a step back and open your ears

and open your fucking eyes and say, "Nobody's fucking accosting me, no one's attacking me."

IF IT DOES SEEM LIKE SOMETHING'S WRONG WITH ME, MAYBE IT'S BECAUSE I'M WORRIED ABOUT THIS PROJECT. I SEE ALL YOUR OTHER RELATIONSHIPS FALLING APART AROUND YOU, AND I SEE A LOT OF THINGS THAT YOU CREATE NEVER GET FINISHED OVER THE PROCESS OF—
Like what?

SONGS, WRITING, THE JANE'S MOVIE, THE WEBSITE. THEY'RE ALWAYS CHANGING AND THEY'RE ALWAYS INCOMPLETE.
Well, the website is going to be continually changing forever.

NOT ONLY YOUR WEBSITE, JUST IN GENERAL WITH STUFF THAT YOU CREATE. YOU DON'T THINK THEY'RE ALWAYS GOING TO BE CHANGING AS YOU GET NEW IDEAS?
If I can make something better and I don't have a deadline, why not? I made my record one way. I have a while until I have to put it out, and I have two hundred thousand dollars left to spend on it. I'd be a moron to not try and better it. I have free money and time, and my manager is suggesting it. So of course I'll do it. What else don't I finish?

I DON'T KNOW.
Well, then as a partner it's your job to carry the parts that your partner can't. That's why people team up. Dude, let me tell you something else. You are lying down with your eyes closed. What the fuck do you care?

DAVE, I'M LYING DOWN WITH MY EYES CLOSED BECAUSE IT'S DAYLIGHT OUTSIDE AND I'VE BEEN HERE ALL NIGHT. I DON'T KNOW WHY ALL OF A SUDDEN YOU'RE PUSHING ME AWAY NOW.
I'm not pushing you away. I told you already that the reason I'm upset is because as a human being, you tend to snap at me because of your own frustrations.

I'VE SNAPPED AT YOU TWICE.
Dude, what's the number of times that it's supposed to be good? How many am I supposed to accept?

YOU NEVER SNAP AT OTHER PEOPLE? DAVE, YOU FUCKING HUNG UP ON ME THE OTHER DAY WHEN I MADE A JOKE ON THE PHONE. DUDE, YOU JUST HUNG UP ON ME. I DON'T TAKE THOSE LITTLE THINGS YOU DO AS INSULTS. I SAY, "YOU KNOW WHAT? HE WAS UPSET," AND THAT'S IT.
Neil, listen to me respond to that, okay? However many people I do snap at isn't the basis for how I feel when I'm snapped at. Second, I'm hanging up on you on the phone when for the third or fourth time I'm trying to express to you the need for an emotional therapeutic group, and it's a hard thing to admit and ask for help with, and you're making jokes with my ex-girlfriend. Yeah, it's a little frustrating.

I'M NOT DISAGREEING WITH YOU.
Okay, so what is the point then? Because those are both cases in which I feel like I had a justified reason.

SO EVERY TIME YOU SNAP AT ME YOU HAVE A RIGHT TO, AND EVERY TIME I DO IT I DON'T.
I'm not saying that, but the time that you illustrated I think I did.

DAVE, YOU THOUGHT IN YOUR HEAD I WAS BELITTLING YOUR IDEA WHEN I WASN'T. I WAS THINKING THAT IF WE HAD A GROUP THERAPY SESSION, WOULDN'T IT BE FUNNY IF WE HAD A PERSON WHO COMPLETELY DIDN'T UNDERSTAND WHAT WAS—
Dude, do you see that through that you're

deciding what I felt? That's not what I felt. I was incredibly disrespected when I was reaching out for help, period.

OKAY, SO YOU INTERPRETED WHAT I SAID INCORRECTLY.
I don't think so, because if you interrupted me with anything else unrelated to what I was asking you for, I would have felt the same way. Whereas here, you're sleeping with your eyes closed. And I understand you're tired, but I don't think I deserve that. And, granted, neither one of us should snap at each other in any case. But I just don't think by sitting here spell-checking on the computer I'm squashing out an emotional weakness for you. I'm not stepping on you reaching out for help when I'm fucking checking apostrophes.

MAN, I DON'T EVEN KNOW WHY WE'RE BLOWING UP.
Dude, go home and pass out. Now we're at the point where I'm—

I CAN'T DO THIS.
What?

DUDE, I CAN'T DO THIS.
What do you mean?

I JUST DON'T UNDERSTAND HOW TO MOVE FORWARD WITH YOU. I FEEL LIKE I'M FUCKING SINKING IN QUICKSAND.
Dude, that's what you should be telling me. I'd much rather hear that flat out. I understand. Because sometimes in the past when it's seemed like we're sinking in quicksand, we've come out of it together with a great idea.

TRUE. SO WHY AREN'T WE DOING MORE THINGS TOGETHER?
Do you want to know what my truthful feeling is? Because (a) you're tired of not sleeping, or (b) you're fearful of how this is going to turn out, and you're letting that get in the way of being a creative artist. That's why.

I DON'T KNOW WHY I WAS YELLING BEFORE. WE GET MUCH MORE DONE HAVING A DISCUSSION. I THINK WE WERE PUSHING EACH OTHER'S BUTTONS ON PURPOSE. I DON'T KNOW. I DO ENJOY WORKING WITH YOU.
I do too, dude, that's why I think it's important for us to do this, talk about this stuff, you know? Your insecurities show themselves in certain ways, and my insecurities do too. Mine are that you don't want to be my friend anymore, that you don't like me anymore. Because my fear isn't that you don't want to do this anymore, my fear is that you're doing it and don't want to do it.

NO, I'M DOING IT BECAUSE I WANT TO. YOU'RE SMART AND PERCEPTIVE, AND EVEN THOUGH THIS HAS BEEN SO FRUSTRATING TONIGHT, IT'S REMINDING ME OF ALL THE REASONS WHY I WANTED TO DO THIS IN THE FIRST PLACE.
And I'm glad you're doing it, dude. So write this down: idea for series—poor loser agrees to write a book about a great man's life, and in the process comes to learn deep values.

VERY FUNNY. I SHOULD KICK YOUR ASS.
That's a line from Woody Allen. Seriously, I should apologize too for not talking to you enough about what's been going on in my life this month. Maybe that's why it seems like you're losing faith. All I can say is I'm sorry, dude. I've been going through a lot of shit. Maybe I'll be ready to talk about it next month.

DUDE, I CAN'T DO THIS.

What do you mean?

feb

ruary

part I

NAVARRO HYPOTHESIS # 9

If 1 through 8 don't work, there's always number 9.

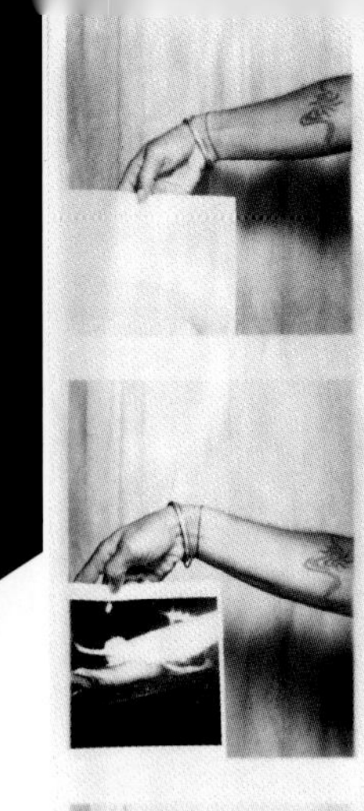

part II A TEMPORARY REPRIEVE FROM DARKNESS

Dave is back! He calls and says he's ready to talk again. "Come over here with a tape deck," he practically shouts. "I'll make up for the past few months."

It's as if at the beginning of each month, his clock resets and everything is back to normal. He has just returned from a short trip to New York to begin mixing his record. And he's done two good deeds already this month: bailing Mary and a prostitute (Sara from the Playboy party night) out of jail in two separate incidents, the first involving a supposedly stolen car and the second culminating in some kind of jailhouse scuffle involving a fork and a human eye.

In addition, Val Kilmer bought him a leopard-print hat in Utah, Cher has become a fan (even inviting him to dinner at her place), the photo booth has been repaired, and a chance meeting with Grandmaster Flash inspired him to buy two turntables and a mixer. (He has given himself the pseudonym DJ Moth after a poem about a moth who gets burned by a flame and learns a lesson about his powerlessness to change things.)

In New York, he also had dinner with Lou Reed. They talked about motorcycles, quad recording, Andy Warhol, Lester Bangs, and Dave's lack of political involvement. A woman who works with Reed described the dinner: "We had the absolute best time, and that was before Lou heard Dave's version of [the Velvet Underground song] 'Venus in Furs.' After he listened to it, Lou called and said it was the best cover version he had ever heard. I said, 'Lou, you never say that.' And he said, 'You're right. I never say that.' You know what Lou's like, but he and Dave liked each other instantly. Lou's a very private person—he doesn't trust anybody—but he even took Dave to his home. I couldn't believe it."

The day after meeting Reed, Dave flew back to L.A. "I always bring a bomb on a plane with me because that way the chances of there being two bombs on the plane are very small," he laughs.

"My philosophy," he continues, "is pessimistic optimism. I expect the worst, and that way I'm always surprised by life. So I view my pessimism as optimism."

Since returning, he has whittled his drug intake down from $300 a day to $150 to $75. "I called my dealer and asked him to come today and he said, 'Sorry, I can't. I'm busy,'" Dave says, running a hand through his shower-wet hair. "And I said, 'What do you mean, you're busy?' And he said, 'I have to go somewhere. And, besides, I was just there.' I said, 'Yeah, but that was yesterday.' He said, 'Look under your left turntable.' I did and there was a package. He left it there for me. He's been trying to help me taper."

As Dave rattles on with rapid-fire excitement in his living room, the Who rock opera *Tommy* flickers across the television screen. Every so often, Dave turns around and watches the movie for a few minutes, rapt. "When I was a kid, I wasn't really into music," he explains during the baked bean scene. "I took lessons for a little while and quit. Then my dad took me to see *Tommy* and I flipped, especially when I saw Elton John in those big boots. At the time, I was slowly losing my hearing. Eventually, I was seventy percent deaf, although I didn't really know it because it happened so gradually." (Two years later, his full hearing returned with no warning or medical explanation.)

"Anyway, I always thought, as most kids do, my parents never listened to a word I said as a kid. I used to fucking mutilate myself and no one would pay any attention to it. So here was *Tommy,* this story about a kid who is blind and deaf. And in order to be heard and get attention he becomes egotistical, loud, blasphemous, self-serving, and alienating. And that's almost what I did when I became an entertainer. Because I also learned that you can get people's attention if you do something that they enjoy and is a fantasy for them. I became an Elton John freak after that, and I loved KISS. They wore things that were costumeish and elaborate and full of showmanship. I realized it was a way to get noticed without saying anything."

Temporarily, at least, the dark cloud brought on by his failing relationship and the drugs seems to have lifted. It has been months since Dave has been this positive, this open, this communicative. "The thing I'm scared about is that Adria leaving my life again just confirms everything I said in the first chapter of the book. And maybe in talking about it we can figure out what role I play in it. Because this always happens, no matter who the girl is."

As evidence of just how bad things got in January, there is a hole in the floor of Dave's studio downstairs. "My shotgun went off and I shot a hole in the floor," he explains. "The gun was in my hands for some reason, and I was really fucked up. I could have killed myself."

He stops and reflects. "This last Christmas was just bad. I got in a huge fight with Adria, and we just cried. I wanted to kill myself."

The two have broken up now, although Dave still isn't sure if it's the right thing or not. Perhaps the two didn't so much break up as push each other away—out of fear, insecurity, doubt, mistrust, self-centeredness, and all those other emotions that wreak havoc on two people's ability to effectively communicate, especially when those two people are emotionally dependent on one another. "I love her," Dave says. "She loves me. I probably would have married that girl. You're shocked to hear me say that, I know. I am too. But the reason why I won't marry her is because she's been doing this tough love thing. And to me, that's not love. It's abandonment."

Yesterday, he wrote her a letter and posted it at a secret URL on the Internet that he sent her in an email. Alongside the letter, he posted a photo-strip montage from months ago of him holding up pieces of paper to form the sentence I . . . AM . . . IN . . . FEAR.

III

Freud assumed that all love is ambivalent in depressives . . . and that hostility towards the love object is turned inwards. Thus a patient who is depressed is mourning for someone who is consciously or unconsciously believed to be lost.

—*LEWIS WOLPERT,* MALIGNANT SADNESS: THE ANATOMY OF DEPRESSION

February 5, 1999

Dear Adria,

One morning like many I stayed in the studio while you went into the bedroom to sleep. I played Neil Young's "Needle and the Damage Done" before I ran into the bedroom and held you as tight as I could while sobbing so fucking hard. I never needed anyone as much as I thought I did on that day, those days, these days, today. (It's almost funny how dramatic that is.)

Anyway, I've been feeling this way for about two months now. This letter is an attempt at cleansing myself, an attempt at letting you know where I am and where I've been coming from. First of all, I commend your admission of treating me with a hint of distance as of late. That is the honesty I've always hoped for from you. However, honesty does not take away the pain. Pain that comes at a time in my life when I have lost just about everyone and everything, not to mention facing the fear and isolation of trying to get clean and starting over an endeavor that was begun originally with love and excitement.

Our distance has hurt me beyond my comprehension. I understand the fear you are faced with. I really do. But I can see no reason why the only option for dealing with this fear was the building of walls between us. I cannot say that the isolation has made these past months harder, because I feel that that would be a cop out, yet I can tell you that it has not made them any easier. I know I have claimed that you have done nothing to be supportive in this, but the truth is that you have continually tried to show me help and guidance. I have only perceived a selfish and arrogant intent behind your help in the form of what is better for you. The inconvenience of my ailment on you has been the result of none other than your insistence on staying around me while dropping the elements of your life that would later lead you to resent me. I have asked for nothing from you during this time while you have only told me what I needed to do. Three times, Adria: New York, Vegas, L.A. I cannot risk the pain anymore. I have failed at the attempts of sobriety I have looked into, I know. But never have you said, "Sorry, Dave, that sucks. It must be hard and you must be in a lot of pain." As if I had made those attempts solely for your benefit.

I realize I may expect too much, that I shouldn't expect a partner to fulfill every single need of mine (especially when I seem to have so many these days). But looking back on the relationship, since we've been apart, our behavior shows no sense of decorum. I thought that our love, or our quest for such a love, was much stronger than that.

[The letter ends here, without a signature.]

part IV LOVE IN L.A. III: INTIMACY AND COMMUNICATION

BY DAVE NAVARRO

Why is it so difficult to maintain true intimacy within a relationship?

A Los Angeles resident explains: "I share everything with my partner: housework, bills, meals, friends . . . We sleep together, wake up together, know each other's secrets [sure you do], and go out socially. We even work together while trying to cope with the everyday stress of life. My partner has become my buddy, which is great! Except . . . I don't really want to fuck my buddies. I get bored."

Bored? Scared.

I, too, have experienced this exact problem. However, when I honestly analyzed these situations in my own life, I usually found that I was either not in love with my partner or a fear of intimacy had taken over.

Lack of communication can be a ruthless killer of intimacy. Defending, arguing, and the illusion of "sides" are just a few of the characteristics that some of us possess when in the throes of conflict. Let's look at the "sides" angle: Because of the fact that men and women are of the opposite sex, they sometimes make the mistake of assuming that they are on opposite sides. Sure, our stories and points of view may differ, but a couple should share a common goal of understanding and harmony.

For example: If I feel misunderstood ("I told you, she's just a friend!") and my girlfriend feels like I'm not listening ("That's not the point. I don't care. It's the way you introduced us. It just made me feel funny. Forget it, you're not hearing me!"), the last thing on my mind should be "winning." When we assume a side, we are therefore attempting to win. The problem is, if I win ("See! There's her boyfriend!") or if she wins ("Why didn't you say, 'This is my girlfriend'?"), one of us loses. If one of us loses, the couple we make up cannot possibly be a winning couple.

"This is my friend Mary. Mary, this is Jane."

"So who's Mary?"

"Mary? She's just a friend."

"Well, if she's just a friend, why didn't you say, 'This is my girlfriend, Jane'?"

"I dunno."

"Did you fuck her?"

There is no way to win. An answer of "no" sounds like a lie and an answer of "yes" will wreak havoc on the rest of your evening. You learn a lesson for the next time. Unless you run into this:

"This is my friend Mary. Mary, this is my girlfriend, Jane."

"So who's Mary?"

"Mary? She's just a friend."

"Well, if she's just a friend, why did you say, 'This is my girlfriend, Jane'?"

" 'Cause you are and I love you and I want the world to know."

"You fucked her, didn't you? You just said 'girlfriend' as a cue to her so she wouldn't say anything!"

Jane's admission of her fears might have saved the evening. Instead of an attack on her partner, a communication of how she was feeling would have assigned no blame. Plus, an opportunity to comfort her would have presented itself to her partner.

When I take the time to examine some of the conflicts I have had in the past, I am stunned by the differences between my behavior with "just friends" and my behavior with my significant other. Nine out of ten times, I am more courteous and willing to find a resolution with my friends than with my girlfriend. Never with my friends do I utter the phrases, "That's not fair!" or "Well, my side is . . ."

Why is that? Well, perhaps the simplest explanation is the fact that most people are not in search of sexual validation from their friends. It is much easier to communicate when there is no danger of rejection or injury to one's self-worth. When our sexual sense of self becomes threatened, our abilities to maintain true intimacy become challenged. Fear takes over and runs the show. When I let fear run the show, the show pretty much sucks. I have found that the best way to avoid fear's control is to confront my fears, not my partner. In fact, sharing my fears with my partner usually takes the power out of them and at the same time opens a door to communication and mutual intimacy. Could it be that our L.A. resident has yet to honestly share everything? Has he been truly intimate?

"Where were you last night?"

Ever ask your partner this question? If so, I'm willing to bet that your inquiry stemmed from some sort of fear, insecurity, or bad thought. I'm also willing to bet that the imagined answer to that question was potentially scary. (Don't worry. If the answer turns out to be as scary as your fear, it is more than likely that your heart will be protected by the lie your partner will eventually tell.) Why would someone even ask his or her partner this question? Just wondering? Couldn't reach him or her? My favorite is "I was worried about you!" (Translation: "I was worried you were having intercourse with someone prettier, funnier, smarter, and sexier than me.") Let's be honest. This situation usually stems from one partner's desire to spend time with the other partner and nothing more. What started out as an innocent intention to have a nice day together can become a nightmare of attacks, screaming, crying, and long phone calls wherein the subject matter dances around the idea of breaking up and character assassinations. Ironically, these conversations can last up to three times longer than any original plan would have.

The internal dialogue that most commonly precedes such an interrogation goes something like this: He/she was with someone else last night. Either that or he/she is mad at me and is trying to punish me by not calling.

It is easy to see why there is no possible answer that can make us feel any more secure. We have set up a circumstance wherein the truth wouldn't even be believable to us. A conflict of major proportions is in the works, all because of a simple little fear that will eventually mean nothing in a week or perhaps even a day.

[To be continued . . .]

part V RUNNING ON EMPTY, SCENE ONE

The time is five A.M. The place is Dave's house. The curtains are drawn. A rough mix of a solo song—"Running on Empty"—plays on the stereo. The lyrics: "I saw her on the street today/I thought she was someone else/Met her last September/I thought she was someone else."

"I wrote that after this girl hurt me really bad," Dave says. "I was driving down Santa Monica and I saw this really hot blonde walking down the street and I thought, 'Fuck, man, maybe there's hope for me being attracted to other women after all.' I slowed down to look, and all of a sudden I realized it was the girl who had hurt me. The actual girl. This is my favorite song I ever wrote."

part

RUNNING ON EMPTY, SCENE TWO

The time is five A.M. The place is Dave's house. The curtains are drawn. But tonight is another night.

Dave fills up a syringe from a spoon. Sometimes it seems like it's always five A.M. it's always Dave's house, the curtains are always drawn. And the syringe, of course, is always being filled or emptied. Even though he's slowed down his intake, he's still shooting coke like it is gasoline and he's a car that can't run without it.

"That analogy is not entirely correct," Dave says as he drives the point into his arm. "Because gasoline doesn't eventually deteriorate your car."

part VII RUNNING ON EMPTY, SCENE THREE

The time is five A.M. The place is Dave's house. The curtains are drawn. But tonight is not just any other night. Tonight, Dave's hair is falling out. And not just on the top of his head: his body hair, his Vandyke, and his eyebrows are all disappearing. Every time he scratches his face, clumps of hair drop off.

Since last week, his skin has turned bright yellow, as have the whites of his eyes. And he is losing weight as fast as hair. He looks like a skeleton with a severe case of hepatitis.

A doctor is called the next day, and she tells him that he is shooting so much garbage into his system that his liver, which serves as a filter, can't process it all.

She returns later that afternoon with an IV drip, which she assures him will cure the degenerative liver failure from which he is suffering and restore his regular weight, skin color, and hair adhesion.

After two weeks of drips, Dave's liver begins to sputter back into action and the jaundice fades from his skin. When the doctor returns, she begins the next stage of her cure: She tells Dave that he needs to stop taking drugs. Dave fires her and gets a new doctor.

Tonight,

HIDE

part

TWENTY THOUSAND LEAGUES UNDER THE C: A JOURNEY INTO THE MIND OF A GIRL CONSIDERING PROSTITUTION

DATE: *Saturday, March 6, 1999*
TIME: *4:49 A.M.*
PLACE: *Dave's living room couch*
BACKGROUND: *There are two kinds of girls in the world: the kind you bring home to mother and the kind you bring to Dave's house. Bonnie and Eve are the kind of girls you bring to Dave's house. Bonnie is a short blond stripper wearing shorts, a sweater, and fake breasts so large they make her appear to be fat. Eve is a short blond stripper wearing shorts, a sweatshirt, and fake breasts so large they make her appear to be fat. They are loud, they are sniffing every drug in sight, they are drinking from a mineral water bottle filled with the drug GHB, and they have a penchant for indulging in antics such as comparing their private parts in the mirror. The intention of these antics is to get them attention, although they fail to elicit the attention the girls obviously think they deserve.*

BONNIE: Why don't you get your business done while we wait and party?
EVE: Yeah, can't you make your phone calls while we party, and then come with us so you can see our apartment?
DAVE: Hey. I just had a great idea. You know what I'm looking for?
EVE: What?
DAVE: What I've had three of and I need one more: an assistant.
EVE: You've had three at a time before?
DAVE: No, no. I've had three who didn't work out.
EVE: Didn't work out? Okay, so you only need one. Which one of us do you want?
DAVE: Now, let's see. Who here would make a better assistant: the person who's been cleaning up my house all night or the person who's been sitting on the couch doing nothing?
EVE: That's because she's tweaked. I want to do it. I don't want to strip anymore.
BONNIE: What would I do?
EVE: Sexual favors?
DAVE: This and that, everything from degrading gruntwork to exciting fucking bullshit. Maybe run around for guitar and computer cable shit, make phone calls, dry cleaning.
EVE: Be his little bitch.
BONNIE: That would be awesome, and I don't live far from you, either.
DAVE: That's really true. Well, let's talk about

it and think about it. I don't like you or trust you, but—

EVE: Why don't you trust us?

DAVE: Now that you've seen my penis, you know too much.*

EVE: It's huge. Pretty close to Tommy Lee's.

DAVE: No.

BONNIE: Yes.

DAVE: Bullshit.

EVE: It is. I bet you that it was the camera angle that made his look that big. If I had a cock your size I'd walk around like I was the shit.

DAVE: You know what, if that were true I wouldn't need drugs. Come on.

EVE: Well, like you said, you're always searching for something more.

DAVE: It's gotten bigger over the past year.

EVE: Your dick's gotten bigger?

DAVE: I swear to God, it's growing.

EVE: Maybe it's like a muscle, and you've been working it out.

DAVE: Maybe it is because I'm using it more. Neil, you're rolling tape, aren't you? You got the whole "huge" thing, right?

EVE: Let's get back to the hooker thing.

DAVE: So you guys really want to become hookers?

EVE: You know what, things always seem different when you're high on drugs.

DAVE: Come on. If the madam called right now?

EVE: Actually, Dave, I really do want to get in touch with her. I want to meet with her.

DAVE: I just paged her.

EVE: What if she doesn't call you back? Could I have her number?

DAVE: No.

EVE: So I have to depend on you to help me?

DAVE: No, you have to depend on her calling me back tonight. Besides, I already helped you by calling her.

EVE: What did you say to her?

DAVE: I said, "Call me back. I have a friend who wants to work with you."

EVE: Oh, okay. Cool. Good answer.

DAVE: "Good answer"? I'm not on a fucking quiz show.

BONNIE: What do you think the job interviews are like with her?

DAVE: What?

BONNIE: What do you think she looks for?

EVE: Your pussy.

DAVE: She looks for a girl who she thinks is pretty and smart but not too pretty or too smart.

EVE: Uh-oh.

DAVE: You have to appear controllable.

EVE: Okay. I get it. You can't be too smart because then you can, like, steal her business.

DAVE: You're not anyway, but, yeah, that's the idea.

EVE: Actually, I'm only going to do it for two months. I swear to you.

DAVE: Not true.

BONNIE: Don't make comments like that.

EVE: Okay, but I know myself. I walk away all the time. It'll get to me.

DAVE: No.

EVE: And all the—

DAVE: No.

EVE: Wait. You don't understand. Money and nice things aren't that important to me. It's just that I want to get out of stripping. And I want to work the minimum amount of time that I have to so that I can spend more time doing what I really want to do. I don't need to have twenty grand in the bank or a nice car. I have my '97 Chevy Blazer and that's fine.

DAVE: Okay, I'm not questioning what you're . . .

EVE: But I want you to be able to talk to me two months from now and I want to be able to say, "Yeah, I'm out in the clear. I even have five

---

*It is important to mention, in the interest of preserving what little remains of Dave's reputation, that no sexual contact of any kind took place between Dave, Bonnie, and/or Eve either before, during, or after this conversation. Dave simply showed them a picture taken of his private part that he posted on his website.

Oh, man, if Cher showed up here, man, I'd be all over her shit.

grand in the bank while I'm looking for another job." I want you to be proud of me. I want to show you.

DAVE: If you say so, I'll put my faith in you.

EVE: I couldn't live with myself if I kept doing it for a year, but I could live with myself for like a month or two.

DAVE: Well, you might hate it, but you might love it. Don't set a time limit yet.

EVE: When I told everyone I was moving to Vegas to go dance, I was there for three days and then I was back.

[*Several cuckoo clocks go off.*]

EVE: I'm sorry, I'm, like, tweaking on the interior. But I'm, like, conscious that I'm annoying people because I can't make any sense.

BONNIE: What would you do if you ordered a prostitute and Eve came over? Would you have sex with her?

DAVE: Probably not. But she wouldn't come over without my knowing it.

BONNIE: Let's just say she did. Say the madam said, "I got a new girl tonight, a hot blond," and Eve had changed her name to Amanda. And you didn't realize it was her until she came over.

DAVE: I still don't think I would.

EVE: Why is that?

DAVE: Because part of the whole game and process and reasoning behind calling them . . .

EVE: . . . is the inonotomy.

DAVE: "*Inonotomy?*" Oh, anonymity. Yeah. I don't want to call and have a girl I know come over and have to say to her, "Wow, isn't this weird? Oh my God. It's you. Ha-ha, isn't that funny?" I'm just looking for an empty experience.

EVE: You want a total stranger.

DAVE: Yeah. My rule is, if the penis comes out of the pants—or if any pants come off—it counts as sex. That's why I don't have intercourse with anybody. Actual intercourse leads to phone calls, whereas anonymous sex doesn't. That's why they call it "intercourse."

EVE: Damn, so I lost out on a potential client.

DAVE: But if I called and asked for you, that's another story.

EVE: Ah, there you go.

DAVE: But basically if someone I knew—not just you—showed up, I don't think I would be into it. Unless of course it was somebody I knew I wanted to have sex with.

EVE: Like Cher.

DAVE: Oh, man, if Cher showed up here, man, I'd be all over her shit.

EVE: Maybe I'll use the name Cher when I start.

DAVE: That is great fucking comedic timing.

EVE: Seriously. Tell me, are you physically attracted to me at all?

DAVE: No.

EVE: You're not, are you? I'm not saying I'm beautiful, but, like, why? What if we went downstairs and I physically aroused you . . .

DAVE: You couldn't physically arouse me right now if you wanted to.

EVE: All I know is that normally I can pretty much get any guy I want, as far as looks are concerned. I'm tweaking and I can't talk, but I'm wondering if there is something in my personality that turns people off. I'm trying to see if there is something wrong with me because I was with this actor, and I brought him over to Bonnie's. And we all started fooling around, then he left me and got with Bonnie and never called me again. And I've never been rejected before.

BONNIE: There's one more thing I want to do: Do you have a mop?

DAVE: It's in the same place as the brooms were. Use your fucking head.

BONNIE: Shut up.

EVE: I still want to kind of talk about the prostitute thing.

DAVE: Well, keep going, come on.

EVE: Okay, you asked me a question earlier, and you said . . .

DAVE: Have you ever shit in somebody's mouth?

EVE: Oh, God, I want to talk about the prostitute thing.

DAVE: One hooker told me that guys wanted her to shit in their mouths.

EVE: Did she do it?

DAVE: No. She's like, "You can get hepatitis from that shit. Why would you want me to shit in your mouth?"

EVE: Oh, he can get hepatitis. Who cares what he gets? If he's taking that risk, he wants it.

DAVE: Yeah, but she just didn't see any reason to do that.

EVE: I mean, some of these guys are, like, intelligent men. They know the risks of eating shit.

BONNIE: I'm an intelligent person. I don't know the risks.

DAVE: Yeah, people get hepatitis. All the time. In fact, I narrowly escaped it.

BONNIE: Very funny. Seriously, though, would someone get it because they had cuts in their mouth? I don't understand how you get it.

DAVE: Because you digest it and it goes into your bloodstream immediately.

BONNIE: Oh, I thought they spit the shit back out. They actually swallow it?

DAVE: No, they chew it first, and then they swallow it. It's kind of like beef jerky.

BONNIE: Do they, like, plan it out with the prostitute in advance, and kind of tell her what they want her to eat?

DAVE: Dude, I don't know.

BONNIE: I've read that sometimes they put Saran Wrap on their face, and they have them do it that way.

DAVE: Oh, come on, that's disgusting. That's so gross.

EVE: So, you asked me if I ever considered the prostitute thing before tonight.

DAVE: I'm just interested.

EVE: I started thinking about it seriously a week ago. I started a job as a masseuse giving finishing touches or whatever.

DAVE: Finishing touches?

EVE: Massaging the penises. And that day, I said, "What's one step further?" Because what I was doing was definitely sexual. I tried to justify it every way I could, saying that it's just a muscle and thinking of it as an extra arm or something. But it still felt sexual. I don't know.

BONNIE: So do you think you could do it?

EVE: Well, if I had clients like him [*pointing to Dave*], hell, yeah, I could do it.

DAVE: But a lot of them will be rich creepy foreign men who will want you to like smell their penises.

EVE: Maybe if the madam girl really liked me,

I could ask her not to send me to Persians or something.

DAVE: The guy's gonna want you to smell his penis. "Smell my penis!"

EVE: That's what turned me off the masseuse thing: my last client was a Persian and he had a huge accent and he was like, "Suck my balls." And I got really grossed out, and I ran away and didn't come back the next day.

DAVE: Did he ask you to smell his penis?

EVE: No, he put my mouth on his balls, and the area between the balls and the anus.

DAVE: "I want you to smell my penis!"

EVE: With the whole prostitute thing, I want to do that for one or two months so that I can focus. I can't focus on anything creative right now because I have fucking twelve messages a day from creditors. I'm very desperate right now. And here I am fucking partying for two days when I could have been making two hundred dollars at the strip club. But I feel like what's two hundred dollars? That's not going to help me.

DAVE: And plus you got to hang out with me.

EVE: Well, I'm enjoying the moment. I live in the moment, that's for sure. But I also hope that the madam thing will work out for me.

DAVE: I really hope not, but I will do what I can. Well, maybe I would rather it work out for you this way than have you look somewhere else and get fucked over.

EVE: That's what I'm saying. I want to have the opportunity to meet someone of your stature and provide a good, reliable service. Because I thought to myself, "If I do this I want to just do it with like high-class, nice people, like celebrities."

BONNIE: Yeah, she'll probably be screwing celebrities, huh?

EVE: How many celebrities really use call-girl services, though?

DAVE: Four out of five recommend them.

EVE: Okay, people, I know this about myself and I think I can do this because I've done things that I normally wouldn't. I can do something awful and turn my conscience off, and separate myself from the act. I'm talking about, like, maybe sex for money. And I won't feel guilty about it the next day because it's almost like I'll forget about it.

BONNIE: Yeah, I remember you telling me about that one thing.

EVE: Yeah, I still don't feel guilty about that. It doesn't bother me. I can just separate myself from the act, which is the same thing a serial killer or murderer does. I have an ability to control my conscience. I can say, "Okay, you're gonna do this, and you're not gonna feel guilty about it." Like I cheated on my boyfriend of four years and actually convinced myself that it didn't happen. I even forgot about it until he found out six months later. And I am still in denial because my imagination is just like whacked. And I think that's the same thing with like Hitler or serial killers: they just separate themselves. And I think a lot of women have that.

[*The doorbell rings. A cab arrives to take the girls home.*]

BONNIE: Is your house clean?

EVE: My house?

DAVE: Well, I had a wonderful time meeting everybody.

BONNIE: I did too.

EVE: Thank you. I hate it though when we bond over drugs like this for hours, and then you never talk to the person again.

DAVE: You're choosing to do that. I'm not bonding over drugs.

EVE: I mean, you know how people feel like they're great friends and then they never really talk again.

DAVE: Oh, I didn't say that you guys were great friends either, did I? I just said I had a really nice time meeting you. You're not my friends. Fuck, what do you think this is? This is not a game. This is my life.

This is not a game.

This is my life.

part II CRACKING UP IN THE CITY THAT NEVER SLEEPS

"I'm going to kill myself."

Dave is calling from New York, where he's been working on his album for the last two weeks, and he's despondent. "It's about Adria," he says angrily. "I've been spending a lot of time trying to comfort a good friend who's very depressed and just moved here. And he let it slip today that he was dating Adria. He thought I knew. We should make this a chapter. If somebody's going to be fucking me over, they shouldn't do it while I'm writing a book."

On top of that, Dave rages, he has been removed as a producer from the Jane's Addiction documentary and no one will tell him why. Since his liver failure last month, he says he has seriously cut down his needle use. But now he wonders what the point of being careful is.

As Dave talks, the line suddenly goes dead. Return calls to his room are met with a busy signal.

I don't hear from him again until the following night. "You know, when I talked to you last night I had a lethal syringe loaded up," he begins. "I called a friend of mine who was at the Academy Awards, and told her that Adria was dating my friend Conrad and that this was it. I was going to do it. And she wasn't able to help me."

As soon as he hung up, help arrived in the form of a call from a producer working on his record. He was worried because Dave had shown up to the studio five hours late that day. "How are you doing?" the producer asked.

"I'm doing really bad," Dave replied. "I don't know what to do."

When Dave told the producer his plans to give up on everything and leave the record half-finished, the producer became hurt and upset. He seemed to really care about the music, which surprised Dave. As the producer talked and talked about the music, Dave slowly came to a conclusion not unlike the one he arrived at the last time he wanted to kill himself (when he made his checkout film and put Montell Jordan in the CD player). And that conclusion was that his work was not yet done.

"It was kind of like with the movie," Dave explains. "Except that with the movie I realized I cared about something I was making, and this time somebody else cared about something I was making."

As the conversation wound down, Dave picked up his lethal syringe, pointed it into the air, and squeezed out the excess heroin, watching it arc into the air in a thin stream and then drop into the carpet. The rest he shot into his arm to put himself to sleep—for the night only.

Letting sleep settle his problems instead of death, he woke up in a different frame of mind. He decided that his friend Conrad was actually being honorable by admitting that he was dating Adria, while Adria was being a liar by continuing to insist she wasn't seeing anybody.

Later that day, Dave decided to stop by Conrad's house to get the whole story. "I've been really depressed lately," Conrad said as Dave entered.

"Yeah, so have I," Dave replied.

"What do you mean you have too? What's wrong with you?" Conrad asked.

"Well, dude, that shit you told me about Adria kind of has me fucked up."

"What are you talking about?"

"The fact that you've been fucking her."

"What?!?"

Dave, it turned out, had completely misunderstood his friend: Conrad had been talking about a time two years ago when Dave had visited his house with Adria on Halloween, but Dave somehow misinterpreted him.

"Oh, so that's what you were saying!" Dave finally exclaimed, reddening as he realized that he almost killed himself over nothing. "I thought that you were telling me she had been over recently."

"Why would I say that to you?" Conrad asked.

"Well, the only reason I'm here is the fact that you said it so matter-of-factly. I thought you were being honest and straightforward with me, while Adria was deceiving me."

"Man, that is so amazing," Conrad replied, on the verge of tears. "I can't believe you would still come here and help me after you thought I was sleeping with Adria. That means so much to me, I don't know what to say."

Conrad grabbed Dave and hugged him, tears rolling down his face. "Enough with the hugs," Dave deferred. "I almost wish that shit with Adria had happened so you'd stop hugging me. Anyway, I didn't come over here to help you. I'm here to see your girlfriend."

While Dave has been helping out Conrad, Conrad hasn't exactly been doing the same for Dave. In fact, he has turned Dave on to a new vice.

"By the way, have I ever told you about the amazing things crack has done for my soul?" Dave says in a phone call later that night.

"What?"

"I like smoking the glass dick."

It turns out that while Dave may have cut down his needle use after last month's scare, he hasn't made a dent in his drug intake. He has simply substituted one addiction for another. And although Dave may sound glib about the crack, it's just a continuation of the willful self-destruction-with-a-smile that has been taking place since June. But the difference now is that even though Dave says he is depressed because he is impatient for his record to come out, the real reason may be because he has been wanting to get clean since September but just can't seem to pull it off by himself. Dave says he's found a place in Antigua to get treatment, and promises that he will check in as soon as the record is finished.

But Dave should do it before the record is finished. It is okay for him to disappear for a few weeks. Anyone who doesn't know what he's doing will think he's off working on something important. And anyone who knows what he's doing will see it as evidence of his seriousness and commitment to his solo career.

"I'll tell you what," Dave says. "I'll check in when I get back from mixing in New York."

He exhales smoke loudly into the phone and, as the conversation continues, he gets woozier and more incoherent until he can't speak anymore. It is four-thirty in the morning on Monday, March 29, when he hangs up, presumably to go to sleep.

part III A SERIES OF ANSWERING MACHINE MESSAGES

MESSAGE #1

Monday, March 29, 6:00 A.M.

"I hope I'm not waking you up. Or taking your face away from some gash, but that producer is suing me. I just picked up my messages, and he called and said he's hurt that I'm not giving him any points on the record so he's filing a lawsuit against me. I called and told him that he quit, he didn't return phone calls to resolve anything, and all the recordings he did are gone, and the arrangements are different. Nowhere on the record does he appear in any way, shape, or form. So, as it stands, I'm prepared if this thing escalates to seriously go public with this. The guy's coming after any money he can get his hands on. He just finished two other projects. I mean, I'm starting all over, alone, with a new label, a new lawyer, a new manager, and these little songs I wrote about my past. And he wants like fifty percent of the income on them forever. Where is he getting this? You saw him come over to my house that time? That was not the guy I knew. And this isn't the guy I knew. He was never like . . ." [*Machine cuts off.*]

MESSAGE #2

Monday, March 29, 6:04 A.M.

"Anyway, as the guy who is my cowriter, I think it's important for you to know that this is going to be a story that has to come out. The truth of the matter is that the project I was doing was quit by this guy. He walked back into his old situation without informing me or asking me or telling me or even having the courtesy to give me a phone call—or even a return phone call. He contributed half a chorus to one song, and I agreed to give him that money. He wants more than that, yet he hasn't done a stitch of work since. He doesn't know what this band is about. He doesn't know who I am anymore. He doesn't know how to be a man or be earnest, and I think I'm ready to do a piece about this somewhere. I think that we should pen this piece, or at least I should. Would you help me out with it? Bye."

MESSAGE #3

Monday, March 29, 10:20 A.M.

"Neil, it's Dave. I'm going to go to rehab. It's, whatever. You have the key to my house, or I guess I'll call you from there. They probably won't let me make calls for like a week or so, in which case do what you have to do at my house. And check on it. I probably won't be able to talk to you for a while. I trust you with the house. If you could check on it. Actually, you have to call my housekeeper and tell her not to come anymore. She's listed on my computer, under Miranda. Sylvia Miranda, M-I-R-A-N-D-A. If you have to, call Jen and she'll tell you what the number is. I don't know what her number is. I'm sorry, but there's really nothing I can do about this. Okay, bye."

MESSAGE #4

Monday, March 29, 1:08 P.M.

"Hey, Neil, it's Dave. I'm at the airport. Call me up. Bye."

MESSAGE #5

Monday, March 29, 7:15 P.M.

"Hey, dude, it's me. I'm almost at the place. Maybe I'll try you from there if I can. Okay, bye."

MESSAGE #6

Monday, March 29, 7:42 P.M.

"Shit, dude, you're still not there. Listen, this is my last chance. I'm in Tucson. I'm so upset right now. I don't know if I can call you again."

HUMAN VOICE #1

Tuesday, March 30, 11:04 A.M.

Finally, Dave calls when I'm home. I've been worrying about him for over twenty-four hours, wondering what is going on. Somehow, between messages number two and three, an intervention of some sort took place. When he speaks, he is clearly in pain. He sounds worse than I've ever heard him, worse even than when he called overdosing in December or turned yellow last month. For the first time, I'm confronted with a dilemma I haven't had to face before: Do I start the tape recorder?

This is the rawest, most real, most anguished state I have ever heard Dave in. And he needs me—not as a documentarian but as the friend I've become through getting so close to his life in the process. If he is reaching out to me as that friend, one who supposedly hasn't betrayed him, I can't start the tape recorder. But, at the same time, I wonder, when Dave's out and clean, will he ask me for the tape? Maybe he is really just calling me so that I'll record it and he can document his state of mind at the moment. Ultimately, the conversation is left unrecorded, just remembered.

Speaking from the pay phone at the clinic, he explains that he is going crazy, that he doesn't know what to do. He feels betrayed. Some of the people on the business end of his record pulled an intervention on him, which is upsetting to Dave because he says he was planning to check into rehab as soon as the record was finished. He feels that they didn't trust him to do it himself, and consequently they stabbed him in the back by springing this intervention on him.

"The work I did was the work I did while I was like this," he groans. "They don't understand that the album means more to me than my life."

But he is backed into a corner: if he completes rehab successfully, his people will think that they did the right thing when he feels they didn't. But if he runs away, they'll feel like he's beyond hope and abandon him and his record. "If I leave here, I lose," he finally decides. "It'll make everybody who doubts me right. So I'm going to stay."

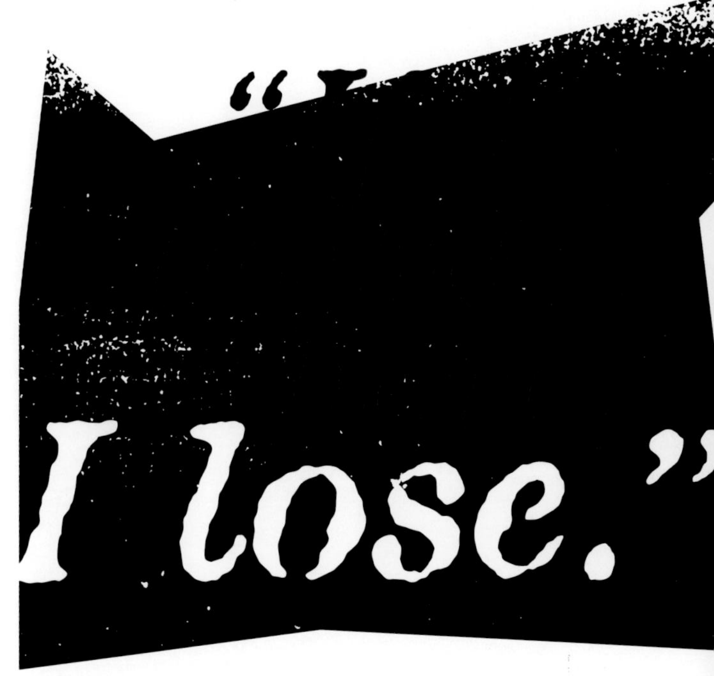

NAUARRO, DAVE
4041950 #13305
AGE 31 3-30-99

part I THE SWEEP

I stop by Dave's house today to help his formerly fired assistant Jen "sweep," as she puts it. Evidently he called her with a mission to search for and either destroy or confiscate all traces of drugs, paraphernalia, and anything reminiscent of his old habits before he returns from rehab.

The needles that Dave melted together and called his artwork. Gone. The shotgun he pointed at the Department of Water and Power workers and the ammunition kept in the safe. Gone. The skull-decorated box he used to transport drug paraphernalia on rare nights out. Gone. The mail-order package full of probably harmless pill containers. Gone. The needles scattered around the living room, the drug residue on the coffin coffee table, and every single spoon in the house. All gone. However, we do not dispose of a singing bird clock and rubber urine bag that arrive in the mail as we sweep because we can't seem to figure out a connection between them and drug use other than the fact that they were clearly ordered while on drugs.

As we throw out every cigarette that is missing its filter, Jen reminisces about the time Dave got sick from accidentally injecting threads from the cigarette filters he uses to absorb melted drug residue. She visited the house to find it freezing cold with Dave sweating madly. But he didn't want to call 911, she explained, because he didn't want to deal with the infamy that would ensue. So she sat up with him all night, watching him sweat more and more, watching the pain increase until the couch was soaking wet. Afterward, he told her, "You saved my life. I can never fire you."

Two months later, he fired her.

"Initially when he would explain the book to people, he was talking about the whole concept of documenting a year in his life and watching people come and go and then come back or go forever," Jen remembers. "And personally that's what I've done. I'm sure that last year we didn't think I'd go a month without talking to him. Then I was gone for over three months. And now I'm back helping him almost exactly a year since this all began."

Jen and I spend hours in the house, looking for drugs that Dave has secretly stashed or that dealers with his house keys have concealed. We know most of the hiding places by now: inside the spout of the drainpipe, underneath the turntables, behind the security camera over his doorbell, in the silver-dollar-shaped slots on the back of his Macintosh computer monitors, and in guitar cases, vases, drawers, pianos, cassette boxes, and coat pockets.

Just when we are about to leave, sure that we've made a thorough sweep, I stand on a chair to see if I should collect any of the books of photo strips lined up on top of the photo booth. There I find a needle, a gun, a bong, and a Virgin Mary altar candle. Inside the candle, the wax has been burned halfway to the bottom: in the empty space above the wax, there is a ball of tinfoil wrapped in black electrical tape. Jen gets very excited when she sees it. It is impossible to tell how long it's been there: weeks, months, years?

Inside the obsessively wrapped package, there is a fingernail-size lump of black-tar heroin and a rock of coke about half the size of a golf ball. So I drive home with several grams of coke and heroin, a handgun, a shotgun, a bong, several boxes of shells, and a biohazard jar that we found full of needles in the trunk of my car. I can only imagine what would become of me if I were pulled over.

I wonder, as I drive home, if Jen and I are really doing any good. We've only taken away the things that are obvious tools for drug use or self-destruction. The problem is that everything in the house is reminiscent of drugs, from the dead-end sign outside to all the modifications Dave made inside while on drugs—the purple-painted walls, the chrome kitchen, the cuckoo clocks.

"I walked up there with Keanu Reeves the other day, and all I could think was, 'Dave did drugs here, Dave did drugs there,'" Jen muses. We all want Dave to come back and stay somewhere else—Laguna Beach, Malibu, wherever. When we talk to him, however, he keeps saying he can't wait to get back to his house. But what's he going to do there? We're going to have to spend twenty-four hours a day with him.

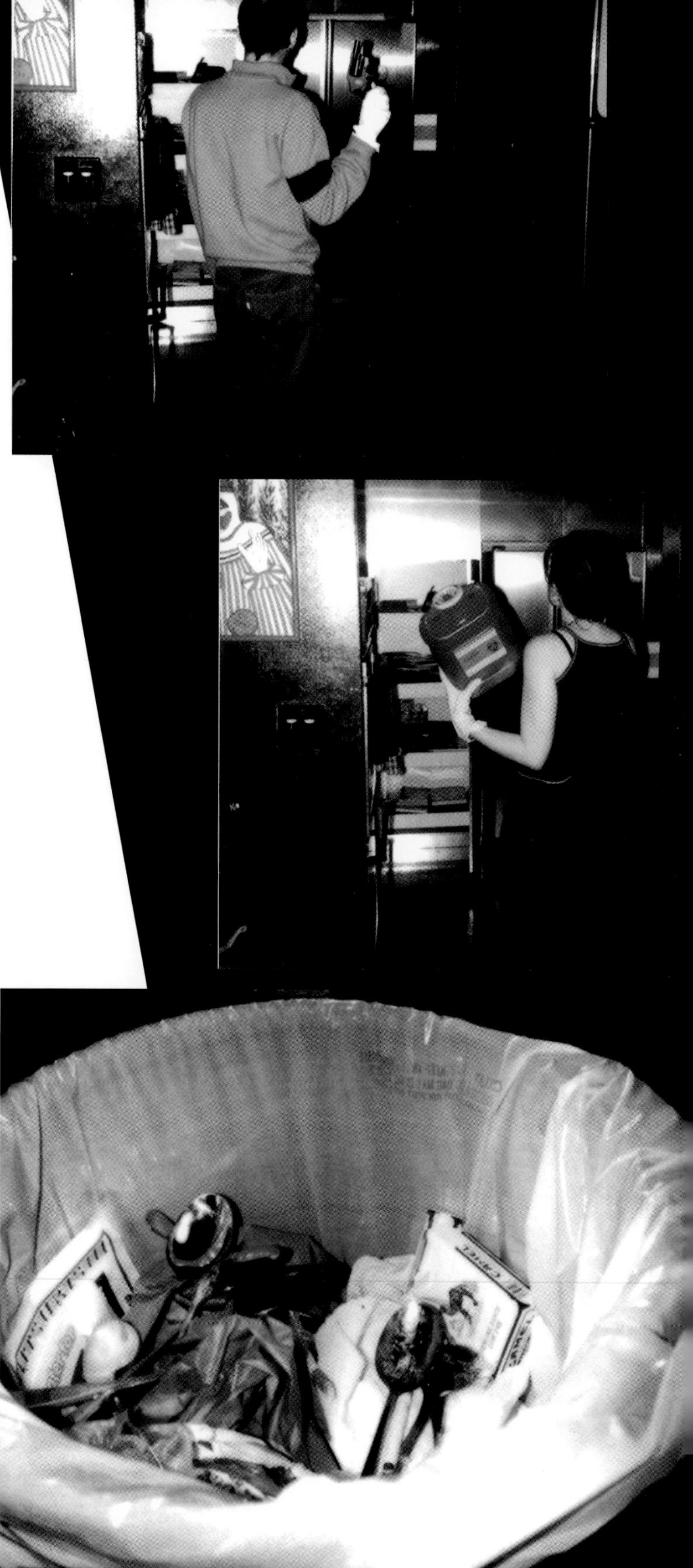

part II THE NOTE

Whenever Dave calls from rehab, he sounds miserable. Every time I try to ask how he is or what he's doing, he becomes quiet and melancholy. "I really hate it here," he says. "I'm trying to get transferred back to L.A. It's just terrible, dude. Tell me some good stuff. I don't want to think about how bad it is here."

Perhaps to keep a plot in his life, he has fallen in love with a fellow patient. "She's the worst fucked-up junkie chick you ever saw, but she's so cute," he says. "She looks like she's totally going to die.

"But," he adds, "no one in here's seen anything like my case either. They say, 'Dude, what happened to your arms?' No one can believe it's tracks. I guess I never really looked at them; they're gnarly."

I ask him about some of the things Jen and I found in the house. "I bought that piss bag because I was going to make an art piece out of it," he explains. "I was going to call it 'Grandpa' and hang it on something. And I liked the bird clock because each hour has a different type of bird chirping."

He wants me to leave a hundred dollars on his computer table for his maid to pick up. When I return to the house two days later, for some reason I check under the doormat. Underneath, there is an envelope from Mary containing a unicorn bookmark and a note saying that she has taken back a delivery of drugs she left him there, since it's been lying beneath the doormat uncollected for several days. The funny thing is, when Jen and I swept the house a week ago, there was nothing under the doormat. He must have called her and ordered the drugs sometime since then. But why?

D—
I had left something on your doorstep but I hadn't heard from you so I came back. Call me when you get here. I'll be up or someone can wake me up. I have something I think you should try. Something different.

I've missed you a lot the last couple months. I feel so helpless knowing that you feel like your life is over. No matter what you decide I'm positive you can make the best of it. Your so good at pulling things together when the going gets tough. There's so many different options for you.

Well, I won't keep going on, but please call so I know your o.k.

Allright?

Love,
M

part III THE CONFESSION

"I went in to talk to this doctor, and I was just trying to get a general sense of what the whole plan was for me here. I was telling him about my CD and how it has a lot to do with the grieving process for my mother, because that's what they've been making me focus on and work on here. And he interrupts me and goes, 'Dave, listen, I'm telling you now, I'm not going to listen to it.'

"But I wasn't asking him to listen to it. I was just telling him what it was about. I got so fucking mad that I stood up and said, 'Fuck you, you're not even listening to me.' I went to my room, packed my bag, called a cab, and signed out A.M.A., which means 'against medical advice.' I got into the cab and said, 'Take me to the airport.' I had a hundred dollars with me. The cab driver looked pretty cool, so I said, 'Hey, where can I get heroin and cocaine in this part of Tucson?'

"She goes, 'Oh, well, we'd have to go down to South Sixth Street, although that's a really gnarly part of town.'

"I said, 'Well, there's a hundred dollars in it for you if we can make that trip.'

"So we drove around to all these places and finally got a toothless black guy and his wife to get in the cab. And they were telling us, 'Turn down here; turn down there; no, slow down; make a left here; slow down; pull up in front of this house.'

"Finally, the guy goes in, gets the drugs. By the time all this was done, I looked at the meter and it was eighty-five dollars. I had just spent my only hundred dollars on drugs and the airport was like an hour away from where we were. So the rest of the day was used up going to Western Union, calling everyone I could think of and begging, 'Wire me some money.' I even went to a bank to get an advance on my American Express card, but they told me they didn't do that there.

"The cab driver was cool because I told her, 'Look, if you can deal with me, I'll give you an extra grand.'

"I kept going back again and again to Western Union, waiting in line and asking if the money came through. But it never did. I finally called my manager, who said, 'What the fuck do you think you're doing? You're going to ruin everything. Everyone is counting on you staying in rehab; you're not going to have a record to come back to if you don't. Put the cab driver on the phone.'

"Apparently, my manager had told everyone not to wire me the money. So he said to the cab driver, 'Look, lady, there is no Western Union money coming in and he's not going to be able to pay you. The only way that you're gonna get your meter is if you take him back to where you picked him up.'

"And she did. It was gnarly having to walk back into rehab. I felt like an outlaw, like the Indian who threw the furniture through the window in *One Flew Over the Cuckoo's Nest.* I had to go through detox all over again. Then I got the flu. It was terrible. But today has been a really good day. My dad came to visit me, I had yoga class, and it seems like there's a chance I just might make it through this."

"I just might make it through this."

may

part I A NOT-SO-TRIUMPHANT RETURN

We failed. The plan was to spend twenty-four hours every day with Dave when he came home from rehab to make sure that he didn't return to old habits. I had to go to New York for business, so Jen and Tori looked after him. He called as soon as he arrived home and sounded depressed. Reading over transcripts from the documentation of the last year, he noticed that all his talk—for example, his Steve Vai argument—was, to him, based on what he thought were deep, profound spiritual principles of live and let live. But the fact is that it was his misinterpretation of those principles that kept him from benefiting from them. He was being, in other words, a hypocrite.

"These principles are here to help you better your life," he said. "And I've misinterpreted and tangled them up in such a way that they've hindered my life."

On Thursday, he left an extremely sad message on my machine, but then never called again when I left him messages the following Friday, Saturday, and Sunday.

On Sunday, Jen calls in tears, sobbing that Dave had kicked her and Tori out of the house, called his dealer, Mary, and started using again. His explanation: he was bored and didn't know what to do. He has hardly called anyone since then, perhaps because he feels like he's let them down.

"I'm glad we took the guns out of the house," Jen says. "He's really upset. I'm worried he might try to kill himself if he can't get straight."

Some of his other friends are less sympathetic. In fact, they're pissed. One calls and rages: "That guy has taken so much more than he's given to me in the last year. All he's done since he's been back is go out and do drugs. He just blew everything he did for the last six weeks."

As I return to Los Angeles to find him, I'm bummed out. We thought this book would have a happy ending, but now it's May 10 and we're right back where we started. He must feel like shit: everything he prides himself on—his mind, his willpower, his control of himself—has proven useless.

Sometimes, though, people just can't help themselves. Even if we're not addicted to drugs—maybe instead it's gorging on chocolate, smoking, masturbating, staying out too late, picking our noses, or simply saying no to other people—we like to think that we're stronger than our compulsions. But when time after time we can't break a habit we so badly want to eliminate, we begin to realize that maybe our willpower and self-control aren't as strong as we thought they were. Maybe we are just as weak as everybody else.

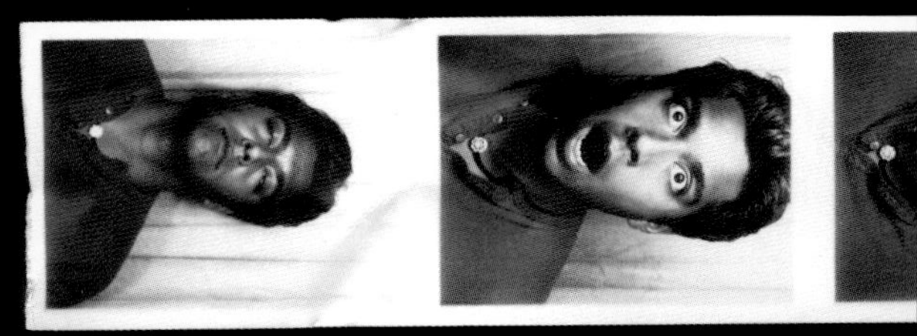

"He just blew everything
he did for the last six weeks."

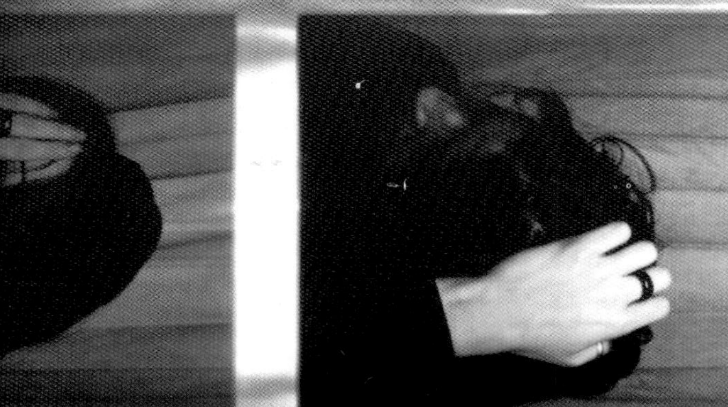

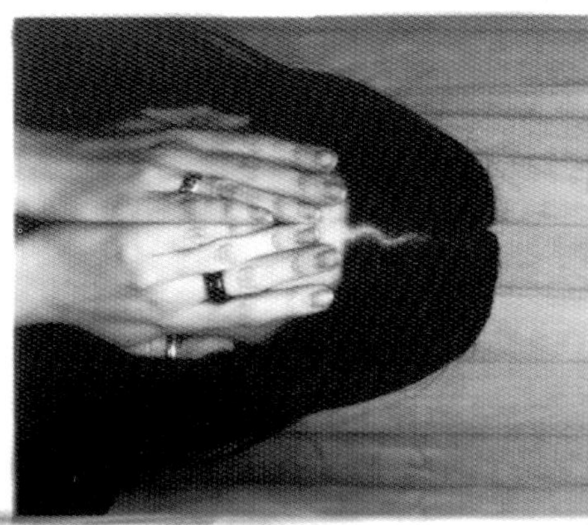

part II TORI'S STORY

Thursday, May 6

DAVE: I was drug-free and had quit everything. But the second I got out of rehab, I bought a pack of cigarettes and started eating chocolate.

TORI: Every vice came back. Addiction started instantly. When I picked him up at the airport, he was nervous. He was shaking from the anxiety of going home. I knew that he was going to have a problem being there. We went back to his place, and Jen was waiting for us. A few things were changed around, but it was still the same place where everything had happened before.

DAVE: There was still a heavy vibe in there.

TORI: When he walked in, he was completely overwhelmed. And Jen was there saying, "Look at this" and "Look at this." I think it took a lot out of him. Maybe he needed to be alone.

DAVE: It was really hard. So I told them to split. I paged Mary, and then I called her. She was the first person I phoned.

TORI: Everybody kept saying, "How could this happen?" And I said, "Because it's not just the drugs that he needs to get away from. It's his emotional stuff that he needs to take care of so he doesn't do the drugs again."

DAVE: So Mary came over and I shot up. It was just like the old days.

TORI: Except a big difference was that now he had to lie to everybody about it. He called me two hours later and said, "Come back up." He was either feeling guilty or wanted someone to be with because he was high again. So I came back and we hung out, although I didn't know he was high. That evening, he asked me to leave because he said he was going to the gym. But Adria came up and they got into a big fight. And that set him off.

DAVE: I knew that going to the gym would be useless.

TORI: I didn't know you didn't go. But when I couldn't get in touch with you all night long I began to get worried that something was wrong.

Friday, May 7

TORI: For Friday morning, I had made him a facial appointment. I called and called and called, then finally I came by. I knew something was wrong. He answered the door and he was wearing a blue crusty face mask that he had obviously fallen asleep in. He was still groggy and couldn't walk because his legs hurt for some reason.

DAVE: I probably slept on them wrong.

TORI: Icky stuff.

DAVE: So she canceled the appointment and I got high again.

TORI: He was really upset that I had woken him up too. He said, "Make it for two in the afternoon." So I did, and then he disappeared downstairs and got high. Again, I didn't really know that, but I had a feeling because when he sneaks off like that he's usually doing drugs. He said, "Oh, excuse me, I'm going downstairs to make a private phone call in the bedroom." Hello! Since when has Dave made private calls?

When he came back upstairs, I said, "You know what, you're not going to go to your two o'clock." I knew he was high again, so I canceled. He said okay. He was having a really bad high. It was only the second time I've seen him have a high that bad, and I was scared enough that I was about to dial 911. He was shaking, and he wasn't doing well at all. He was nodding out instantly, and he couldn't walk.

When he bent over to pick up something, he fell forward and hit the ground. And I was like, "D, I'm kind of scared right now." And he went over and started playing on the piano, and he nodded out on the keyboard and fell asleep. I was like, "Fuck, I've been here before. What do I do?" I tried to talk to him to see how he was and where he was, and all of a sudden he started throwing up on the piano. And it wasn't like food throw-up. It was like green mucus-y, pus-y body acids or something. And I got scared. I said, "D, I'm going to call someone right now, so you tell me who to call because you need to get help. You're not any better." He didn't say anything, so I said, "I'm going to call Johnny. Is that okay?" And he said, "Yeah, call Johnny."

DAVE: Johnny's my cousin.

TORI: So he gave me the number and I called Johnny. Johnny said to just hang out with Dave for a little while and let him sleep. So I said, "D, come over to the couch." And as he was coming over to the couch, he started throwing up all over the floor and all over the bathroom. He was sweating so much, and I started getting really scared. Then he came and laid on the sofa, and he was like gurgling, making some kind of fluid-y sound in his throat. I thought he was going to choke.

But he pretty much slept the entire day. During that day, there were hundreds of phone calls. And everyone who called was really upset.

Then his manager called and was really mad. He said, "You know what? First of all, he shouldn't have had a six-day span like this with no treatment whatsoever."

DAVE: Yeah, they had set up a therapist, but here's what happened. I had it all lined up for when I got out of the center in Tucson, but I did so well—exceptionally well—in Tucson that despite my escape they let me out early.

TORI: And that's another reason why everyone was so mad. They said, "I can't believe Dave manipulated them into letting him out early. What kind of a facility would let him out?" And they were right. When they let him out, they gave him a window. He had six days before he was going to get any kind of therapy. Can you imagine?

DAVE: Yeah, but I fucked up too. I do think that I contributed to it.

TORI: I stayed with him through the night. During that time, he started drying out. He didn't do drugs and slept most of the time. On Friday night, Johnny came up, we had dinner, and we hung out together and made sure Dave stayed sober and talked to him about what he wanted to do.

Saturday, May 8

TORI: On Saturday morning he woke up, and I knew he was going be uncomfortable again and was going to want to get high. I didn't think he would. But he did, and he lied to me. I don't know where he got the drugs from, because I was with him the whole time. I asked him at about two in the afternoon if he was high, because I could tell by his behavior and the scratching. He was also rubbing his eyes like he does when he's high. So he looked at me like he didn't want to have to lie but said anyway, "No, I'm just anxious about what's happening."

I said okay, but I kind of had a feeling. Then a couple of hours later I asked him

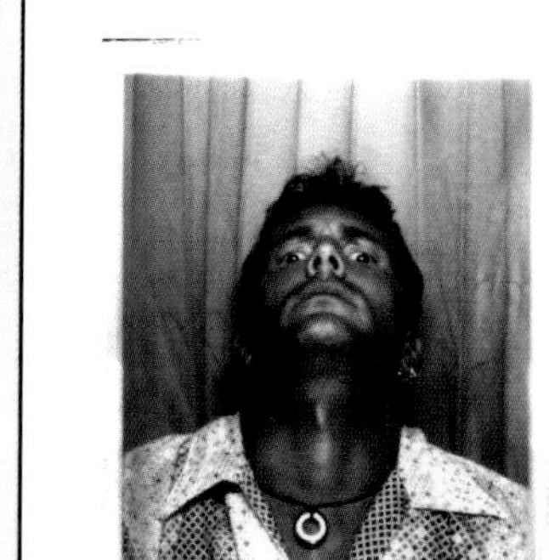

again because he started getting mean like he gets when he's high. And he said no again.

However, half an hour later, a friend from rehab called and asked Dave how he was doing. And he told his friend that he had relapsed and lied to me twice saying he was sober. It was interesting that he would lie to me but be honest with someone who was coming out of rehab, which is actually pretty honorable.

DAVE: I think that my friend from rehab was in less of a position to do something about it. And by that time, I assumed Tori knew.

TORI: I had a feeling, but I didn't think he'd lie to me—twice.

DAVE: Come on, I was, like, organizing the photo strips for about seven hours.

TORI: Anyway, once he said it and I heard it and it was out in the open, I went into total panic mode. I thought, "Well, at least if I'm here, he'll have to hide it. He can't go all-out and be sitting on the living room couch with the spoon and needle." I kept saying, "Oh, I'm going inside to get a drink," and I'd be like opening up the drawers in the kitchen and the cabinets looking for the drugs. He did a really good job of hiding them because the whole weekend I was in the house, I couldn't find anything.

DAVE: Do you know where they were?

TORI: Where?

DAVE: They were underneath the studio computer keyboard.

TORI: See, see? Yeah.

DAVE: I copped drugs three times.

TORI: Yeah, he walked my dog Lucy, which he would never do. He's only done it once since I've known him. But all of a sudden, he said, "I think I'll walk her now." I'm like, "Okay."

DAVE: That's not when I scored.

TORI: No, but he took his phone with him. I just know that those things were clues that he was looking in the mailbox or under the mat or down the road for something. But I kept thinking optimistically because I couldn't find anything in the house. I figured if he had a stash, he was probably about to run out. I thought he really wanted to sober up.

By Saturday evening, I started getting on his nerves because he wanted to get really high, I think. And we had been together for two days straight. So he goes, "Jimmy's coming over." And I was like, "Fuck."

DAVE: Jimmy isn't a bad influence.

TORI: No, he's a great guy and he doesn't do drugs. But he's kind of passive, and probably wouldn't care if Dave did something in front of him. And that really upset me. I didn't say a word to Dave.

DAVE: She just gave me the evil eye.

TORI: I did, because on top of the fact that he had just lied to me and was getting high and was probably going to get even more high after I left, I was really tired. I hadn't slept because I was watching him the whole time. At one point, I was lying on the back of his sofa, holding his arm because his veins were pumping so hard. I was crying and he was just sweating and it made me really upset. But anyway, Jimmy came over and I went downstairs. Dave would come down, purposely, just to see how I was reacting. And then he started calling me a bitch. He's like, "You're a fucking bitch, Tori. What are you giving me the evil eye for? You're a fucking bitch. Fuck you, Tori."

It's the kind of behavior that appears when someone feels guilty for lying. He started saying, "Fuck you, get the fuck out of my house. I don't want you here anymore."

And I said, "You know what, D? I am a bitch, you're right. I'm a fucking bitch, D. And you know what? I'm not leaving. So what are you going to do? Call the cops? I think they'd be more interested in you than they would be in me."

So Jimmy hung out, and then they went into the studio downstairs. I was trying really hard to have the biggest ear I've ever had in my whole life to listen to the conversation. And he was talking to some chick on the phone, going, "We're coming down."

DAVE: Oh, I forgot about that. We went to the Whiskey Bar.

TORI: So he comes up to me and goes, "Oh, Tori, I'm going out with Jimmy for a little while."

I go, "Dave, I just heard you on the phone. You're going to meet someone."

And he said, "Yeah, we're going to the Whiskey Bar. So what? I think it's time for you to go home now."

DAVE: Did you think that I was going to score drugs or meet a girl?

TORI: I thought you were going to do both, which is probably what happened.

DAVE: No, that's not what happened, because, see, I had already scored three times. I had a system. Mary stopped coming because she felt so terrible about my condition that she refused to sell me drugs anymore. She took my cell phone number off her caller list. We made a deal that I'd stop, and then I said, "Okay, give me another one."

And she went, "That's not part of the deal." It was pretty cool. So I had another guy, and I would page him and he would put it somewhere. Then he'd call when he was on his way down the hill afterward.

TORI: You're kind of scared to tell me where he put it right now, aren't you?

DAVE: I know. I want it to be a secret.

TORI: Then who was the girl?

DAVE: I didn't even know her. In fact, I'd never even seen her before. I'm terrible. Some girl just called and said, "Hey, I would really like to meet you." That's why I went down to the Whiskey.

TORI: So Dave and Jimmy go out to the Whiskey Bar, they come home later, and I'm so tired and cranky that I want to kill him. I'm in tears. And now I hear him talking on the phone to Jack, the little actor guy with the monocle who hangs out at the Whiskey. He's saying, "Come on over." And I'm like, "No fucking way."

But Jack comes over anyway, and I'm really pissed now. I'm downstairs sleeping in the bed, and Dave's like, "Get up and get into the other room." He just did not want me there at all. And Jack proceeded to stay.

Sunday, May 9

TORI: The next morning, Sunday, Dave and I had plans to spend Mother's Day with his dad at the Bel-Air Hotel. We were supposed to meet him for an eleven A.M. lunch. But Jack ended up staying until ten-thirty in the morning, chattering away, playing music.

This is what I don't understand about his friends—they know he's just gotten out of rehab, they know he's loaded, and they know he's tired and probably hasn't slept. He's so high he's speaking with his eyes closed and he can't even get whole sentences out. Half of it is mumbo jumbo about "my guitar is red in the other room and it's got a blue ribbon around it." He doesn't have a fucking clue what he's saying because he's so high and tired. And Jack is having a conversation with him about nothing, you know? It freaked me out that he wouldn't leave. I wanted to kick him out, because I knew Dave would do more drugs to stay up with Jack, but I knew that if I did Dave would be so pissed. Finally, Jack left just in time for us to meet Dave's dad.

At lunch, Dave and I had a blast. We had a lot of fun. It was upsetting, though, because Dave's dad knew that he was high and that was obviously a big problem for him.

DAVE: Toby was there with her dad and her friends too. And I was sitting there at the Bel-Air Hotel loaded.

TORI: Loaded! But we had fun. His dad loosened up and was enjoying Dave's company. And Dave was really fun with Gabe, and Toby's dad kept cracking us up. I think Dave and I laughed a lot more than we have in a long time.

DAVE: Yeah, we did. We had a good time.
TORI: After that, we drove back to the house. I remember Dave borrowed my cell phone on the way back to check his messages.
DAVE: Yeah, and the message was: "Dave, I just want to let you know that I got this new CD. It's called *Check the Drain by the Garage.*"
TORI: That's just great. Then Jerry Cantrell [of Alice in Chains] came over, and I said, "I'm going home to change out of these clothes. You guys go have dinner." I thought he'd be safe. But then he said that he was going to meet Twiggy and he'd call when he got back to the house. He called a few hours later and said, "Jimmy's going to babysit me tonight." And I wasn't thrilled about Jimmy again.
DAVE: But all we did was go to Crazy Girls.

Monday, May 10

TORI: Then on Monday he was sad. We talked on the phone a lot, and he decided to check into rehab. I wondered if he was actually going to do it or not, and I was thrilled that he did.
DAVE: I know. I called and I packed and I came. I can't believe it myself. I just knew that I couldn't finish my record if I wasn't sober. I have a whole company behind me ready to work, and I know that I can't do drugs if I want them to put it out. I've been working on it too hard to throw it away. And this time it's not just another quick dry-out thing. I'm going all the way.

Loaded!

But we had fun.

part III A TRIUMPHANT RETURN

The previous conversation took place at a rehab clinic in Venice Beach. After four days of unanswered messages, Dave finally phoned the day he checked in.

"Dude," he said, excited. "We're going to have a happy ending, but a happy ending with a twist. This is it: I went to the place that my businesspeople put me in and it didn't work. So I did it myself. I'm in an inpatient facility for two weeks, and then I'll be in an outpatient program for three months."

He paused. "You know I wouldn't let this book not have a happy ending."

The treatment center is in a residential-looking house with a front lawn and a large garden in back where the patients can lounge around picnic tables. On my first visit, Dave is wearing a black T-shirt and jeans. The painful part—the withdrawal Dave likens to the chronic ache that the elderly must feel every waking moment—is over for him. He looks weary, but great. He is bright and funny and brimming with excitement—not the edgy excitement that accompanies drug intake but a genuine happiness to really be seeing the world through unclouded eyes.

He sleeps in a small dormitory room that he shares with another patient. Above his blue-blanketed bed is a drawing he made of a trash can containing the things he wants to get rid of in his life: there is a crayon rendering of the spoon we saw in June (symbol of the nourishment of both his youth and his recent past), a frowning face with a line drawn through it (no more unhappiness), a rainbow not unlike the one in the unicorn painting that hangs above his computer (a sign of the impossible dreams he wants to banish), and a telephone (representing miscommunication).

Last night, his rehab group went on a field trip to see an IMAX movie. In it, the camera slowly zoomed away from the earth and showed the immensity of the universe; then it slowly returned to the ground, moving closer and closer until it was magnifying the tiniest fragment possible to display a world of life inside a microscopic speck. Afterward, Dave had to talk to his counselor. The movie made him feel insignificant and, more to the point, made him doubt the very principle he needs to cling to in order to get clean: a firm belief in a higher power that can restore his sense of self. The counselor told Dave that he plays a part in this massive universe. Just like our body depends on a vast network of cells and molecules and DNA that all must be perfectly arranged and operating for us to function, so too is the universe a living system dependent on the ability of all of its parts to function.

At dinner in the clinic's kitchen that night, Dave sits around a large wooden table eating salad and lasagna with his fellow patients, who take turns cooking and cleaning each night. They laugh and talk about their visitors and exchange the stories that led to their ending up at this dinner table today. They are single mothers, record executives, and drifters. And then there is Dave, sitting on the end of the table, talking about his record and his book and his website, smiling like I've never seen him smile before.

I
YOU
D!
xo.

part IV THE OUTPATIENT

They let Dave out of the clinic without a chaperone now. He calls to meet for breakfast at ten A.M. on May 27 at Swingers.

Walking around sober, he seems like a fish out of sea. He is still jittery: tapping the table with his fingertips, wolfing down his sandwich, fidgeting impatiently as he waits for the check. It is almost as if his body still needs to readjust to real time, which includes three meals a day, a cycle of sleep once every twenty-four hours, and a lot of waiting around doing nothing. Drugs, much like love affairs, have the advantage of providing a plot in our lives, distracting us from the oppression of ordinary, everyday existence. Without drugs and without Adria, Dave still must supply a plot for his days in order to make it through this transition.

After lunch, he races to a studio in the Hollywood Hills to meet Mötley Crüe drummer Tommy Lee, who called Dave to ask him to play on his Methods of Mayhem project. This is the first time that Dave has been out and about sober in a year. We gather in the kitchen with Tommy's crew. Between the tattoos on the arms of Dave, Tommy, a white dreadlocked rapper named TiLo, and the studio engineer, there is enough ink to start a publishing company. When Tommy sees Dave's arms, he flips out. Not over the tattoos, but over the severity of the track marks running through them.

"They've discolored my tattoos a little right here," Dave says, showing a spot of white in the green on the bend of his elbow.

"But that's not because you shot heroin," the studio engineer says. "Shooting coke every ten minutes will do that to you."

"Man, I can't believe now how much I did," Dave says. "Probably like a hundred shots a day."

"I'll never forget it when I was shooting up," Lee says. "It got so bad that Nikki [Sixx, Crüe bassist] and I were in a hotel room, and we were out of coke and heroin, so we filled a cap with Jack Daniel's and shot that up. I can't believe that now."

"That sounds like Nikki's idea," TiLo says.

"It was."

In the studio, Dave picks up a guitar and adds a few tracks to the music as Tommy films him with a video camera. It is as if the documentary torch is being passed to a new musician, who, like Dave, is also stepping away from drugs and his musical past in order to attempt his first solo project. The connection deepens when Dave shows Tommy pictures from the June and July chapters. Tommy knows nearly every one of the women. Hollywood is a very small town, and the same girls always seem to find their way to the arm of each rock star.

Afterward, Dave goes to see the movie *Trippin'*. It is so bad and Dave's so fidgety that he leaves after fifteen minutes. He's sick with a cold and wants to get permission from the clinic to crash out for the night at his dad's. He says he feels ungrounded and compares himself to an ice cream cone with no scoop on top. But, he says, on the bright side, there is actually ice cream inside the cone. May is over in four days, bringing a year of documentation to an end, and it seems like he's going to make it this time.

Reassurance comes a few days later, on May 31. He has spent the past few nights at his dad's house, getting caught up on sleep and pampered. Finally, he seems happily sober when I see him at a tattoo parlor on Sunset, getting his arm touched up. He is spoon-feeding himself tuna fish from a can.

"I went to a trainer this morning and worked out," he says, grinning. "The monster is back. I can even pick you up with one hand."

He shovels another spoonful of tuna into his mouth. "I'm so excited about my life right now."

A healthy regimen of high-protein food, weight lifting, and therapy has become his new addiction, and he is as obsessive about them as he was about drugs. Physical fitness has become the plot to ease his transition into sobriety. He suggests starting a new book documenting the forthcoming year. It will begin, he says, with the line, "Do you know what to do when somebody goes to too many therapists?"

"Oh," he adds as he leaves the tattoo parlor. "Did I tell you I'm getting a new house?"

He returns to rehab just as the pay phone in the hall rings. It's Perry Farrell, calling with good news: he and the movie crew want to give the Jane's Addiction movie back to Dave and reinstate him as producer. Even Anthony Kiedis is back in Dave's life. Kiedis left him a supportive message the previous day, and Dave phones back today, thanking him for calling and caring. "I've got all these people back in my life," he says with a big smile. "Maybe we should modify our thesis."

So what is the thesis now? "This book is about a drug addict who has negative beliefs about life and buys a photo booth to prove and document those beliefs. But in the process he comes to learn that many of his beliefs are inaccurate and he gets sober."

Dave walks into the dormitory kitchen and picks up a broom: it's his turn to clean up today.

june 2000

part I

"WHAT WAS I THINKING?"

The following conversation took place on June 1, 2000, exactly two years since the documentation of Navarro's life began and a year since it ended. The location was Real Food Daily, a health food restaurant in Beverly Hills.

I DON'T THINK YOU'VE BEEN LOOKING FORWARD TO THIS CONVERSATION.
To be honest, I haven't. Because what I'm supposed to do is analyze a part of my life that I'm not proud of.

LET'S BEGIN WITH THE FIRST QUESTION POSED IN JUNE: WHAT *DO* YOU DO WHEN SOMEBODY SHOOTS UP TOO MUCH?
The answer is: Call 911 from your cell phone as you're getting the fuck out of there. And definitely don't get sucked into writing a book about it!

HOW ABOUT IN THE BIGGER PICTURE. I HAD TREMENDOUS GUILT THROUGHOUT THE YEAR BECAUSE I WATCHED YOU HARM YOURSELF WITH DRUGS TO THE POINT WHERE YOU COULD HAVE EVEN DIED. AND I ALWAYS WONDERED IF I COULD HAVE DONE SOMETHING MORE, LIKE CALL AN INTERVENTION OR HAVE YOU ARRESTED OR—
There's really nothing you could have done that would have stopped me from doing what I wanted to do. What could you have done? Told me it's bad for me? An intervention didn't help me; I escaped. People in greater positions of power over of my life tried to do the very same thing, and there was nothing they could do. They threatened to take my music away and that didn't stop me. No one had that power but me. If a guy is running away from his fears, what human power is going to make him face them?

IT'S INTERESTING HOW OPEN YOU WERE DURING THAT YEAR, BUT NOW YOU SEEM MUCH MORE CLOSED OFF, LIKE YOU USED TO BE BEFORE YOU STARTED TAKING DRUGS AND DOCUMENTING YOUR LIFE.
All I can really tell you about all of it is that I fed myself a lot of bullshit to self-destruct because I was unhappy with a lot of things. And I think a lot of the bullshit that I fed myself with was based on making large generalizations because of past experiences. I think my whole trip was that I was living in absolutes, and there aren't really absolutes. So it was a very delusional time for me. And to be honest with you, I was on a path of self-destruction in which the only way to remain on the path was to live within delusion. Plus, like I said in the conversation with Tori, self-disclosure can be a very deceptive yet effective way of concealing some inner truths regarding our insecurities and most intimate fears. I could intellectualize a lot of things to the point where there wasn't much anybody else could say to me. Fortunately or unfortunately, I have an intellect. In fact, I would even go so far as to say that it isn't so much an intellect as it is a gift for manipulation.

COMPLETELY. BECAUSE I DIDN'T EVEN REALIZE UNTIL I LOOKED OVER THE TEXT FROM THE ENTIRE YEAR THAT—AND I DON'T WANT TO COME OFF AS HARSH OR ANYTHING—BUT EVERY TIME SOMETHING WENT WRONG, YOU PUSHED THE BLAME ON SOMEONE ELSE. WHEN YOU AND ADRIA BROKE UP, IT WAS HER FAULT. WHEN YOU DIDN'T FOLLOW UP WITH ANGELYNE, IT WAS MY FAULT. WHEN YOU COULDN'T THINK

OF A SONG TO PLAY TO GABE'S KINDERGARTEN CLASS, IT WAS YOUR PARENTS' FAULT. WHEN ANYTHING ELSE WASN'T DONE, IT WAS JEN'S FAULT.
I know. It's fucking funny when I look back on it. If it's everybody else's fault, then why am I the guy who's dying?

EXACTLY.
It occurs to me that a lot of what I was going through at the time of making all this stuff was me living in so much fear and being so afraid of who I was and my experiences that I was basically forcing them on everybody else. By doing so I thought that I'd be looking at them too. But really what I was doing was amplifying everything I didn't like about myself and then avoiding having to deal with it, as bizarre as that sounds. I think there was a lack of acceptance on my part about where I was coming from. And I don't want to say that I regret any of this stuff, because it has been incredibly self-realizing for me and I've grown a lot. But I've also damaged myself a lot in the process. I have to admit, however, I had some really fun times.

BUT THAT'S YOUR MEMORY SPEAKING. WHAT'S INTERESTING IS THAT IF YOU HADN'T DOCUMENTED ALL THIS, MAYBE AFTER A WHILE ALL YOU'D REMEMBER IS THE GOOD TIMES, AND YOU'D FORGET THE ARGUMENTS AND THE PAIN AND THE UGLINESS.
I think in a weird way the documentation has helped me stay together this past year, because reading it kept me from remembering it in a glamorized way. My memory gets really selective: I remember having strippers in the booth; I don't remember that I was in the bathroom the whole time smoking ice. And the truth is, we could have all that again now without the drugs. But we wouldn't want to. The problem is that my brain became so clouded with chemicals that all the random, nonconnected interactions with people seemed somewhat tolerable. The truth is that after all has been said and done, I don't really feel that I actually experienced a single true memorable and life-altering moment. Certainly none that were beautiful, and definitely none that I was truly present for.

EXACTLY. YOU LET THEM COME IN AND SUCK UP A LOT OF TIME IN WHICH YOU COULD BE DOING SOMETHING MORE MEANINGFUL.
I had to be completely whacked out of my head to be able to stand it for five minutes. Granted, the conversation we had with those wannabe hookers was really funny, but now I can realize how desperate they were. Now I find it sad. I'd much rather find humor that isn't at the expense of the desperate.

HOW DO YOU FEEL NOW ABOUT YOUR RELATIONSHIP WITH ADRIA IN THAT TIME?
I think that I made some bad choices, and maybe getting back together with somebody was one of them. And I have to accept responsibility for that. Getting fucked up is all about pointing fingers and, when you're not fucked up, it's all about accepting responsibility. That's why I stayed fucked up: I wouldn't accept any responsibility.

LET ME ASK YOU SOMETHING, THEN, AND YOU HAVE TO PROMISE NOT TO GET MAD AT ME. BUT LOOKING BACK ON YOUR MTV INTERVIEW JUST BEFORE YOU LEFT THE RED HOT CHILI PEPPERS—THE ONE YOU GOT INTO THE ARGUMENT WITH ADAM ABOUT—DO YOU THINK YOU BROUGHT IT ON YOURSELF?
Is that one of your questions?

YES.
You know what, I thought about it a lot, and I've pretty much come to the conclusion that I accept full responsibility. I'll send Adam a box of chocolates in the morning.

WHAT IS YOUR RELATIONSHIP WITH THE BAND NOW?

I talk to them once in a while, and really like their new record. I think I told Adam that they had taken away my ability to have fond memories of having been with them. But I do have fond memories, and for me to say that my memories hinge on somebody else's actions is really an immature way of thinking.

WHEN YOU SAW THIS ACCOUNT OF THE PAST YEAR, THERE WERE SOME SECTIONS THAT YOU JUST COULD NOT BRING YOURSELF TO READ. WHY WAS THAT?

God, it was hard. I looked at some of it and thought, "Who the fuck is that guy?" I actually have to hand it to you for seeing this thing through, considering who your partner was.

I WASN'T ALWAYS AS SUPPORTIVE AND RATIONAL AS I COULD HAVE BEEN EITHER.

But I was a fucking monster. If there's ever a day I'm thinking about getting high, all I have to do is look at that argument with Adam Schneider to change my mind. I think that I was dealing with a lot of pain that needed some course of action, and the only course of action I could think of was one that was destructive to others. There were times when I would rather see certain people go down than live. Which is really unbelievable, because I would get just one-dimensional, where my sights were so narrow I couldn't see anything else. There was no big picture. My manager refers to my life back in those times as "the small reality."

It's funny, because I was driving around with Conrad last night and two hookers drove by and said, "Yo baby, wassup? You want a date?" And we said no thanks and left.

As we were driving away, Conrad asked, "Do you realize that if this was two years ago, we'd all be up at your house looking at little films that you made on your computer?" I would have just brought them into that little fucking world. And I would have told them, "You guys gotta get in the booth!"

In a weird way, the booth was initially supposed to be a way to capture people who would eventually leave my life. Is that right?

YES.

But what it might have been, more than that and unbeknownst to me, was a way to get people in my life.

BECAUSE YOU WANTED TO MAKE YOUR PLACE INTO THE FACTORY?

Yeah, and also because if you have a bunch of freaked-out, fucked-up, drug-addled prostitutes and strippers and IV drug users in your house all the time, it's really hard to focus on how fucked up your own life is. There were a lot of really intense, underlying messages in the project that I wasn't aware of.

AND TO THINK, NO ONE SEEMED TO BE MORE SELF-AWARE AT THE TIME THAN YOU, AND NO ONE SPENT MORE TIME RECORDING AND ANALYZING EVERYTHING THEY DID. BUT YOU STILL WEREN'T FULLY AWARE OF YOURSELF.

I used self-awareness as a way to remain unaware. Lately, I've been trying to live with the knowledge that it has always been my awareness of self that causes most of my problems. Actually, I think I was more self-centered than self-aware.

WHY DO YOU THINK IT WAS SO IMPORTANT FOR YOU TO HAVE THE VIDEO CAMERAS AND THE PHOTO BOOTH AND DOCUMENTATION GOING ON ALL THE TIME? OBVIOUSLY, YOU DON'T STILL DO THAT.

As delusional as I was, I was still pretty aware that I was destructing. I fooled myself pretty well sometimes, though. Like when the doctor was coming over and giving me IV drips, I was thinking, "Look, I'm taking care of myself. I've got vitamins." That's why my head was so dangerous, because I truly believed I could figure out or afford a way out of almost any problem.

AT THE BEGINNING, WE NEVER MEANT FOR THIS TO BE A DOCUMENTARY ABOUT DRUG ADDICTION, BUT IN MANY WAYS IT BECAME ONE. DO YOU THINK THAT IN DOCUMENTING IT DRUGS ARE GLAMORIZED IN ANY WAY?
Absolutely not. In no way are we glamorizing drugs. Perhaps drugs have been glamorized so much already that anything having to do with them seems glamorous, no matter how negative the message ultimately is. For this book, the message that I read into it is simply that I can't do them. I guess if I had died, the book would have done a better job of dissuading people from doing drugs.

WELL, A LOT OF THE BOOK ISN'T THAT GLAMOROUS ANYWAY.
Exactly. Life may suck sometimes, but back then it sucked most of the time. I mean, the types of people that want to hang around while a guy's killing himself have got to have some major issues of their own. "Ooh, this is fun. Let's go over to this guy's house—he's killing himself. Let's go watch it." I mean, there were times you couldn't hang out with me. And it wasn't all fun and games for you.

TOTALLY. ALSO, A LOT OF TIMES I DREADED COMING OVER TO YOUR HOUSE, BECAUSE I KNEW IT WAS SIX P.M. OR NINE P.M. WHEN I CAME OVER. BUT YOU'D KEEP ME THERE UNTIL THE NEXT AFTERNOON, OR LATER. AND I WOULDN'T DO DRUGS AND I'D WANT TO GO TO SLEEP, AND I WOULDN'T BE ALLOWED TO GO TO SLEEP OR LEAVE.
Probably because we were too busy arguing.

MAYBE ARGUING, MAYBE SITTING AROUND, MAYBE PUTTING UP WITH PEOPLE. BUT IT WAS EXHAUSTING, AND IT WAS CONFUSING AND STRESSFUL BECAUSE THERE ARE NO RULES FOR A DOCUMENTARY LIKE THIS. ON ONE HAND, I WASN'T SUPPOSED TO INTERFERE WITH YOUR LIFE BECAUSE THEN I WOULDN'T BE A GOOD DOCUMENTARIAN. BUT THEN, ON THE OTHER HAND, IF I STOOD BY AND WATCHED YOU DIE, I WOULDN'T BE A GOOD HUMAN BEING.
I don't know how I survived. I really don't. I did it for so long I can't believe I look like a human being again.

WOULD YOU SAY YOU'RE HAPPIER NOW?
Yes, much happier. Actually, come to think of it, I honestly feel like I never really knew back then what it was like to feel anything besides compulsive excitement or fear-driven anger, resentment, and overblown self-serving suffering. Happy really wasn't an option. So now I feel much happier when I am happy, because it is actual happiness. The hard part is the rainbow of emotions that come along with life that I never had a chance to experience. I'm not able to avoid certain emotions and things, but on the other hand, instead of hanging onto the anger for a year, I hang on to it for a day. I think that it's hard to measure your level of happiness when you're living under a cloud. Now, living in reality, I definitely think that I'm on a shorter road to inner peace.

IT WAS BRAVE OF YOU TO OPEN UP YOUR LIFE LIKE THIS.
I disclosed a lot of shit because I never thought in a million years I'd survive long enough to see this book come out. So I hope it helps someone. And, besides, when I get this book in front of me, I'll have hard evidence of what I have to apologize to a lot of people for.

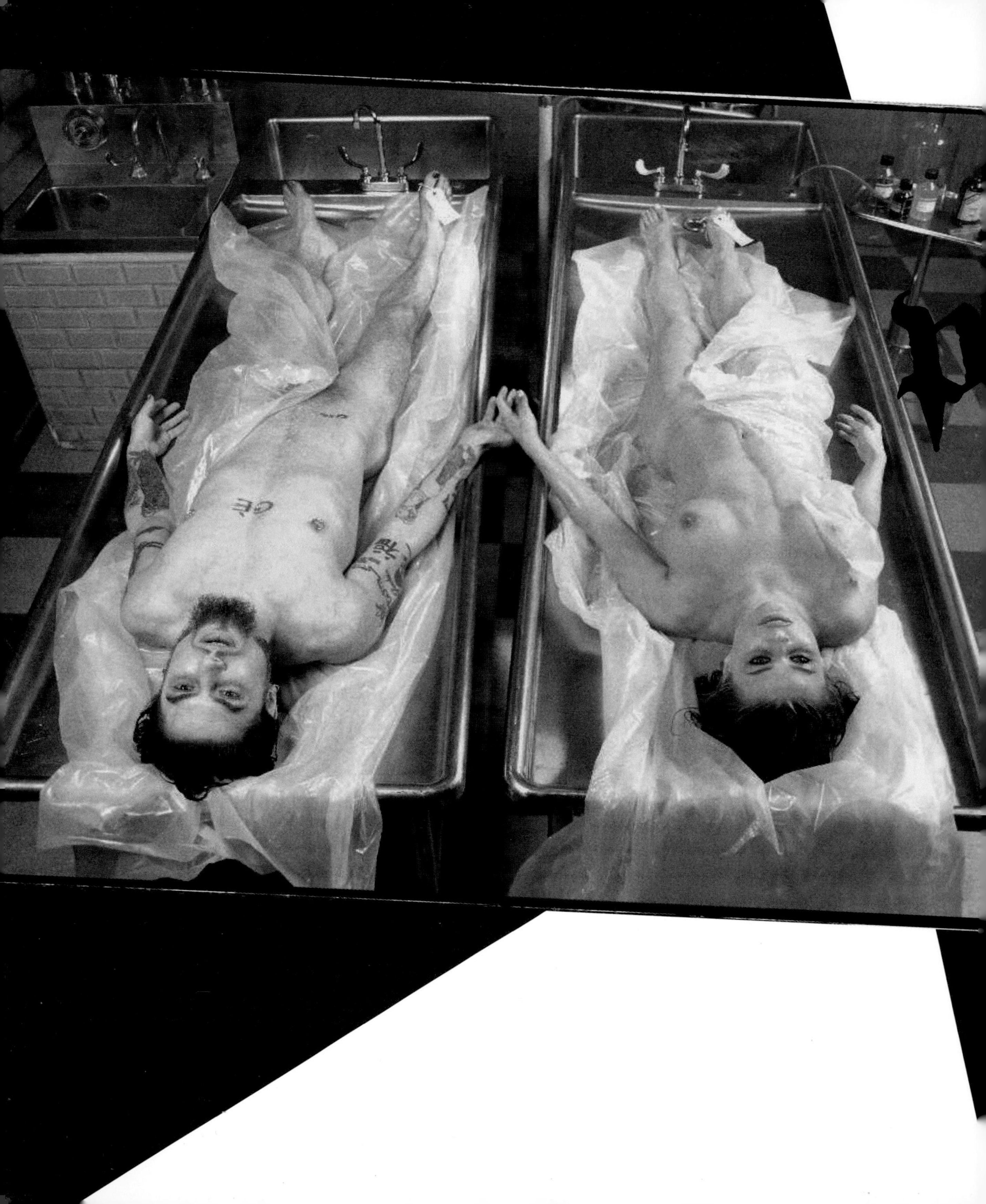

part I GOOD-BYE TO HOLLYWOOD

The canyon road dips and winds to Navarro's new home overlooking Beverly Hills. It is not at the end of a dead-end street, it does not have thick black curtains to blot out the sun, and there is not a single cuckoo clock on the walls. Parked in the driveway are a black Hummer, on permanent loan for his MTV reality show *'Til Death Do Us Part,* and a black Grand National, a gift from his wife, Carmen Electra.

The door to his garage is open. There are no cars inside, only piles of discards: cardboard boxes, a pink bicycle, rusting drum sets, empty Coke cans, a Prince wall calendar, faux presents hand-wrapped by his interior designer to go under the Christmas tree, and a self-portrait that Angelyne gave Dave to hang on his wall.

One item in particular stands out: pushed flush against the wall, it is covered with dust and partially blocked by percussion instruments and wardrobe boxes. I recognize it immediately because I spent a year living with it. It is the photo booth.

In the glass frame on the outside of the booth are five photo strips. One strip came with the booth: it depicts a beaming, all-American couple. The pair reeks of innocence and purity, especially in comparison to the photo strips around them. Three of the other strips are of Dave's former houseguests. Dave inserted them into the frame randomly years ago. Since then, however, the women pictured have either passed away or been institutionalized.

The first strip features Where's My Purse from June, a Penthouse Pet who since died of an overdose. The second strip shows the breast puppeteer from September. She is now in a mental institution, which isn't all that surprising considering her idea of fun. And the third is of Jen Syme, Dave's former assistant. Driving to a party at Marilyn Manson's house around dawn, she crashed into a row of parked cars and was thrown from her Jeep. Her injuries were fatal. Dave was one of the pallbearers at her funeral.

The fourth strip shows an unshaven, emaciated Dave. In all probability, he should have been among the ranks of the crazy and the dead. Instead, he now has much more in common with the smiling, happy, generic couple.

"You couldn't ask for a better location to keep the photo booth to imply how over it I am," Dave says when he greets me in the garage. He has a gym bag and two salads from KooKooRoo in his hands.

We walk into a house decorated so immaculately that it looks like the lobby of an Ian Schrager hotel. "I think that a lot of people who knew me before are very surprised to see how happy and free I am now," he says as we sit down on the couch.

It has been four years since our last interview, and, truth be told, I expected that this book would have been out long ago. But when Dave reread it prior to publication, he flipped out. The past was still too close for comfort. It was then that I learned the only reason he had allowed me to document his life: he didn't think he'd be alive to deal with the consequences.

As the years passed by, there wasn't a day that I didn't think about the book. And there wasn't a day that Dave didn't think about the book either. The only problem was that he was too afraid to read it: he didn't want to be reminded of his year of living dangerously. And then, one recent afternoon, we sat together over lunch and cracked it open again. And he realized not only that enough time had passed that he could see himself with some perspective, but that the book was incomplete.

"With this much clarity and distance, I really have a black-and-white sense of before and after," he said. "And the conclusion, I realize, is not getting off drugs, but getting a life. There's no reason to get off drugs if you're going to get bummed out. I needed to change my whole life. And I have."

All the projects Dave was working on back then that he never completed—his solo record, the Jane's Addiction documentary, this book—came into being only after he cleaned up. And then there are new projects that he never dreamed of that have come about from his ability to get out of the house and think clearly: meeting Bill Clinton and performing with Michael Jackson at a Democratic Party fundraiser; playing on Christina Aguilera's *Stripped* album; starting a rock side project called Camp Freddy; and jamming with childhood heroes from KISS to Steven Tyler of Aerosmith. He even reunited (but didn't relapse) with Jane's Addiction for a tour, a CD, and the Lollapalooza festival. And then there's *'Til Death Do Us Part*, his wedding-preparation show with Carmen, which had the highest-rated premiere in the history of MTV.

Between the show and the paparazzi, he says, "My life gets documented so much that I don't need to do it myself anymore. I don't need to own a camera when everyone else has one."

In fact, his cleaning ladies are gone, his drug dealer is gone, and, since he moved, the pizza and Pink Dot delivery people have changed. In the meantime, however, Adam Schneider, Heather Perry, Chad Smith, his father, his stepmother, Adria, and all his other friends and family members are still in his life.

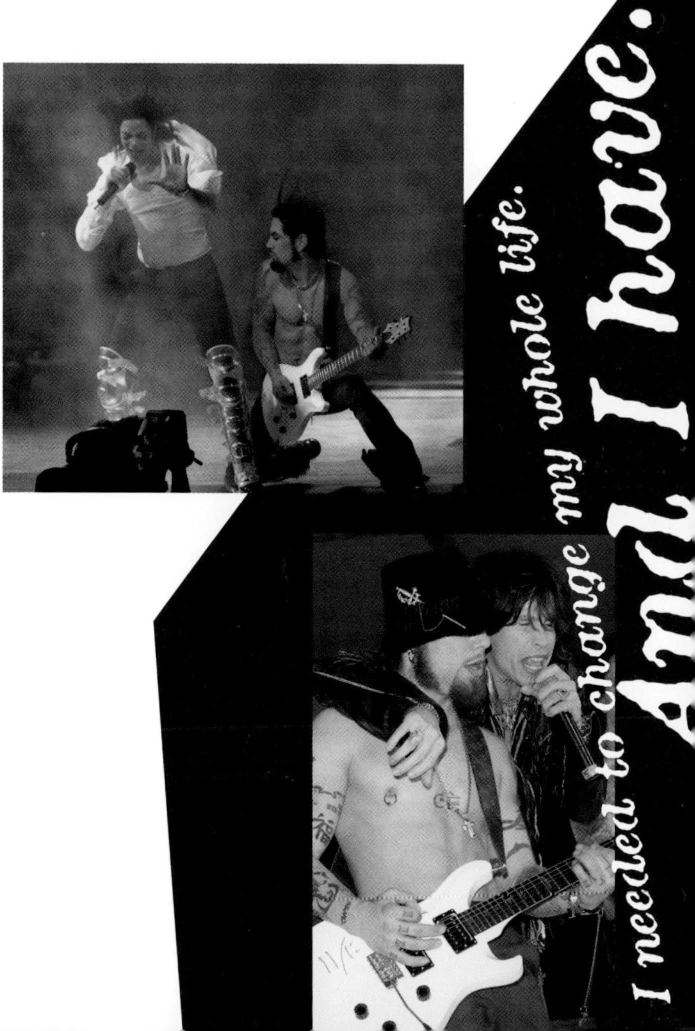
I needed to change my whole life.
And I have.

"It blows me away how sick I was," he says. "All the people that I was whining about are still hanging around. They never went anywhere. The problem was that the more consequences I wasn't willing to face up to, the more fucked up I accused everybody else of being. I was never willing to take responsibility for anything."

Two years ago, after Carmen and Dave got engaged, they moved to this new home—allowing Dave to change his environment, as people like Jen and Tori had been begging him to do for years.

"I didn't want this new relationship dwelling in a place full of old baggage," he explained, lighting a cigarette, his only vice besides watching reality TV shows. "I realized that the little projects from the old house that I thought were going to change the world were just a bunch of shit nailed to a piece of wood. So I threw out tons of stuff and made a clean break. I wanted to start over—clean—and not be attached to any of the things that I thought defined me.

"So we found a house that was the polar opposite from where I'd been. And I took it upon myself to hire the designers to make it look clean and sparse and bright—like a home. It just feels like a new lease on life."

When Dave's statuesque, black-haired stylist arrives—looking like a healthy version of Mary—with free shirts and clogs for him, he continues, "I guess there's a similarity between this house and my old house—except she's dropping off clothes and not heroin."

Dave, of course, is still an addict: he is addicted to the gym, to high-protein meals, to sobriety meetings, to cleanliness, to being a husband, to the bands he plays in, to *The Apprentice.* One of the biggest differences I notice is that no one is walking on eggshells around him anymore; he has stopped picking fights with people over minor faux pas or turns of phrase. He seems to have learned one of the greatest secrets to a happy existence: not to take things personally, a hard dictum to follow when under the delusional thrall of cocaine.

Carmen is in her bedroom, wearing a powder blue sweat suit and packing for a trip to London. There is a question that Dave and I are dying to ask her: Looking back on Dave's past, how does she feel about it?

"I think that it makes him the person that he is now," she says without hesitation. "And I love that person."

Dave beams and throws himself onto her bed. "And I love that he's done everything and been through it all," she continues. "There is something very wise about Dave because of all of his experiences. And his knowledge and spirituality help me with things that I get stuck on."

She drops onto the bed next to him and puts her hand over his. "The thing about Dave and the drugs and whatnot is that he never intentionally tried to hurt anyone. He was just hurting himself. He's a sweet person. He has a sweet soul. So in a way it was his own little beautiful darkness. It was a self-tortured little sadness that I could relate to in my own way. He was a poor little piggly wiggly, because he has a piggly-wiggly tail."

Oh, God. Baby talk. Things really have changed.

"Now get out of my room," she snaps, scrunching up her nose. "I have to be out of the house in fifteen minutes."

I leave the room. Dave follows.

"Is it too late to make a change to the book?" he asks.

Maybe. What do you want to do?

"I just have one request," he says. "Can we change the name Dave to Steve?"

part II

LOVE IN L.A. IV: LOVE DOESN'T HAVE TO CRUSH YOUR HEART LIKE A COKE CAN

BY DAVE NAVARRO

Forever and ever. I had this idea in previous columns of forever and ever. Where did that come from? I mean, 'til death do us part is an awesome goal, but where does it say that for love to be successful, it has to last that long? I know so many people who are discouraged by love because it fails to be everlasting. In fact, I was one of those people.

I now say, "Why does it have to? Hasn't the experience been a good one? Haven't we grown as individuals? Have we had fun, laughter, erotic sex, and lots of experiences we can use in the future and with new relationships? It felt like love, but since it didn't last till the end of time, it wasn't? Bullshit."

Everlasting love is a great goal, but it's not the only path to happiness with someone. Sometimes when we say, "We moved on," we feel like what we are really saying is, "We failed." But perhaps we actually succeeded. We don't know what life has in store for us. I can tell you that I am a better partner now as a result of my relationship with Adria. I have learned so much from her and other past relationships. They are all a part of who I am today, the man my wife loves. And conversely, it is also true that my wife's past loves are a part of who she is. And I am grateful for that. A cliche that holds true for me is that it is all about the journey, not the destination. There is no ride into the sunset and fade to black. No finish line.

Open to the idea. I suppose that being open to the idea is really the point. For me, as soon as I stopped trying to figure out what love was supposed to be or look like and just decided to be open, my whole life changed. I am now happily married to a woman I not only love dearly, but who is also my best friend. I have often been asked, "What's the key, then?"

Well, for us, I think there are several. There are of course the obvious ones: space, individual lives, career direction, and so forth. Honesty and communication are also essential. We don't really expect one to "fix" the other when there is an issue, but we verbalize the issue without making it personal. It's hard to do but worth the effort.

Beyond these, there a couple of huge things that have worked for us. We have learned to love each other's defects. Remember how the idea of a spilled glass of wine used to drive me nuts? Well, it still does. My wife, God bless her, has a tendency to leave Coke cans everywhere in the house. Half-empty Coke cans—and let me tell you, whether I view them as half empty or half full, they invariably spill all over the place. What I have done is learned to love the Coke cans and love the way she leaves them everywhere. It took time, but I am there . . . at least, most of the time. It's about acceptance. I accept her and love her for who she is, who she was, and what she does or doesn't do. It's a process. I figured out that it's much easier just to deal with stuff than to try to change someone.

It's hard. I won't deny that. Love requires work and discipline, just like anything else. If you want to get stronger, you go to the gym—but it is hard. If you want to learn an instrument, you have to practice—but it is hard. Eventually, though, the challenge becomes fun and the rewards begin to show. The blues scale that you learned on Saturday just might not work on Tuesday, but you could end up being a much better player on Wednesday. The funny thing is that these examples only require an individual effort and they are still hard, yet somehow we feel that love, which requires two people, should be easy and free. So, have I finally found the one, you ask. Well, which one? This one? That one? Someone? What did I mean by "the one" in the first place? I guess I was hoping for the one to be a person who completed me perfectly; who took away all my defects of character; who made me funnier, smarter, more interesting, and more attractive. An "ornament to my vanity," as Neil called it once. A partner who never had a problem with me, and if I had one with her, I would be right. A woman I could ride off into the sunset with. A woman who would never cease to be a sexually engaging animal. Basically, a void, challengeless blank canvass that I could paint over from time to time as I desired.

> **"All people are nuts, so you might as well find the hottest one you can and learn to deal."**

The answer is no—I never found that one. And thank God for that. I don't think that one exists anymore, and I wouldn't want it anyway. I have figured out that I would much rather be challenged, grow as a human being, and learn as much as I can about life, love, patience, honor, and gratitude. I let go of the idea of the one years ago. As a result of letting go of the one, I found the one. My wife is funny, smart, beautiful, talented, sexy, honest, loyal, and a real pain in the ass. And you know what? I'm a pain in the ass too. Who isn't? As my friend Duff McKagan once said, "All people are nuts, so you might as well find the hottest one you can and learn to deal."

I endorse that statement to a degree. My wife and I are nuts, but we deal and we have become the closest of lovers and friends. We weren't born with the ability to know how to do this love thing. We weren't even given the ability to know how to do this life thing. So, ultimately, if she leaves an empty Coke can on the coffee table, well, I suppose I can deal.

[Not to be continued.]

part III

THIS IS HOW WE DID IT BREAKING THE ICE

DAVE: So what made you get in touch with me in the first place?

CARMEN: Actually, it was weird, because your name was brought up through a friend. Actually, it was Dennis [Rodman].

DAVE: Really?!

CARMEN: Yeah, this was at the end of our relationship. Dennis and I were still friends, and he called me and said, "I know someone that wants to meet you."

And I said, "Really, who?" You never know what to believe with Dennis. And he said, "My friends were at a record release party, and Dave Navarro was there and he wants to meet you."

DAVE: Wow!

CARMEN: So it sparked a little curiosity. I remember saying, "Wow, he's a good-looking guy!"

Then I remember Dennis saying, "Yeah, he's your type." So that planted a little seed in the back of my mind.

DAVE: What's strange is that I only met Dennis one time at a Chili Peppers show, but your name never came up. I don't think he had even met you yet.

CARMEN: I don't think you said it to Dennis directly. You probably said it to someone he knew.

Anyway, some time went by. I was getting my hair done by a guy named Brandt, and the VH1 *Behind the Music* special on the Red Hot Chili Peppers came on. And I said, "Damn, he's fine." Those were my exact words.

Then Brandt said, "Oh my God, you guys would make the best couple. I'm friends with Dave. He's actually broken up with his girlfriend right now; so he's single."

He wanted to call and set up a dinner for all of us. I was a little hesitant, because I'm the kind of girl who likes to be chased after. I'm not a chaser. I would never put myself out there to get played, because I'm just way too insecure.

Brandt and I then had a long talk about being single. I had been single for a while by that time. I had been doing some work on myself, and wanted to find the right person. But I wasn't in a rush; I was going to let it happen.

So, as time passed, I started thinking about you more and seeing you in things. But I didn't hear anything from Brandt. Eventually I saw him and he said, "I talked to Dave. He's not into it."

DAVE: It wasn't that I wasn't into it. I was into it, but I had just gotten out of my relationship with Adria. So I was too emotionally raw, and wasn't ready to date anybody or put my heart on the line.

I didn't know much about you. I knew you were beautiful, but I had never met you and I knew about Dennis. So I figured, here's a girl with a wild persona coming along when I'm trying to recover from my wild period. I was basically fearful. So I declined.

I told Brandt, "You know what? That's really sweet. Thank you for offering, but I'm going to have to say no to your offer."

I had never been approached by a woman like that. I had never been contacted on behalf of somebody. And I kind of thought that is how Hollywood relationships happen. And then of course I thought, "Well, why haven't I been called before by other Hollywood girls? What's wrong with me?"

CARMEN: All the coincidences about Dennis and Brandt were weird. But when he told me you weren't interested, I blew it off. I figured we weren't meant to meet each other. Of course, I felt a little rejected, and I was a little bit mad at myself for putting myself in that position. I felt really stupid.

So about a year went by, and I was shopping on Melrose. I went into a store and a girl there mentioned something about the Chili Peppers getting back together and you were going to play guitar.

DAVE: It was Jane's Addiction.

CARMEN: That's right, it was Jane's Addiction.

DAVE: I love that you don't know all the history and you don't give a shit. You'll ask, "Who did that dog-barking song?"

CARMEN: That "Jane Says" song is the only one I know.

DAVE: Just like Angelyne.

CARMEN: So when the girl in the shop mentioned your name, I said, "He's so hot." And she said, "Oh, my girlfriend knows him really well. Do you want to meet him?"

I said, "No, absolutely not. He's not interested."

And she said, "No, no. I'll call."

And I begged, "Please don't. I'm going to be so embarrassed. I'm going to look like some stalker."

She promised me that she wouldn't say anything. And she broke her promise. But I guess you were into it this time.

DAVE: I *was* into it. I was playing poker down at the Commerce Casino, and I got a call on my cell phone from this girl Taylor, who's friends with Amanda, the girl from the store. And Taylor said, "I was talking to Carmen and your name came up. She'd like to meet you. Would you be interested in going on a date with her?"

And I said, "I would love to."

At this point, it was a year later, and I had been single the whole time. I had always been interested, but before I wasn't ready. This was going to be my first blind date, so I was freaking out.

CARMEN: It was mine too!

DAVE: I didn't know what to expect. I honestly thought you were like six foot five, and would like get drunk and dance on the tables. I thought you were a screamer. I just had my idea of Dennis, and then put it into a girl.

THE BLIND DATE

DAVE: So I set up a time to meet you at Jones Restaurant in Hollywood for dinner. I was so excited and nervous that I showed up early. The maitre d' took me to the biggest table in the place. I'm sitting at one end and there were like six empty seats. About fifteen minutes later five girls walked in: you and like four of your best friends. You were like this little bunny wrapped up in fur. You were so petite and quiet and sweet and just beautiful. The second I saw you, I was just sunk. But I was also totally uncomfortable because I'd never met any of your friends before, and it felt like they were basically there to check me out and take notes.

CARMEN: I brought them because I was scared. I had never done anything like this before. I remember pulling up in the car and looking at the clock. I was on time, and I was so afraid that I would be the first one there that I drove around the block a couple of times. So I walked in like five or ten minutes late. I wasn't expecting you to be there. But there you were, on time.

DAVE: I was on time, but I was petrified.

CARMEN: I assumed you would have some friends with you, but you were all alone.

DAVE: What I did to get over the uncomfortableness is that I directed my attention to your friends right away. "Hey, you look great . . . Nice to meet you . . . What do you do? . . . Great." But when you and I started chatting, everyone else just disappeared. I liken it to the scene in the film of *West Side Story* when Tony and Maria are at the dance and all the other people in the room go out of focus. I didn't even notice we were with anybody after that.

CARMEN: We immediately started discussing our moms. We really connected right away.

DAVE: I don't know how it happened, but we got into the fact that we had suffered losses in our family. It was really real. *[Note: Dave uses the exact word—"real"—that he made fun of the Baywatch blond in September for using to describe her relationship.]*
CARMEN: It's weird because I almost felt like I knew you. Though you lived your life completely opposite to the way I lived my life, the thing I could relate to was being in so much pain, and not knowing what to do with it.
DAVE: I definitely relate to you on those levels. You lost your mom to brain cancer, and I lost my mom. We've both just had—
CARMEN: —we've had a lot of tragedy.
DAVE: After Jones we went to Cherry, which is like a half-gay, half-glam club. It was very uncomfortable, because I'm not used to people coming up to me based on who I'm hanging out with.

We actually ran into Adria that night, and said hi to her. You were really nervous, so you didn't say much the whole time. And I was pretty nervous, but you know what I do when I'm nervous: I talk too much. So, you did a lot of listening to me.
CARMEN: My friends came along too. We only stayed at the club a little while.
DAVE: I remember after Cherry, I wanted to move it to another location, so I go, "Uhh, how would you like to go get some tea?" And you just looked at me and said, "I don't like tea." So I said, "Oh, okay. 'Bye." And we just went home.
CARMEN: But you were so sweet: you had forgotten to say 'bye to one of my friends, so you ran across the street to say 'bye to her. You were such a gentleman. That was a good sign. I knew everything was going to be okay.
DAVE: What did your friends say afterward?
CARMEN: They said, "Oh my God; I think he really likes you." They were talking to you all night trying to get information from you, and then telling me.
DAVE: I was like, "Dude, I'm totally into her." You were nothing like I thought. Not that I had a bad idea of you—I just didn't know. It was intense.
CARMEN: You assumed that I wanted a guy who was partying and wild, probably the way you were a few years ago. So you were thinking that you weren't exciting enough. And I was thinking the same thing. I didn't think I'd be exciting enough for you because of where I was at. I had been through so much with Dennis and now I had calmed down. I didn't want to be with someone who was drinking or someone who wanted to go out all the time. I wanted to have a normal healthy relationship.

THE FIRST KISS

CARMEN: I couldn't stop thinking about you after the date. And you were so sweet: you

called the next day.
DAVE: I couldn't stop thinking about you either. My friends were like, "You should wait to call her." And I'm like, "For what? What if I get hit by a bus today? I want to talk to her." So we made a date to go see a movie.

"What if I get hit by a bus today?
alk

CARMEN: Remember, we went to the Ivy for lunch before the movie? You picked me up. I'm the kind of girl who loves to have music on all the time. I thought, "Hey, he's the rock guy. He'll play loud music in the car, and that will help get rid of the uncomfortable silence that happens when you get to know someone." And no—there was no music. None at all. You wanted to be the interesting, let's-talk guy.

DAVE: Well, first of all I wanted to get to know you, and it's hard to talk with music bumping. But at the same time, I felt like I would have to do this on personality. I just wanted to get in your heart. And I didn't think I could do that with Jay-Z cranked up to 9. Whenever you picked me up in your car after that, there was always hip-hop on—loud.

CARMEN: And then you took me to the Ivy, which was the last place I wanted to go.

DAVE: Well, it's better to go to the Ivy than the IV. And I thought taking you to the Ivy was a classy move. I just thought it was a cute little spot on Robertson with good shrimp. But then I came to learn that for you, it's too Hollywood. And it's a paparazzi hangout, which was a bad idea for like our second date.

CARMEN: I think that lunch was one of our most uncomfortable moments. We talked about *Three's Company.*

DAVE: Afterward, we went to see *Requiem for a Dream,* which is about a topic I know a little something about. But the truth is that I was so excited and nervous about who was sitting next to me that it could have been any movie. And thank God I was feeling like that: maybe a movie about drug addiction would have been hard to watch otherwise.

CARMEN: It was the perfect film for me, because those are the kind of movies that I like—edgy, documentary style.

DAVE: Your favorite movie is *Gummo.*

CARMEN: Well, it's one of them. I was raised not too far from Zenia, Ohio, where it took place.

DAVE: I was so surprised by Carmen's likes and dislikes and interests. We're both into weird, dark, edgy stuff. But during the movie, my focus was elsewhere. Do I make the move? Do I put the arm around her? Do I hold her hand? And I didn't.
CARMEN: I thought we did hold hands a little bit.
DAVE: We did? I was so paranoid I didn't know what we were doing. Somewhere in the back of my head I was still worried about the friend issue. You know, I didn't want to be the big brother or the friend. But at the same time I didn't push it. I wasn't like, "So do you want to come up to the house and see my Basquiat?" I'm not that guy.
CARMEN: So the next thing was, you leaned right in for a kiss.
DAVE: This was in the car, when I was dropping you off.
CARMEN: And I was so happy.
DAVE: It was amazing, and I knew right then and there that this is probably the one. I don't know how to explain it because every first kiss with someone you are into is great. But somehow this one was different. It was scary too. I just said, "Fuck it. What have I got to lose? Let's just give this a chance. Maybe there is something to this love thing."

TROUBLE IN PARADISE

DAVE: How about the Hawaiian shirt story you told me? I found it terrifying.
CARMEN: Did I tell the Hawaiian shirt story on our second date?
DAVE: I think it was on the second or third date.
CARMEN: During the time I was single, I went on a date with a very handsome guy with great hair. He was funny and sweet, and I was extremely attracted to him.
DAVE: Everything you could want in a guy, right?
CARMEN: It was summertime and he invited me to a barbecue. He came to pick me up, and he was wearing a Hawaiian shirt, he had cut off all his hair, and he was wearing flip-flops. And that was it: I was done.
DAVE: When you told me that story, I was thinking, "I have to get my personality across, because what if I wear something strange or cut my hair funny?"
CARMEN: Like when you broke out and you had a zit on the end of your nose (*laughs*).
DAVE: That was almost the end for us. That was the one time when things almost didn't work out.
CARMEN: What happened was we continued to go on a few dates, and everything was great. I had fallen head over heels. I was trying not to, because I was so afraid. But I couldn't control it. One night, we were sitting at the Whiskey Bar having a drink and this girl runs up, yelling at you, "How could you do this to me?"

I told you, "You need to go outside and talk to her." She was freaking.
DAVE: This was one of the girls that I kind of had a thing with, but she wasn't a girlfriend.
CARMEN: When the girl started yelling at you, I thought, "Okay, now I get it. I see what's really going on here." I was hurt, so I just changed my whole way of thinking. I became really distant and closed up a lot.
DAVE: It turned out that this girl was drunk and, whatever. Everything has been fine since then. We've all said hi. But right after that, I got a zit right on the end of my nose, and there was nothing I could do. I would still try and call you, but I wouldn't go see you or ask you out. So you were probably thinking, "Oh great, he's got all these girls out there in Hollywood."
CARMEN: I figured, "He's a player, and he's out doing his thing."

So there was someone at the time who had been wanting to go out with me. And I would run into him in different restaurants and clubs. We had a mutual friend who was also trying to hook us up. And there was this big party in New York around Christmastime, and I knew this person was going to be there. I thought he was a nice guy, though my heart was still with you. So, purely out of pain, I decided to go to New York and go to the party. Then, I think it was the night before I was leaving.

DAVE: It was actually the night you were leaving.

CARMEN: It was? No, you called the night before and said, "Is there an elephant?"

DAVE: An elephant is therapy talk for a huge issue that two people aren't bringing up. It's a metaphor for miscommunication.

CARMEN: I was thinking, "He has nerve to call and ask me if there's an elephant when he's got the Crier out there."

DAVE: We have nicknames for everybody.

CARMEN: You have the Crier and I have the Hawaiian shirt guy. Whatever.

DAVE: I also have the Bulimic Fish.

CARMEN: We also call her the Grouper because she looks like a fish.

DAVE: I don't see it. She doesn't look like a fish to me.

CARMEN: The Crier was beautiful.

DAVE: I know some Ostriches.

CARMEN: I do too. I even had a brief fling with a Rhinoceros. So anyway, I did go to New York, and right when I was about to leave for the airport, you show up. You called and said, "I have a Christmas present for you." And I didn't even get you a Christmas present because I honestly thought it wasn't working out between the two of us. So you showed up with a heart-shaped chocolate cookie, handcuffs, and a whip from Agent Provocateur. I got all confused. Maybe you were telling the truth: after all, now that I thought about it, you did say in the beginning that there were a couple of girls you were dating.

DAVE: There were three girls that I was dating, not even seriously. When we met, I called each one of them and said, "I met someone that I'm really serious about and pursuing."

And I had called that girl, but we met her on a night when she had been drinking and it blew up into this big dramatic thing.

CARMEN: So I go to New York to try to forget about you. But after you dropped by, I couldn't get you off my mind. I was only there one night. I didn't even want to go to this party. I was so overwhelmed thinking about you. So I flew right back, and we started seeing each other again.

DAVE: But then I got a taste of my own medicine because you went to the party.

CARMEN: I actually didn't.

DAVE: Didn't you go somewhere? Because Conrad called me and said, "Dude, I'm really sorry about the Carmen thing not working out." And I go, "What do you mean?"

CARMEN: I went out with a couple of his friends, so he joined us for dinner. But it was so uncomfortable. It was awful. I just kept thinking about you.

DAVE: Well, Conrad heard that you were seen with some other guy. So when I saw you after you came back from New York and learned that everything was on the up and up, I decided to go for it. I had been through the drugs; I'd been through the rock and the touring; I had been through the wild sleepless party nights; I had been through losing loved ones to drugs; I had been through enough relationships. And I didn't want to deal with any of that anymore.

THE MUSHY STUFF

DAVE: We have a real good understanding of where each other comes from and what makes us tick and what makes us insecure and what makes us feel strong. You know everything I've done and everything I'm ashamed of and everything I'm proud of. I just knew it back then. There's nobody out there who is better for me. I honestly haven't looked back since.

CARMEN: When I found out your insecurities and certain things you had a problem with, I couldn't believe it. When I look at you, I see the most handsome man in the world—well maybe not right now. But in general you're so sexy and you've got an incredible body and you play guitar and you're talented, and you're so smart and funny. I couldn't believe that you didn't think all of those things also. It tripped me out.

DAVE: Do you think having such a public relationship and marriage has made it more challenging for us?

CARMEN: It's been great. It's like night and day compared to my last situation, and I think that's because we love each other and we even love each other's flaws. I think in our TV show people can see that, and it gives hope that you can find love—and that you can change your life and be a better person and be inspired by people you love.

DAVE: Even though I resisted the idea when MTV first pitched it to me, I loved doing that show. It wasn't intrusive. I think it gives a lot of hope, and it's nice to have something public that is positive.

As for the marriage itself, I never thought it would happen. But we really took our time with it. We dated for a year before we got engaged, and we remained engaged for almost two years.

CARMEN: By that time, you pretty much know it's right. I loved the invitations to our bachelor party.

DAVE: We had a joint bachelor/bachelorette party, and we had strippers and porn stars doing shows and things. And they were only into you. There was a bowling alley room at the party, and I was just in there bowling. I got no play.

CARMEN: I can laugh at that now. I used to be the kind of girl who was like, "Show me a sign. Let me know that he's cheating, or lying, or doing something." I was always waiting for the other shoe to drop . . .

DAVE: I was like that too. But after hanging in there with each other, I'm not looking for that other shoe. Are you?

CARMEN: No, I'm not.

I just knew it back then. There's nobody out there who is better for me.

I honestly haven't looked back since.

part IV

TEN REASONS *NOT* TO TIE OFF

"When I was growing up and reading fucked-up druggie novels like *Junkie* and *Less Than Zero,* I never got the message. Those books should have been red flags for me, but they weren't. I had the mind of an addict. So, in case you missed the subtext, consider this your red flag."

1. Because you don't want to deteriorate into a hairless, liverless green sack of pockmarks and bones. This is actually worse than just dying, which in itself is bad enough.
2. Because you think you're being productive, but you never accomplish any of your goals. You end up just chasing your own tail.
3. Because self-destruction is a magnet for negative energy, not just from yourself but also from others.
4. Because it's a financial disaster. You spend money not just on drugs but also on all kinds of other crap that doesn't enrich your life at all—whether it's hotel rooms or weird items off QVC.
5. Because it's a prison sentence: you have no option each day except to drag around the ball and chain of your habit.
6. Because you become a source of pain for your family and the people you care about.
7. Because life passes you by and you cease to have experiences, other than the dull, dark, lonely, paranoid monotony of addiction.
8. Because by removing yourself from the ability to contribute to things, it's very difficult to find a sense of self and purpose.
9. Because you lose the gift of laughter when the joke's on you.
10. Because of pages 1 to 231.

part
A FINAL IMAGE

I think about all that Navarro has learned in the past five years—the lessons he's been able to apply, the huge life changes he's made, the fully functioning human being he's become today. Tonight, he is performing with one of his bands, Camp Freddy, a Los Angeles supergroup of sorts that also includes members of Guns N' Roses and the Cult. A cavalcade of the rock elite is scheduled to get onstage and sing with the group.

But unfortunately, I will not be able to attend. As I type this in the kitchen of my Hollywood home, I am trying not to make too much noise: I don't want to wake up my houseguest. Her name is Courtney Love. She has fallen on hard times financially and has temporarily moved in with me.

Courtney said she would perform a song with Camp Freddy tonight, but I was unable to get her out of the house (not unlike when Navarro missed the Manson show he wanted to perform at). While Dave has changed so much, it seems the only lesson I have learned is to have the rock star come to me. It saves on gas money—and, if I want to "lie down with my eyes closed," as Dave said in January, I can do it on my own bed.

The next morning, I receive an e-mail from Dave letting me know what I missed in the real world: "Last night I rocked with Chad Smith," he writes. "Adria was there as a friend and in support. Even Dennis Rodman, Carmen's ex-husband, made an appearance. It's all good. Everything is good when you have faith in your life."

Now, if only Courtney and I can get a van up to Dave's house to pick up that photo booth.

2. According to the **Myth of the Cave,** *the process of getting out of the cave is:*

A. Disorienting, painful, frightening, gradual.
B. Clear, pleasant, fun, quick.
C. Something each individual must do completely alone, in isolation.
D. An act that curious humans do quite naturally.

—Question from a test in "The Examined Life," devised by Wadsworth/ Thompson Learning

ACKNOWLEDGMENTS

THANKS TO JILL BERLINER, EMILY HAY, SARAH LAZIN, SUNJA PARK, JEREMIE RUBY-STRAUSS, IRA SILVERBERG, DANA ALBARELLA, ALIZA FOGELSON, JUDITH REGAN, LARISSA FRIEND, AND THE NAVARRO FAMILY.

SPECIAL THANKS TO JASON BRODY, FOR HIS TIRELESS TRANSCRIPTIONS OF INCOHERENT LATE-NIGHT SHENANIGANS, AND TO MARILYN MANSON, IN WHOSE BEDROOM THIS BOOK WAS CONCEIVED.

THIS BOOK IS ALSO DEDICATED TO ALL THOSE WHO VISITED THE HOUSE DURING THE YEAR, AND TO ALL THOSE WHO STAYED AWAY.